Flora of the San Juans

A Field Guide to the Mountain Plants of Southwestern Colorado

MAP OF THE SAN JUAN MOUNTAIN REGION

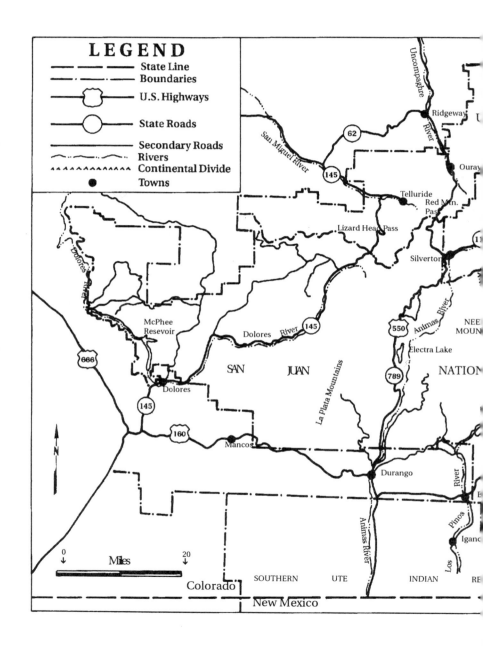

LEGEND

State Line
Boundaries
U.S. Highways
State Roads
Secondary Roads
Rivers
Continental Divide
Towns

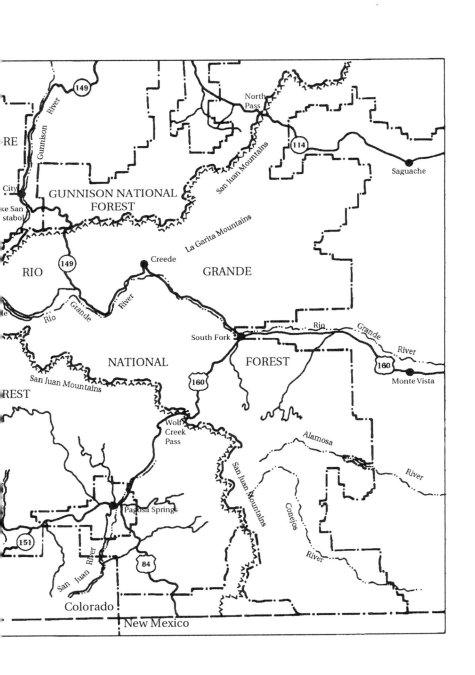

❧ DEDICATED TO THOSE WHO SEEK TO EXPAND THEIR AWARENESS ❧

Flora of the San Juans

A Field Guide to the Mountain Plants
of Southwestern Colorado

Susan Komarek

Sue Komarek

KIVAKÍ
PRESS

Front Cover: *Castilleja integra, Corydalis caseana,*
view from Handies Peak
Back Cover: *Penstemon hallii*
Cover Photographs by Susan Komarek
Author Portrait by Kevin Tonkin
Map © 1994 Amelia Budge
Illustrations and Photographs © 1994 Susan Komarek
Film Processing by Twilight Photography
Book Design by Greg Cumberford and Olive Charles
Cover Design by Olive Charles
Indexing and Production Assistance by Pippa Thomas

Kivakí Press
585 East 31st Street
Durango, Colorado 81301
(303) 385-1767

Library of Congress Catalog Number: 94-076631

Publisher's Cataloging in Publication

Komarek, Susan.
    Flora of the San Juans : a field guide to the mountain plants of
southwestern Colorado / Susan Komarek.
      p. cm.
    Includes index.
    Preassigned LCCN: 94-076631.
    ISBN 1-882308-06-9

    1. Botany—Colorado—San Juan Mountains. 2. Plants—Identification.
I. Title.

QK150.K65 1994   582'.09788'3
                    QBI94-1272

First Edition
First Printing, 1994

Printed in the United States of America
on recycled paper
1 2 3 4 5 — 99 98 97 96 95 94

ACKNOWLEDGMENTS

Many thanks to those who inspired this work and to those who lightened it. I am grateful to Professor Weber for generously sharing his time and vast knowledge. Thanks to Cindy, Kim, Shawna and many others who shared their ideas and words of encouragement. A special thanks to Kevin for embracing my dreams and always being open to the possibilities. Most of all, my gratitude to Sedge for sharing in the travels.

PREFACE

My experience learning flora revealed a lack of field guides for the amateur botanist, especially for the mountains of southern Colorado. Various picture books are available—however, they have drawbacks. They address very broad areas, being only partially applicable to specific locations and they do not impart basic botanical terminology or taxonomic associations. There are several technical floral guides that encompass southern Colorado. The most recent of these guides are William A. Weber's two-volume series, Colorado Flora: Western Slope and Colorado Flora: Eastern Slope. The only limitation to these complete floral guides is the user's commitment to learning them. Perhaps this field guide can be a stepping stone to learning these more complex volumes.

I gathered information on the distribution of plants in the San Juan Mountains for two field seasons. I believe, the more one looks, the more one finds. The challenge is to keep alert and discover for yourself; you may observe plants or distributions previously unknown.

SCOPE

Area

This field guide covers the San Juan Range and close surrounding foothills. From a floral standpoint the area is bounded on the south and west by the mesa and canyon desert flora, roughly the New Mexico State border and Dolores River Canyon respectively. The north side is rather abruptly defined by the southern extent of the intermountain park flora that begins at the forest edge approximately ten miles south of State Highway 50. The Continental Divide, however, is more subtly defined. North Pass was the chosen boundary as a matter of convenience though quite likely this guide is applicable far beyond that point. The east side is bounded by the San Luis Valley with its high alkaline basin flora. See map, pp. 2-3

Content

I have chosen to cover conspicuous flowering plants, those with notable flowers, large size, uniqueness of form or those found in abundance. All trees, shrubs, ferns and common grasses are included as well. The vast majority of introduced weeds at lower elevations are not included. If one is serious about learning weeds, *Weeds of the West*, a cooperative publication illustrated with photographs, is a useful text.

Medicinal and edible uses of wild plants have not been included in this guide for two reasons. One is the sheer volume (and weight!) that would be added to a guide whose primary purpose is identification in the field. There are plenty of good arm-chair books on the subject. The second and perhaps more significant reason is to avoid encouraging an assault on the flora for food and medicine without having full knowledge of what one is doing. Plants could easily be decimated by uneducated practices. Learning identification is basic to any of these other pursuits. Again, there are books that cover these topics specifically.

THE SAN JUAN FLORA

The San Juan Mountains have very diverse flora due to a complexity of factors influencing plant distribution: rock substrates, moisture, sun and wind exposure, geologic history and others. There is quite a noticeable difference between the eastern and western slopes, delineated by the Continental Divide. As a nearly continuous high ridge and peak area, the Continental Divide forms a barrier that influences weather patterns. Storms predominantly come from the west, dropping most of the moisture they carry on the western slope, a strong factor in its high floral diversity. In contrast, the eastern slope lies in the rain shadow and receives very little moisture, consequently, diversity is lower. Grasslands, requiring very little moisture, predominate on areas too dry or high to support trees on the eastern slope. Shrubs and herbs, requiring more moisture, predominate in most treeless areas on the western slope. In addition to higher moisture levels, western slope floral diversity is also directly related to the wide variety of rock substrates, ranging from sandstone and limestone to those of volcanic origin. The eastern slope has a more consistent rock subtrate of volcanic extrusives. Elevational ranges are greater on the western slope as well.

USING THE FIELD GUIDE

Keys

Keys are used to identify plants. They are dichotomous, composed of opposing statements. Reading the first pair of statements and choosing the one that best fits the plant at hand leads the user to the next pair of opposing statements. This process continues until a name is reached. An example is given in Appendix I p. 225. Maximum benefit of this field guide is derived by using the keys. They develop an understanding of plant relations and the ability to distinguish relative differences. Once this knowledge is gained plant identification becomes much easier.

The keys in this book, based on characteristics visible to the naked eye, are designed for easy field identification. Due to plant variability, a small degree of accuracy may be sacrificed for certain plants. However, these keys apply to the majority of plants encountered. The descriptions and illustrations will help with identification.

A key based only on vegetative characteristics is given for woody plants although those with conspicuous flowers also appear in the regular keys. A key is also provided for non-woody plants with inconspicuous flowers as well.

In this field guide, the Key to Major Groupings (p. 12) delineates the first level of plant relatedness. Through various keys these are separated into families, then genera (singular, genus), and finally species. Many plants could be narrowed further to subspecies. However, most of these distinctions are based on technical characteristics not visible to the naked eye or require in-depth experience to recognize the differences. This endeavor is beyond the intentions of this guide.

Descriptions
Family characteristics are described for families with more than one genus represented. These characteristics are listed in a consistent order for easy review. Genus descriptions should be reviewed along with species descriptions when learning a species. The most distinquishing characteristics or differences are listed first in these descriptions.

A Word on Variability
Try as we may to fit things into neat categories, plants are less inclined to be rigidly defined. Within a given species there will be some variation in form as one travels across its range encountering different populations. Sizes, leaf shapes, and degree of hairiness are characteristics that often vary drastically. Through hybridization, variations in habitat, or any number of influences, the characteristics of members of a species can grade softly into one another from one area to the next. Some species will vary widely in relative close proximity to one another while others differ very little around the world. In the San Juan Mountains, eastern slope plants are generally smaller than western slope plants due to the moisture differences. A range of heights accompanies each species.

Names
A plant's name is given in two parts, the genus followed by the species name. Once a genus name has been given, succeeding species of that genus will be referred to by the first letter of the genus name and then the species name (i.e. Thalictrum sparsiflorum and T. fendleri).

Common names are not stressed in this guide as they are often misleading. For example, several plants may have the same name whether or not they are related. They are often not descriptive and instead contrary and confusing. It is useless to learn them. Learn the botanical names. They are standard and indicate relatedness. When changes have been made in botanical names it is customary to include the previous names (these are given in brackets beside the current name in this guide). Most of them are also descriptive. Learning the meaning of a handful of Latin words can prove to be quite useful. I believe the deterrent to using botanical names is not knowing how to pronounce them. Basically, the botanical names should be pronounced in a manner that is easily discernible to the listener. This can be accomplished with the help of a few guidelines and the given accents. (Note: Accents on family names always fall on the second to the last "a.") The accents are true to Latin except when surnames or stem words are involved. In these cases surnames and stem words are kept intact for easier interpretation. Names based on surnames are pronounced like the surnames. Otherwise, all vowels are pronounced separately except for the combinations given below. Guidelines are also given for a few consonants.

ae	e as in *meet*
au	aw as in *awe*
ei	ei as in *height*
eu	u as in *flute*
ii	e as in *meet* (may be pronounced twice)
oe	e as in *meet* (except *Boechera* is based on a Danish surname and therefore is pronounced as book-er-a)
oi	oy as in *toy* (or may be pronounced separately with the i long, as in hide)
ua	in some cases ua as in *aquatic*
ui	ui as in *ruin*
y	most often pronounced i as in *pit*
c	c as in *car* when preceding a, o or u
	c as in *center* when preceding e, i, or y
ch	k as in *kite*
g	g as in *game* when preceding a, o or u
	g as in *ginger* when preceding e, i or y

Symbols and Abbreviations
East and West symbols, **E** and **W** respectively, denote on which side of the Continental Divide the plants are found. An occurrence on either side is inferred when a symbol is lacking.

Family names have a three-letter abbreviation in the keys, such as CCT for Calochortaceae. They also appear in parentheses next to the family names in the text. A list of the abbreviations is given in Appendix II, p. 228

TERMINOLOGY

A pictorial glossary is provided on the inside covers of this book. These terms are very basic to floral taxonomy and save lengthy descriptions in the text.

Relative Abundance
These terms refer to the quantity of a species relative to other species within their shared habitats.

Abundant   found in great numbers, primarily determining the appearance of the landscape

Locally abundant	may be abundant in some locations but not all locations of a certain habitat
Common	found in large numbers but not primarily determining the appearance of the landscape
Uncommon	low in number

Plant Types

Evergreen	leaves are green and functional year-round
Deciduous	leaves are shed for winter
Annual	plants live for only one season; usually have sparse, hair-like roots; often bloom for extended periods
Biennial	plants live for two years; bloom only during the second year
Perennial	plants live for many years; bloom every year
Herbs	stems die back to the ground for winter
Woody	stems do not die back to the ground for winter

Vegetation Zones

Some plants are confined to areas with certain growing conditions whereas others can range over a variety of conditions. The amount of moisture seems to play the most influential role in the distribution of plants. In general, aside from streams, lakes, bogs and the like, the amount of moisture available to plants increases with elevation but is also strongly influenced by sun and wind exposure, depth and type of soil, drainage patterns, and a number of other intricacies. For our purposes, vegetation zones will be equated with moisture zones and defined visually by the dominant tree species (or lack of). The distribution of plants in this book are referred to by their relative zone(s) as follows:

Foothill

| Lower | These areas are dominated by Piñon Pine, Utah Juniper, and sagebrush on the western slope and by grasslands on the eastern slope. |
| Upper | These areas are dominated by scrub oak on the western slope and Piñon Pine on the eastern slope. |

Montane

| Lower | These areas are dominated by a mixture of conifers. On the western slope, the drier areas are dominated by Ponderosa Pine and Rocky Mountain Juniper. The more moist areas, such as drainages, are dominated by a mixture of White Fir, Western White Pine and Douglas Fir. On the eastern slope these areas are dominated by Bristlecone Pines and Limber Pines on harsh south-facing slopes and Douglas Fir on north-facing slopes. |
| Upper | These areas are dominated by aspen. |

| Subalpine | These areas are dominated by Englemann Spruce and Subalpine Fir. |
| Alpine | These are the areas above tree-line. |

Site

Sites or habitat may encompass a number of factors that provide for the flora present. Throughout this guide, basic sites are denoted: cliff, meadow, bog and so on. Soon you will acquire an eye for these and know what to expect to find there. Most are self-explanatory. Those that may need clarification are as follows:

tundra	high alpine with dry, thin soil characterized by low mat or mound plants.
scree	rock slide areas
disturbed	areas changed by human activity

KEY TO MAJOR GROUPINGS

1a.   Woody shrubs or trees with evergreen needles or appressed triangular scales .... **GYMNOSPERMS**, p. 24

1b.   Not as above (2)

2a.   Woody shrubs or trees without evergreen needles or compressed triangular scales ... see **VEGETATIVE KEY TO WOODY PLANTS**, p. 13

2b.   Herbs or may be woody shrubs or trees with conspicuous flowers (3)

3a.   Reproduce by spores on the underside of leaf-like fronds; each frond directly attached to root crown (no main stem); frond axis (stipe) wiry, not juicy or green; plants without a strong odor .... **FERNS**, p. 26

3b.   Not as above (4)

4a.   Stems cylindrical unbranched or with whorled branches; leaves are reduced to whorled united stem sheaths with tiny teeth .... **FERN-RELATED**, p. 33

4b.   Not as above (5)

5a.   Grass, grass-like or plants with flower parts in threes or sixes and with parallel-veined leaves .... **MONOCOTS**, p. 34

5b.   Not grass-like; flowers with parts in fours, fives, or multiples thereof; leaf veins not parallel (6)

6a.   Flowers inconspicuous ... **INCONSPICUOUS-FLOWERED DICOTS**, p. 222

6b.   Flowers conspicuous (7)

7a.   Flowers with petals united to one another (sometimes only near the base) .... **UNITED-PETAL DICOTS**, p. 64

7b.   Flowers with petals separate .... **FREE-PETAL DICOTS**, p. 148

VEGETATIVE KEY TO WOODY PLANTS

(For those with evergreen needles or scales, see GYMNOSPERMS, p. 24.)

1a.	Leaves absent; stems succulent and spiny .... **CAC**, p. 151
1b.	Leaves present (2)
2a.	Leaves minute and overlapping; large shrubs to small trees .... **TAM**, p. 152
2b.	Leaves not as above (3)
3a.	Leaves opposite (but not necessarily the leaflets of compound leaves) (4)
3b.	Leaves alternate (17)
4a.	Vines (5)
4b.	Shrubs or small trees (7)
5a.	Stems climb into trees .... **CLEMATIS**, p. 193
5b.	Stems creep over the ground or sometimes over shrubs (6)
6a.	Leaves and stems rough .... **HUMULUS**, p. 223
6b.	Leaves and stems smooth .... **ATRAGENE**, p. 193
7a.	Small trees (8)
7b.	Shrubs (9)
8a.	Leaves lobed or divided .... **ACER**, p. 16
8b.	Leaves ternately compound .... **NEGUNDO**, p. 16
9a.	Leaves compound .... **SAMBUCUS**, p. 130
9b.	Leaves simple (10)
10a.	Leaves silvery-gray .... **SHEPHERDIA**, p. 16
10b.	Leaves green (11)
11a.	Plants low .... **PAXISTIMA**, p. 18
11b.	Plants tall (12)
12a.	Leaves rather large, elliptic, acute (13)
12b.	Leaves smaller, tip rounded or if acute then linear (15)
13a.	Leaves smooth (14)
13b.	Leaves rough .... **DISTEGIA**, p. 130
14a.	Leaves olive and shiny .... **RHAMNUS**, p. 154
14b.	Leaves not olive nor shiny .... **SWIDA**, p. 154
15a.	Leaves linear .... **FENDLERA**, p. 154
15b.	Leaves broader (16)
16a.	Bark on older stems shredded .... **SYMPHORICARPOS**, p. 132
16b.	Bark not shredded .... **LONICERA**, p. 130

17a.	Leaves compound (18)
17b.	Leaves simple (25)

18a.	Leaves ternate (19)
18b.	Leaves pinnate (20)

19a. Leaflets rather large and shiny; plants low with creeping or erect stems .... TOXICODENDRON, p. 18
19b. Leaflets small; plants tall and many-branched .... RHUS, p. 18

20a. Leaflets spine-tipped .... MAHONIA, p. 154
20b. Leaflets not spine-tipped (21)

21a. Leaflets tiny and crowded appearing palmate PENTAPHYLLOIDES, p. 160
21b. Leaflets not as above (22)

22a. Stems thorny or spiny (23)
22b. Stems not thorny or spiny (24)

23a. Leaves whitish underneath .... RUBUS, p. 160
23b. Leaves not whitish underneath .... ROSA, p. 160

24a. Small trees .... SORBUS, p. 160
24b. Shrubs .... RHUS, p. 18

25a. Leaves silvery-gray (26)
25b. Leaves green (27)

26a. Small trees .... ELAEAGNUS, p. 16
26b. Shrubs with sage odor .... SERIPHIDIUM, p. 91

27a. Leaves lobed (28)
27b. Leaves not lobed (32)

28a. Leaves pinnately lobed .... QUERCUS, p. 18
28b. Leaves palmately or ternately lobed (29)

29a. Leaves palmately lobed (30)
29b. Leaves ternately lobed (31)

30a. Leaves large (nearly the size of your hand) .... RUBACER, p. 160
30b. Leaves smaller .... RIBES, p. 156

31a. Leaves basically ovate to oval in outline .... CRATAEGUS, p. 160
31b. Leaves wedge-shaped, lobed at apex .... PURSHIA, p. 162

32a. Stems with spines or thorns (33)
32b. Stems without spines or thorns (35)

33a. Large shrubs to small trees .... CRATAEGUS, p. 160
33b. Smaller shrubs (34)

34a.   Stems with many three-parted spines .... **BERBERIS**, p. 154
34b.   Stems with few single spines .... **CEANOTHUS**, p. 154

35a.   Leaves coarsely toothed to finely serrate (36)
35b.   Leaves entire (46)

36a.   Large trees .... **POPULUS**, p. 18
36b.   Small trees to shrubs (37)

37a.   Leaves coarsely toothed (38)
37b.   Leaves finely toothed or serrate (40)

38a.   Leaves elliptic; cones persistent .... **ALNUS**, p. 22
38b.   Leaves broader; not as above (39)

39a.   Bark dark and shiny with white specks .... **BETULA**, p. 22
39b.   Bark not as above .... **CRATAEGUS**, p. 160

40a.   Bark with white marks .... **PADUS**, p. 160
40b.   Bark not as above (41)

41a.   Teeth mostly above the middle on leaf edge (42)
41b.   Teeth along entire leaf edge (43)

42a.   Leaves blunt at tip, thin, dark green .... **AMELANCHIER**, p. 164
42b.   Leaves not as above .... **CERCOCARPUS**, p. 162

43a.   Leaves small (44)
43b.   Leaves larger, elliptic (45)

44a.   Leaves round; twigs with wart-like bumps .... **BETULA**, p. 22
44b.   Leaves elliptic; older stems with peeling bark .... **HOLODISCUS**, p. 162

45a.   Trees; bark rough .... **ULMUS**, p. 24
45b.   Shrubs; bark smooth .... **SALIX**, p. 20

46a.   Leaves dark green and shiny; low growing ...... **ARCTOSTAPHYLOS**, p. 132
46b.   Not as above (47)

47a.   Leaves linear, tiny (48)
47b.   Leaves broader (52)

48a.   Leaves gray or fuzzy below (49)
48b.   Leaves some shade of green (50)

49a.   Leaves fuzzy below .... **ERIOGONUM**, p. 219
49b.   Leaves grayish .... **TETRADYMIA**, p. 91

50a.   Tall shrubs; stems with a white film .... **CHRYSOTHAMNUS**, p. 91
50b.   Low shrubs; stems without a white film (51)

ACERACEAE (ACE)   **Maple Family**
Small trees. Leaves are opposite, simple or palmate to pinnate. Flowers with petals inconspicuous or absent. Sepals four to five or more. Fruits are two, united, winged seeds.

Ácer glábrum .... Rocky Mountain Maple, 6-30', see no. 1
Form many-stemmed clumps. Leaves three to five-lobed or three-parted. Late in the season the leaves develop crusty, bright red patches (caused by a mite). Leaves turn yellow in autumn. Young twigs are dark red. Common in moist, shady, montane forests.

Negúndo aceroídes [*Acer negundo*] .... Box Elder, 10-25', see no. 2
Form many-stemmed clumps. Leaves ternate; leaflets are long-pointed. In spring, pendulous tufts of stamens are obvious, soon followed by clumps of winged seeds. Leaves turn yellow in autumn. Abundant in the lower valleys along rivers and streams.

ELAEAGNACEAE (ELE)   **Oleaster Family**
Shrubs or trees. Leaves silvery or scaly; alternate or opposite, simple and entire. Flowers lack petals; axillary. Fruits are drupe-like.

Shephérdia .... Buffaloberry
Shrubs that bear either pollen producing flowers or seed producing flowers.
1a.   Tall shrubs abundant along rivers and ditches of the lower valleys. Leaves
         opposite; silvery, oblong-elliptic. Branches thorny. Fruit gold to
         scarlet. .... *S. argéntea*, 6-12' or more, **W**, see no. 3
1b.   Medium height shrubs found in dry, rocky, montane and subalpine
         forests throughout the range. Leaves opposite; large and elliptic;
         leathery; rust-colored dots on the undersides. Fruits orange-red.
         .... *S. canadénsis*, 3-5', see no. 4

Elaeágnus angustifólia .... Russian-Olive, 10-20', **W**
Small trees that have escaped from cultivation along the lower valleys. Branches thorny. Leaves are silvery; alternate; variable in size and shape. Flowers are extremely fragrant in spring. Fruit is relished by birds; silvery.

1: *Acer glabrum*

2: *Negundo aceroides*

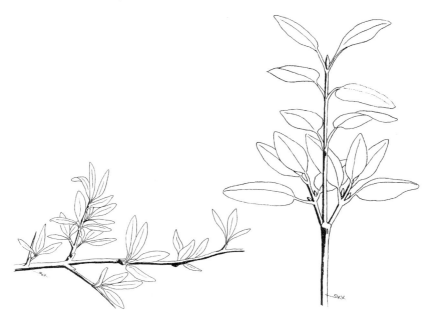

3: *Shepherdia argentea*

4: *Shepherdia canadensis*

CELASTRACEAE (CEL)   **Staff-tree Family**

Paxístima myrsinítes .... Mountainlover, 8-20", see no. 5
Low shrubs with branches arching or ascending. Leaves are shiny, dark green; opposite; elliptic to lanceolate and finely toothed. Flowers small and inconspicuous with four to five petals and sepals. Fruits are capsules. Common to abundant in shady, montane forests; sometimes in open areas of montane and subalpine.

ANACARDIACEAE (ANA)   **Sumac Family**
Shrubs or vine-like. Leaves alternate, pinnate, or trifoliate. Flowers very small in axillary or terminal panicles. Fruits are dry drupes.

Toxicodéndron rýdbergii .... Poison Ivy, 4-36", see no. 6
Stems single and erect or vine-like, trailing over the ground and low vegetation. Leaves shiny, dark green, turning scarlet in autumn; trifoliate. Flowers are inconspicuous in axillary clusters; yellow-white. Fruit whitish. Often abundant in rocky, moist areas and stream bottoms of foothills and lower montane.

Rhús .... Sumac
1a.   Leaves small; trifoliate; turn brilliant orange to red in autumn. Shrubs
           dense and rounded; pungent odor. Flowers tiny and inconspicuous
           in tight clusters; yellowish; blooms before leafing in spring. Fruits red
           and sticky when fresh. Common in rocky foothills and dry, open
           montane. .... *R. aromática* [R. trilobata], Skunkbush, Three-leaf
           Sumac, 3-6', see no. 7
1b.   Leaves large; pinnate; scarlet autumn color. Spread by underground
           rootstalks forming often large, loose patches. Flowers small,
           arranged in dense terminal clusters; greenish. Locally common on
           steep, rocky slopes and embankments of lower montane; mostly on
           the western slope. .... *R. glábra*, Smooth Sumac, 1-3' or more, see no. 8

FAGACEAE (FAG)   **Oak Family**

Quércus gámbelii .... Scrub Oak, 3-25', see no. 9
Form brushy thickets or occasionally very old, magnificent trees. Leaves are alternate, simple and lobed; size and shape are quite variable. Spread by underground roots so that a whole area may be one clone and thus the leaves are all similar. From one area to the next, plants may have very different-looking leaves. Flower parts separate; pollen-bearing parts in pendulous catkins and seed-bearing parts clustered a few together (acorns). Abundant primarily in the upper foothills but also found scattered or in pockets at lower or higher elevations on suitable sites; mostly on the western side of the range.

SALICACEAE (SAL)   **Willow Family**
Trees or shrubs. Leaves alternate and simple. Flowers are catkins, solitary, and axillary among bracts; seed-bearing catkins and pollen-bearing catkins are on different plants. Fruits are capsules that open to release the seeds, attached to cottony hair.

Pópulus
Large deciduous trees.
1a.   Bark thin and smooth (in very old trees the very base is rough and

5: *Paxistima myrsinites*   6: *Toxicodendron rydbergii*

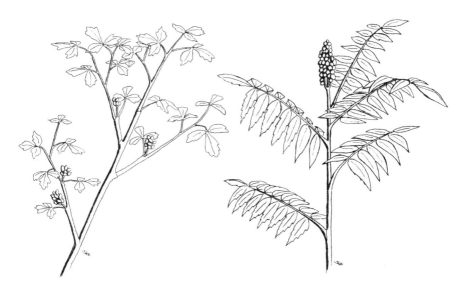

7: *Rhus aromatica*   8: *Rhus glabra*

grooved); white to green or yellow-tinged. Leaves roundish with flattened petioles that cause them to flutter in the slightest breeze; turn brilliant yellow or orange in autumn before dropping. Spread by underground rootstalks forming whole areas of clones. Different clones are often indicated by the different shades of color in autumn. Found primarily in a belt across upper montane, though may be scattered or patchy at lower or higher elevations on suitable sites.
.... *P. tremuloídes*, Aspen, to 90', see no. 10

1b.   Bark thick and deeply-grooved (2)

2a.   Leaves linear-lanceolate; turn yellow to brown in autumn. Crown rather narrow and erect. Found in lower valley bottoms to upper montane drainages.
.... *P. angustifólia*, Narrowleaf Cottonwood, to 60', see no. 11

2b.   Leaves broader (3)

3a.   Leaves triangular; coarsely toothed; turn brilliant yellow in autumn. Crown very broad and spreading. Found in the lower valleys.
.... *P. deltoídes* , Rio Grande Cottonwood, to 90', see no. 12

3b.   Leaves lanceolate. Hybrid of the previous two species, having mixed characteristics. Found where their habitats overlap.
.... *P. x acumináta*, Lance-leaf Cottonwood, to 75'

Sálix .... Willow
Mostly shrubs. This is a large confusing genus. Identification of most species requires noting certain characteristics throughout the entire season. A simplified key is given below.

1a.   Shrubs dwarfed, creeping on the ground; less than 4 inches tall; alpine (2)
1b.   Shrubs taller and erect (3)

2a.   Leaf veins forming a network (most apparent on the underside). Leaves with rounded tips. Plants very small, easily overlooked.
.... *S. reticuláta*, Snow Willow, 1/2-1"

2b.   Leaf veins not forming a network. Leaves mostly acute. Common on tundra. Noticeable. .... *S. árctica*, Rock Willow, 1-4"

3a.   Found away from water, on dry ground; usually montane and subalpine (see also *S. bebbiana* below). Leaves dark green; some hairs on undersides are reddish; obovate to oblanceolate. Blooms before leafing. .... *S. scoúleriana*, Scouler's Willow, 9-12'

3b.   Found near water or on very wet ground (4)

4a.   Leaves linear. Found in wet sand of lower valleys.
.... *S. exígua* [S. interior], Sandbar Willow, 6-12' or more, see no. 13

4b.   Leaves broader (5)

5a.   Stems usually single with a bushy crown. Leaves very thin and strongly veined; obovate. Blooms while leafing. Foothills to subalpine (occasionally away from water).
.... *S. bébbiana*, Bebb Willow, 6-24', see no. 14

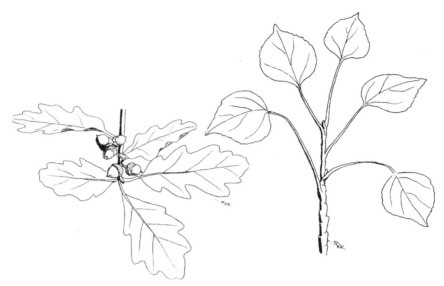

9: *Quercus gambelii*   10: *Populus tremuloides*

11: *Populus angustifolia*   12: *Populus deltoides*

5b.   Stems numerous (6)

6a.   Twigs yellow to orange while blooming, later turning yellow-green.
         Blooms before leafing. Leaves acute and rather narrow. Intricately
         branched. Very common in valley bottoms of montane.
         .... *S. montícola,* Yellow-twigged Willow, 7-15'
6b.   Twigs not as above (7)

7a.   Twigs with blue-white, waxy coating (8)
7b.   Twigs without a blue-white, waxy coating (9)

8a.   Leaves only slightly lighter on undersides. Catkins on short, leafy pedicels.
         Streamsides montane and subalpine.
         .... *S. géyeriana,* Geyer Willow, 7-12'
8b.   Leaves much lighter on undersides. Catkins sessile. Streamsides upper
         montane and subalpine.
         .... *S. drúmmondiana* [S. subcoerulea], Blue Willow, 3-9'

9a.   Catkins sessile. Leaves slightly hairy above and dull; light on undersides.
         Twigs bright chestnut to black. Subalpine bogs (plants less than 3'
         tall) and stream bottoms of subalpine (plants much taller).
         .... *S. planifólia,* Planeleaf Willow, 1-9', see no. 15
9b.   Catkins on short stems. Leaves and stems fuzzy when young (10)

10a.   Leaves with some hair when mature. Older stems yellow-brown to gray.
         Form low thickets on lower edge of tundra and taller stands along
         subalpine streams. ..... *S. brachycárpa,* Barrenground Willow, 1 1/2-6'
10b.   Leaves without hair when mature. Older stems red-brown and shiny;
         young twigs yellow to orange. Form thickets in alpine basins.
         .... *S. wólfii,* 1-3'

BETULACEAE (BET)   **Birch Family**
Trees or shrubs. Leaves alternate and simple. Flowers are catkins; seed-bearing catkins
are cone-like and pollen-bearing catkins are elongate and pendulous. Fruits are
nutlets.

Álnus incána ....Alder, 15-30', see no. 16
Small trees. Leaves elliptic and coarsely toothed. Cones persist for years; tiny and dark
brown. Found along streams and rivers from the lower valleys to subalpine.

Bétula .... Birch
Twigs have wart-like bumps.
1a.   Low shrubs found in meandering stream valleys of subalpine. Leaves
         small, round with small even teeth.
         .... *B. glandulósa,* Bog Birch, 3-6', see no. 17
1b.   Small trees in many-stemmed clumps found along rivers of the lower
         valleys. Leaves ovate to oval; coarsely toothed. Bark shiny, dark with
         white marks.
         .... *B. fontinális* [B. occidentalis], River Birch, 15-36', **W**

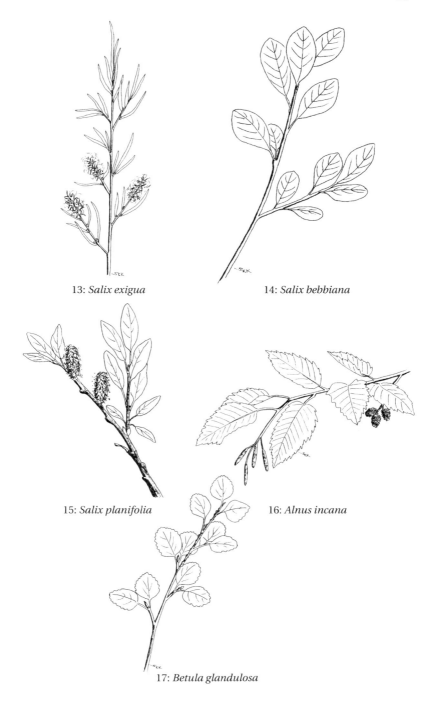

13: *Salix exigua*

14: *Salix bebbiana*

15: *Salix planifolia*

16: *Alnus incana*

17: *Betula glandulosa*

ULMACEAE (ULM)   Elm Family

Ulmus púmila .... Chinese Elm, 20-40'
Introduced, weedy tree. Leaves alternate and simple; elliptic and serrated; blades
unequal at the base. Flowers are inconspicuous. Blooms and produces great
masses of green, round, winged seeds before leafing in the spring. Disturbed areas
of the lower valleys.

GYMNOSPERMS

Trees or shrubs with evergreen needles or appressed triangular scales.

Key to Families

1a.   Plants with needles lighter on the underside or with appressed triangular
        scales; cones berry-like .... CUP p. 24
1b.   Plants with needles the same color on both sides; cones with woody or
        papery scales .... PIN p. 24

CUPRESSACEAE (CUP)   Cypress Family
Shrubs or trees. Leaves are evergreen, either bicolored and needle-like or triangular
and scale-like. Young foliage is entirely different, prickly and needle-like. Seed-bearing
and pollen-bearing flower parts are on different plants. Cones are berry-like.

Juníperus commúnis .... Common Juniper, 12-40"
Sprawling shrub. Leaves are short, needle-like and bicolored (lighter on the undersides); three together at a node. Montane and subalpine.

Sabína [Juniperus]
Trees. Leaves are appressed, blunt, triangular scales. Trunks have bark that peels off in
long, fibrous piecies.
1a.   Leaves thick and tightly clumped; olive-green. Trunks usually single and
        erect but sometimes multiple and spreading. Crown rather rounded
        and broad. Abundant tree of dry lower foothills; codominant with
        Piñon Pine. (2)
1b.   Leaves thinner and looser, generally lacy in appearance; green to blue-
        green. Trunks single, straight. Crown more pointed and narrow.
        Common upper foothill and montane.
        .... *S. scopulórum*, Rocky Mountain Juniper, 15-36'

2a.   Fruit dry and mealy inside.
        .... *S. osteospérma* [J. utahensis], Utah Juniper, 8-18', **W**
2b.   Fruit with liquid resin inside. .... *S. monospérma*, Oneseed Juniper, 8-18', **E**

PINACEAE (PIN)   Pine Family
Resinous trees. Leaves are evergreen needles. Seed-bearing and pollen-bearing flower
parts are separate on the same plant. Seed-bearing parts are conspicuous cones with
woody, papery or fleshy scales. Pollen-bearing parts are rather inconspicuous.

Key to Genera

1a.   Needles bundled several together at base .... **PINUS** p. 25
1b.   Needles not bundled, spread singly along stems (2)

2a.   Needles curved toward the top side of the branch to some degree
     .... **ABIES** p. 26
2b.   Needles point in all directions (3)

3a.   Needles stiff and angular, set on knobs along the twigs .... **PICEA** p. 26
3b.   Needles soft and flat, not set on knobs .... **PSEUDOTSUGA** p. 26

Species

Pínus
Needles are bundled together at the base by a papery sheath. Cones have woody scales.
1a.   Needles bundled two or three together (2)
1b.   Needles bundled five together (4)

2a.   Needles long (4-7 inches); mostly straight. Grow to large outstanding
          trees. Bark thick, of compressed jigsaw puzzle-like segments;
          orangish in older trees. Cones 3 to 4 inches long. Common dry lower
          montane; form magnificent continuous stands of predominantly
          large trees in some areas, such as around Pagosa Springs and north
          of Dolores. .... *P. ponderósa*, Ponderosa Pine, 45-135'
2b.   Needles much shorter and somewhat curved. Cones small (3)

3a.   Trunk many branched. Needles dark green. Abundant; codominating the
          lower foothill zone with "Utah" or "Oneseed" Juniper. Cones 1 to 2
          inches long; seeds are large and provide an important food source
          for birds and other animals. .... *P. édulis*, Piñon Pine, 15-45'
3b.   Trunk straight and unbranched. Needles olive-green. Cones bristly; one
          inch long; remain closed until opened by heat. Form continuous
          stands to the exclusion of all else; even the understory is sparse when
          stands are dense. Montane to subalpine. Naturally occurring near
          Cochetopa Pass, elsewhere used for reseeding old burns such as at
          Molas Pass. .... *P. contórta*, Lodgepole Pine, 60-90'

4a.   Needles short and curved; crowded; dotted with tiny white resin drops.
          Cones bristly; 2 to 3 inches long. Long lived. Dry, harsh, rocky,
          windblown sites of upper montane and subalpine.
          .... *P. aristáta*, Bristlecone Pine, 15-45'
4b.   Needles longer; straight to slightly twisted (5)

5a.   Trunk straight. Found in montane forests.
          .... *P. strobifórmis*, Mexican White Pine, 40-100'
5b.   Trunk branched; not straight. Found on rocky, open sites of montane and
          subalpine. .... *P. fléxilis*, Limber Pine, 30-45'

Ábies
Needles are flat, blunt at the tips, stiff and smooth; all curve upward making the branches appear flat-bottomed. Cones are erect on the upper sides of the branches, near the top of the tree. They break apart rather quickly while still on the tree leaving only the central axis.
1a.   Needles thick and smooth; blue-green (especially new growth). In dry areas the needles are greener and shorter (most on the eastern slope appear this way). Thick bark; grooved on older trees. Large attractive trees in ideal habitats. Moist montane. .... *A. concólor*, White Fir, 60-105'
1b.   Needles thinner; green (2)

2a.   Bark rather thin. Abundant; codominant with Engelmann Spruce in subalpine forests. .... *A. lasiocárpa*, Subalpine Fir, 60-120'
2b.   Bark thick and corky with a checkered appearance. Montane near Wolf Creek Pass. .... *A. arizónica*, Corkbark Fir, 30-60', **W**

Pícea
Needles are diamond-shaped in cross-section. They are set on knobs along the twigs, these persisting after the needles are gone. The pendulous cones are narrow with slender, papery scales.
1a.   Needles prickly sharp-pointed and stiff; usually bluish (especially new growth); pungent odor when crushed. Moist drainages and valleys of montane. .... *P. púngens*, Colorado Blue Spruce, 75-90'
1b.   Needles less stiff and less sharp pointed; green. Abundant; codominant with Subalpine Fir in subalpine forests.
.... *P. éngelmanni*, Engelmann Spruce, 60-120'

Pseudotsúga ménziesii .... Douglas Fir, 60-180'
Needles are very soft and thin, about 1 inch long, straight, bright green and fragrant. Trunks of old trees have thick, furrowed bark. Cones are pendulous and have obvious three-toothed bracts protruding beyond the papery scales. Common montane.

FERNS

This group consists of many families that are represented by only one or two species. It is unnecessary to mention the family names here. Ferns reproduce by spores on the undersides of leaf-like fronds. Each frond is directly attached to the root crown by a stipe (there is not a main stem). Stipes are wiry, not juicy or green. Nearly all of these plants are threatened by collecting.

Key to Genera

1a.   Fronds of two kinds on one plant .... **CRYPTOGRAMMA** p. 27
1b.   Fronds all similar (2)

2a.   Fronds linear, grass-like; may be forked at the tip .... **ASPLENIUM** p. 28
2b.   Fronds not as above (3)

3a.   Fronds pinnately divided or lobed only once (4)
3b.   Fronds divided more than once (6)

4a. Frond divisions with sharp points at the tips .... **POLYSTICHUM** p. 27
4b. Frond divisions rounded at tips (5)

5a. Frond divisions very small and round .... **ASPLENIUM** p. 28
5b. Frond divisions larger and oblong .... **POLYPODIUM** p. 28

6a. Fronds are huge and broadly triangular; form extensive patches
.... **PTERIDIUM** p. 28
6b. Fronds are smaller, or if large, not broadly triangular, nor forming
extensive patches (7)

7a. Frond divisions in a fan shape, these divisions further pinnately divided
.... **ADIANTUM** p. 28
7b. Frond divisions not as above (8)

8a. Fronds large, more than 8 inches long (9)
8b. Fronds smaller, less than 8 inches long (10)

9a. Fronds narrower at the base; papery brown bracts on stems, especially
near the base .... **DRYOPTERIS** p. 28
9b. Fronds broadest at the base; no papery bracts on stems ...... **ATHYRIUM** p. 28

10a. Frond divisions many, very tiny and roundish, arranged in a zig-zag
pattern .... **ARGYROCHOSMA** p. 28
10b. Frond divisions not as above (11)

11a. Fronds rather thick, fuzzy or scaly .... **CHEILANTHES** p. 28
11b. Fronds thin and green (12)

12a. Ultimate frond divisions broadest above the middle; fronds very small
and delicate .... **WOODSIA** p. 31
12b. Ultimate frond divisions broadest below the middle; fronds larger (usually
more than 5 inches long) (13)

13a. Fronds three-times pinnate or simply pinnate and further lobed or
toothed .... **CYSTOPTERIS** p. 31
13b. Fronds bipinnate .... **GYMNOCARPIUM** p. 31

Species

Cryptográmma acrostichoídes .... Rock Brake, 2-12", see no. 18
Fronds are of two types. The spore-bearing type are tallest and have ultimate divisions that are linear. The infertile fronds have ultimate divisions that are rounded and toothed. Plants tufted in often large thick clumps. Rocky areas from montane to alpine.

Polystíchum lonchítis .... Holly Fern, 4-16", see no. 19
Fronds are erect and stiff; pinnately-divided or lobed. The divisions have sharp, holly-like points and are thick, leathery, shiny, and dark green. Uncommon among boulders of subalpine and alpine.

Asplénium
Two very different-looking species.
1a.   Fronds undivided; grass-like; may be forked at the tips. Uncommon on
         montane rock outcrops.
         .... *A. septentrionále*, Grass Fern, 2-8", see no. 20
1b.   Fronds pinnate; divisions tiny and rounded. Tufted. Stems dark. Uncom-
         mon on montane rock outcrops.
         .... *A. trichománes*, Maidenhair Spleenwort, 2-9", see no. 21

Polypódium .... Polypody
Fronds are pinnately-divided or lobed with the divisions oblong and rounded at the
tips. Montane rocks and cliffs.
1a.   Fronds nearly an even width the entire length.
         .... *P. saximontánum*, 3-10", see no. 22
1b.   Fronds wider at the base. .... *P. hésperium*, 3-10", **W**, see no. 23

Pterídium aquilínum .... Bracken, 1-7'
Large coarse plants. Fronds are triangular in shape and three-times pinnate. Plants
spread by underground rootstalks forming extensive patches. Turn rust-colored in
autumn after frost. Abundant in dry montane forests.

Adiántum pedátum .... Maidenhair, 3-24", **W**, see no. 24
Fronds are divided into finger-like sections arranged in a fan-shape. Plants are scattered along creeping rootstalks. Uncommon in lush subalpine forests.

Dryoptéris fílix-más .... Male Fern, 9-40", **W**, see no. 25
Fronds are twice pinnate, narrower at the base; several to many together. Stipes have
pale, rust-colored, papery bracts at the base becoming more hair-like further up.
Rather uncommon in moist shady areas of montane canyons.

Athýrium fílix-fémina .... Lady Fern, 10-48"
Fronds are two to three-times pinnate and oblong-lanceolate. Plants with several
fronds together. Similar in appearance to Dryopteris but lacks the papery bracts on the
stipe. Uncommon in montane woodlands and brush thickets.

Argyrochósma féndleri [Notholaena] .... Cloakfern, 2-10", see no. 26
Fronds have very tiny, roundish divisions arranged in a zig-zag pattern. Plants form
thick clumps in rock crevices of dry foothills areas.

Cheilánthes .... Lip Fern
Frond divisions are rather thick-textured.
1a.   Fronds with white, fuzzy hairs on top making them dull, gray-green;
         undersides with red-brown hairs. Stems dark and shiny. Tufted. Dry
         cliffs and overhangs of foothills and lower montane.
         .... *C. feéi*, Slender Lipfern, 2-8", **W**, see no. 27
1b.   Fronds without hair; undersides scaly. Fronds scattered or sparsely tufted.
         Granite cliffs. .... *C. féndleri*, 3-8", **W**

18: *Cryptogramma acrostichoides*

19: *Polystichum lonchitis*

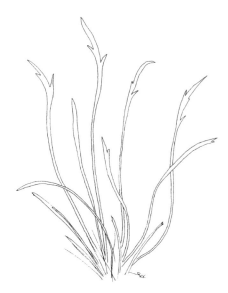

20: *Asplenium septentrionale*

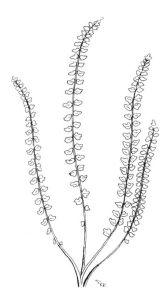

21: *Asplenium trichomanes*

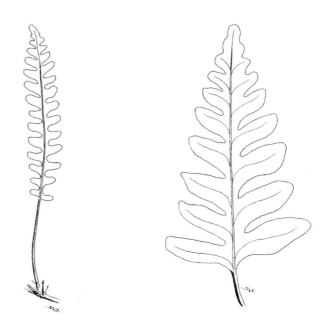

22: *Polypodium saximontanum*   23: *Polypodium hesperium*

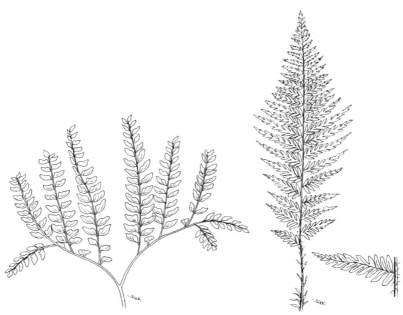

24: *Adiantum pedatum*   25: *Dryopteris filix-mas*

26: *Argyrochosma fendleri*   27: *Cheilanthes feei*

Woódsia

1a. Fronds hairy. Stems with papery bracts at base. Form thick clumps. Shady
     canyons. .... *W. scopulína*, 3-12"
1b. Fronds not hairy; twice pinnately divided, segments toothed. Stems lack
     papery bracts at base; straw-colored. Tufted. Found in cracks in
     rocks of montane and subalpine (2)

2a. Stems dark at base. .... *W. oregána*, 2-10", see no. 28
2b. Stems brown at base. .... *W. mexicána*, 2-10"

Cystoptéris .... Brittlefern
1a. Fronds triangular; scattered along creeping rootstalks. Rocky soil in moist
     subalpine forests. .... *C. montána*, 4-16", **W**
1b. Fronds not triangular; bipinnate to three-times pinnate (2)

2a. Fronds three to four times as long as wide. Lower stems red-brown to
     darker. Tufted. Most common fern from montane to alpine.
     .... *C. frágilis*, 6-12", see no. 29
2b. Fronds about two times as long as wide. Lower stems straw-colored.
     Mostly on rocks of montane. .... *C. ténuis*, 2-8"

Gymnocárpium dryoptéris [Phegopteris] .... Oak Fern, 3-20", see no. 30
Fronds triangular; bipinnate. Plants spread out along creeping rootstalks. Found in
shady, moist areas of montane and subalpine.

28: *Woodsia oregana*

29: *Cystopteris fragilis*

30: *Gymnocarpium dryopteris*

31: *Equisetum arvense*

FERN-RELATED

EQUISETACEAE   **Horsetail Family**
Stems are unbranched or have whorled branches. Leaves are reduced to whorled, united bracts that form toothed sheaths around the stems. Reproduce by spores from terminal flower cones.

Equisétum .... Horsetail
Plants bright green. Stems have whorled branches that are linear to thread-like.
1a.   Branches ascending; four-angled. Common in wet areas of the lower
                   valleys to subalpine. .... *E. arvénse*, 4-20", see no. 31
1b.   Branches spreading horizontal or curving downward; three-angled. Less
                   common in wet areas of subalpine forests or moist montane
                   drainages. .... *E. praténse*, 4-12", see no. 32

Hippochaéte [Equisetum] .... Scouring-Rush
Plants deep green. Stems are unbranched, jointed, hollow, and vertically grooved.
1a.   Stems slender with five to twelve grooves. Sandbars. .... *H. variegáta*, 6-20"
1b.   Stems robust with sixteen to forty-eight grooves (2)

2a.   Stem joints with a dark band at the base. Flower cone pointed at the apex.
                   Common wet areas of lower valleys to montane.
                   .... *H. hyemális*, 20-40", see no. 33
2b.   Stem joints without a dark band at the base. Flower cone rounded at the
                   apex. Less common in wet areas from lower valleys to subalpine.
                   .... *H. laevigáta*, 8-40", see no. 34

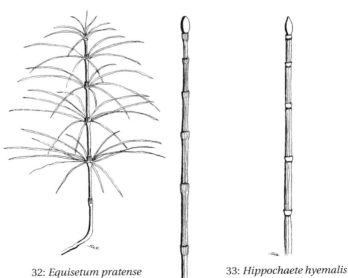

32: *Equisetum pratense*   33: *Hippochaete hyemalis*

34: *Hippochaete laevigata*

MONOCOTS

Plants grass-like or with flower parts in threes or sixes and with leaf veins parallel.

Key to Families

1a.	Leaves grass-like and fibrous (2)
1b.	Leaves not grass-like or if appearing so, then not fibrous (4)

2a.	Stems round in cross-section; leaves present, though may be small (3)
2b.	Stems usually triangular in cross-section or if round then lack leaves .... **CYP** p. 35

3a.	Stems jointed .... **POA** p. 35
3b.	Stems not jointed .... **JUN** p. 34

4a.	Plants large and stout; inhabit marsh or pond edge; flower clusters are brown, tight cylinders .... **TYP** p. 54
4b.	Plants not as above (5)

5a.	Flowers irregular .... **ORC** p. 55
5b.	Flowers regular (6)

6a.	Petals and sepals differentiated .... **CCT** p. 56
6b.	Petals and sepals look alike (7)

7a.	Leaves thick, rigid, and sharp pointed; flowers large, bell-shaped, white, in large terminal clusters .... **AGA** p. 56
7b.	Not as above (8)

8a.	Flowers blue-purple; leaves flat and sword-like .... **IRI** p. 56
8b.	Flowers not blue-purple (9)

9a.	Plants with leaves very large, cupped and pleated or narrow and grass-like; flowers in racemes, white .... **MLN** p. 58
9b.	Plants not as above (10)

10a.	Plants with leaves grass-like and fleshy; onion odor; flowers in umbels .... **ALL** p. 60
10b.	Plants not as above (11)

11a.	Leaves all basal or flowers very large and orange .... **LIL** p. 60
11b.	Leaves on stems; flowers not very large and orange (12)

12a.	Flowers bell-shaped (though petals reflexed backward), single or few .... **UVU** p. 62
12b.	Flowers star-shaped, many .... **CVL** p. 62

JUNCACEAE (JUN)   **Rush Family**
Plants grass-like in appearance. Stems round in cross-section and not jointed.

Flower clusters are small and sessile or panicled with three petals and sepals that appear as brownish scales. Many of the species have a bract that appears to be the continuation of the stem beyond the flowers. There are two genera: *Júncus* lacks hair and *Lúzula* has a few hairs on the leaves. There are many species of *Júncus* (see no. 35), all quite similar in appearance. Most are dark green and often indicate very moist areas. There are several species of *Lúzula*, the most conspicuous being *L. parviflóra* (see no. 36) with wide leaves and nodding panicles, common in moist montane and subalpine forests.

CYPERACEAE (CYP)   Sedge Family
Plants are grass-like in appearance. Stems usually triangular in cross-section and not hollow. Leaves often taper to a narrow point at the tip that is withered and dried. Flowers are tightly clustered in spikes, these vary from narrow to globose. Spikes single or several together either sessile or pediceled in tight terminal clusters or in more loose racemes or flower spikes. There are a number of genera and numerous species. Genera that are most encountered in the mountains are *Cárex* (see no. 37) and *Eleocháris* (see no. 38). One can learn to distinquish these quite easily; separating them into species, however, takes a commitment that is beyond the intentions of this guide.

POACEAE [Gramineae] (POA)   Grass Family
Leaves are linear; flat, folded or rolled longitudinally; fibrous. Stems are jointed. Flowers are in tiny, tight clusters (spikelets). Each spikelet consists of two outer bracts (glumes) and one or more flowers within (see glossary). Spikelets are variously arranged.

Key to Groups

1a.	Spikelets grouped together among fuzzy, white hairs	GROUP I p. 35
1b.	Spikelets not as above (2)	

2a.	One flower within glumes	GROUP II p. 37
2b.	More than one flower within glumes (3)	

3a.	Spikelets all attached to one side of the stem and sessile or with very short pedicels	GROUP III p. 43
3b.	Spikelets not as above (4)	

4a.	Spikelets sessile on alternate sides of a flattened stem	GROUP IV p. 44
4b.	Spikelets variously arranged (5)	

5a.	Glumes as long or longer than the lowest flower in the spikelet	GROUP V p. 46
5b.	Glumes shorter than lowest flower	GROUP VI p. 48

GROUP I - Spikelets grouped together among fuzzy, white hairs

Hilária jámesii .... Galleta, 6-24", **W**, see no. 39
Spikelets are clustered in groups set in conspicuous white hairs. Flower spikes narrow. Leaves curled. Nodes of the stems have tufts of white hairs. The stems zig-zag among the flowers, evident when the stems persist after flowers have dropped. Spread by underground rootstalks often forming large patches. Common in dry, rocky areas of the lower foothills.

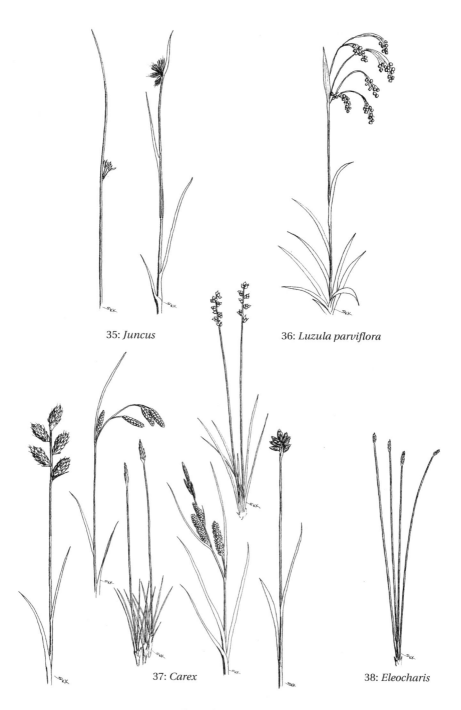

35: *Juncus*

36: *Luzula parviflora*

37: *Carex*

38: *Eleocharis*

GROUP II - Spikelets one-flowered

Key to Genera

1a.   Plants tall with tight cylindrical spikes or shorter subalpine plants with
        more elliptical spikes .... PHLEUM p. 37
1b.   Plants not as above (2)

2a.   Awns long and three-parted .... ARISTIDA p. 39
2b.   Awns lacking or not as above (3)

3a.   Plants rather sprawling; panicle many-branched; flowers numerous, tiny,
        elliptic .... SPOROBOLUS p. 39
3b.   Not as above (4)

4a.   Flowers with hard points at the base (pull out of glumes to see) (5)
4b.   Flowers not as above (6)

5a.   Points very sharp (can puncture skin); awns long and stout on large,
        narrow flowers or awns short on small, broad flowers that are in
        spreading, branched panicles .... STIPA p. 39
5b.   Points less sharp; awns shorter and delicate; panicles narrow and sparse
        .... ORYZOPSIS p. 39

6a.   Dry sites (7)
6b.   Moist sites (8)

7a.   Spikelets in open and diffuse panicle; many, tiny, elliptic; no awns
        .... BLEPHARONEURON p. 39
7b.   Spikelets in interrupted spikes to narrow panicles; if more open, then
        spikelets awned .... MUHLENBERGIA p. 39

8a.   Base of each flower with tufts of hair (pull flower out to see)
        .... CALAMAGROSTIS p. 41
8b.   Base of flowers without hair (9)

9a.   Leaves broad (up to 1/2 inch or more) .... CINNA p. 41
9b.   Leaves narrower .... AGROSTIS p. 41

Species

Phléum .... Timothy
Plants tufted. Flower spikes dense.
1a.   Tall grass with narrow, tight, cylindrical flower spikes. Introduced as a
        pasture grass from Eurasia. Escaped to roadsides and fields. Also
        used in reseeding disturbed areas in the mountains.
        .... *P. praténse*, 16-36", see no. 40
1b.   Shorter grass with short, elliptical flower spikes. Common native of
        subalpine meadows. .... *P. commutátum* [P. alpinum], 8-24"

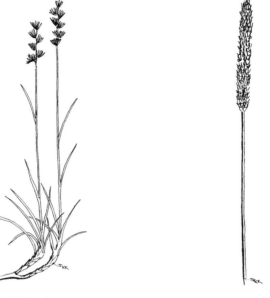

39: *Hilaria jamesii*

40: *Phleum pratense*

41: *Aristida purpurea*

42: *Sporobolus cryptandrus*

Arístida purpúrea [A. fendleriana and A. longiseta] .... Purple Three Awn, 6-12", see no. 41
Flowers have three-parted awns. Panicles are diffuse and few-flowered. Form varies from tight tufts of narrow, curled leaves to a much looser arrangement of straight leaves. Common in dry areas of foothills.

Sporobólus cryptándrus .... Sand Dropseed, 8-32", see no. 42
Plants mostly sprawling; tufted. Panicles are partially wrapped within the stem leaves; emerging somewhat at maturity; many branched. Spikelets tiny and elliptic. Leaf nodes are hairy. Common in dry grasslands and along roads of the foothills.

Stípa .... Needlegrass
Plants tufted. Flowers with very sharp, hard points at the base; awned. Panicles rather few-flowered. Base of panicle often still partially enclosed in leaves.

1a.   Awns 3 to 6 inches long. Abundant foothill and montane grasslands.
        .... *S. comáta*, 12-30", see no. 43
1b.   Awns about 1 inch long or less (2)

2a.   Awns very short. Flowers short and broad in an open, diffuse arrangement; dry to light blond. Seeds dark and round with fuzzy tufts of hair at the base. Plants densely tufted. Form varies due to hybridization with the other species. Open, dry sites of foothills and montane, especially sandy soil.
        .... *S. hymenoídes* [Oryzopsis], Indian Ricegrass, 8-24", see no. 44
2b.   Awns longer. Flowers long and narrow (3)

3a.   Base of leaf blade hairy. Foothill and montane roadsides and dry disturbed ground. .... *S. virídula*, 20-40"
3b.   Base of leaf blade not hairy (4)

4a.   Leaves tightly rolled. Very dry ground of montane forests.
        .... *S. léttermanii*, 12-24"
4b.   Leaves not tightly rolled. Dry montane forests.
        .... *S. nélsonii* [S. columbiana], 12-32"

Oryzópsis .... Ricegrass
Plants with sparse, narrow panicles. Flowers have short, weak awns.

1a.   Loosely tufted with few, wide, sprawling to erect leaves. Stems prostrate. Shady montane woods. .... *O. asperifólia*, 8-28"
1b.   Densely tufted. Stems erect. Shady rocky slopes of foothills and montane.
        .... *O. micrántha*, 6-28", see no. 45

Blepharoneúron tricholépis .... Hairy Dropseed, 8-24", see no. 46
Panicles diffuse and delicately-branched. Spikelets dark gray-green when fresh. Flowers have fuzzy veins (seen best with a hand lens). Plants tufted. Undisturbed, dry, rocky, open montane woods and meadows.

Muhlenbérgia .... Muhly
The species vary widely in appearance.

1a.   Leaves less than 2 inches long (2)
1b.   Leaves more than 2 inches long (3)

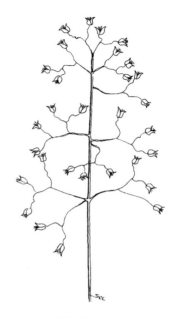

43: *Stipa comata*

44: *Stipa hymenoides*

45: *Oryzopsis micrantha*

46: *Blepharoneuron tricholepis*

2a. Plants spread by underground rootstalks forming mats. Panicle narrow and interrupted or spike-like. Common on rock ledges and gravelly areas of foothills and montane. .... *M. ríchardsonis*, Mat Muhly, 2-20"

2b. Plants tufted, though in rather broad, low, mat-like clumps with the center dying out leaving a ring-like form. Panicle very slender and spike-like. Dry gravelly montane parks and meadows. .... *M. filimicúlmis* , Slimstem Muhly, 4-12", **E**

3a. Leaves flat. Plants spread by underground rootstalks. Panicle spike-like. Rocky areas among sagebrush to upper montane. .... *M. racemósa*, 16-32", see no. 47

3b. Leaves folded or rolled. Plants tufted (4)

4a. Panicles narrow and loose. Delicate awns. Common undisturbed, dry, open, montane forests and meadows. .... *M. montána*, Mountain Muhly, 12-24", see no. 48

4b. Panicles spike-like; interrupted. Densely tufted. Common sandstone ledges. .... *M. wríghtii*, Spike Muhly, 10-20", **W**, see no. 49

Calamagróstis ....Reedgrass
Plants tufted and spreading by underground rootstalks. Flowers have tufts of hair at the base.

1a. Panicles loose and open. Leaves lax. Common wet areas, pond borders montane to subalpine. .... *C. canadénsis*, Bluejoint, 20-40", see no. 50

1b. Panicles narrower. Leaves stiff. Found among willows in wet areas of subalpine. .... *C. strícta* [C. inexpansa and neglecta], 12-40"

Cínna latifólia .... Drooping Woodreed, 12-36"
Plants with single stems or a few together. Leaves broad, up to 1/2 inch or more wide. Panicle lax to drooping. Found in wet woodlands from montane to subalpine.

Agróstis .... Bentgrass
Plants with delicate panicles, the branches very long and slender and spikelets very small.

1a. Leaves 1/4 to 3/8 inch wide. Spreads by underground rootstalks. Cultivated for pasture. Escaped along ditches. .... *A. gigantéa* [A. alba], Redtop, 12-40"

1b. Leaves narrower (2)

2a. Plants spread by above-ground runners. Streamsides of foothills and montane. .... *A. stolonífera* [A. palustris], Creeping Bent, 8-20"

2b. Plants tufted (3)

3a. Panicle branches widely spreading, very delicate and forked above the middle. Various sites from foothills to subalpine. .... *A. scábra*, Redtop, 8-24", see no. 51

3b. Panicle branches less spreading, less delicate and forked near the middle. Meadows of subalpine. .... *A. idahoénsis*, Idaho Redtop, 4-12"

42

47: *Muhlenbergia racemosa*

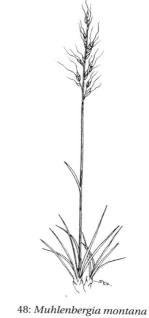

48: *Muhlenbergia montana*

49: *Muhlenbergia wrightii*

50: *Calamagrostis canadensis*

GROUP III - Spikelets sessile or short-pediceled along one side of stem

Species

Boutelaúa curtipéndula .... Side-oats Grama, 10-32", **W**, see no. 52
Spikelets are delicate and pendulous on short pedicels along one side of the stem. Leaves often curled in thick, low tufts. Spread by underground rootstalks. Common in dry, rocky, open areas of the lower foothills.

Chondrósum grácile [Bouteloua gracilis] .... Blue Grama, 6-24", see no. 53
Spikelets sessile in tight comb-like spikes that curl with age and persist. Leaves are curled in thick, low tufts. Common in rocky soil of dry, lower foothills.

Dáctylis glomeráta .... Orchardgrass, 20-40", see no. 54
Densely tufted, large grass. Spikelets clumped in groups on one side of the stem branches of the panicle. Introduced from Eurasia as a pasture grass. Escaped cultivation and now spread along ditches.

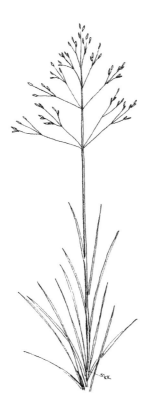

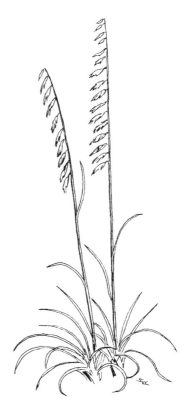

51: *Agrostis scabra*   52: *Bouteloua curtipendula*

GROUP IV - Spikelets sessile on alternate sides of flattened stems

Key to Genera

1a.   Stems weak; weeds of moist disturbed ground .... CRITESION p. 44
1b.   Stems wiry and stout or not on moist disturbed ground (2)

2a.   Plants tufted (3)
2b.   Plants spread by underground rootstalks forming patches of sparse, evenly-spaced plants (5)

3a.   Flowers stacked tightly in wide, lanceolate to oblong spikes
.... AGROPYRON p. 44
3b.   Flowers more loosely arranged or in narrower spikes (4)

4a.   Glumes square at tip .... LOPHOPYRUM p. 44
4b.   Glumes pointed at tip .... ELYMUS p. 44

5a.   Glumes taper from base to tip; leaves bluish, sharp-pointed, rough; dry ground of foothills .... PASCOPYRUM p. 46
5b.   Not as above .... ELYTRIGIA p. 46

Species

Critésion [Hordeum]
Plants tufted with rather weak stems.
1a.   Spikes erect, narrow and compact with short awns. Introduced weed of fields in the lower valleys.
.... *C. brachyanthérum*, Meadow Barley, 4-24", see no. 55
1b.   Spikes nodding, plumed with long awns; attractive when fresh but upon drying the barbed awns become a nuisance, lodging in clothing and fur. Abundant in moist fields, pastures and along ditches.
.... *C. jubátum*, Foxtail, 8-28", see no. 56

Agropýron cristátum [A. desertorum] .... Crested Wheatgrass, 14-40"
Introduced for revegetating rangeland. Plants densely tufted. Spikes are broad, lanceolate to oblong, the spikelets with a neatly stacked appearance; short awned.

Lophopýrum elongátum .... Tall Wheatgrass, 20-40"
Introduced for revegetating rangeland. Plants tufted. Spikes are narrow. Glumes square-tipped.

Élymus .... Wild Rye
Plants tufted.
1a.   Spikelets one per node. Spikes narrow. Along roads and in meadows throughout the mountains. .... *E. trachycaúlus* [Agropyron], 16-40"
1b.   Spikelets more than one per node. Spikes rather broad (2)
2a.   Awns one to two times the length of flowers and rather erect. Aspen woodlands. .... *E. glaúcus* Blue Wild Rye, 16-40", see no. 57
2b.   Awns much longer and widely spreading (3)

53: *Chondrosum gracile*

54: *Dactylis glomerata*

55: *Critesion brachyantherum*

56: *Critesion jubatum*

3a. Glumes narrow, extending into long spreading awns. Common meadows and open woods of foothills and montane. Several species of which the most abundant is .... *E. elymoídes* [Sitanion hystrix], Squirreltail, 4-20 ", see no. 58

3b. Glumes not as such (4)

4a. Spikes 4 to 10 inches; nodding. Large grasses along fencerows in the lower valleys. .... *E. canadénsis*, Canada Wildrye, 2-5'

4b. Spikes smaller; erect or nodding. Stems decumbent. Smaller grasses of dry tundra. .... *E. scríbneri* [Agropyron], 8-20", see no. 59

Pascopýrum smíthii [Agropyron] .... Western Wheatgrass, 12-32", see no. 60 Spread by underground rootstalks forming large patches of evenly and rather sparsely distributed few-stemmed plants. Leaves are stiff, rough, sharp-pointed and usually bluish-colored. Locally abundant in dry foothills.

Elytrígia [Agropyron]
Plants spread by underground rootstalks. Spikes narrow.

1a. Glumes blunt or rounded. Introduced for revegetating disturbed ground. .... *E. intermédia*, Intermediate Wheatgrass, 12-30"

1b. Glumes pointed (2)

2a. Introduced weed of fields. .... *E. répens*, Quackgrass, 12-40"

2b. Native grasses of mountains. Awns short or absent, except for a subspecies that has long spreading awns and is found on rocky slopes. Common along roads and trails. .... *E. dasystáchya*, Thickspike Wheatgrass, 6-36"

GROUP V - Glumes as long or longer than lowest flower in spikelet

Key to Genera

1a. Spikelets large (3/4 inch) .... DANTHONIA p. 48
1b. Spikelets smaller (2)

2a. Spikelets in dense spike-like panicles, pearly sheen (3)
2b. Spikelets in loose panicles, very shiny (4)
3a. Spikelets with delicate awns .... TRISETUM p. 48
3b. Spikelets without awns .... KOELERIA p. 48

4a. Spikelets rather broad and few, arranged in pyramid-shaped panicles; leaves fragrant .... HIEROCHLOE p. 48
4b. Spikelets narrower and numerous, arranged in nodding to spreading panicles (5)
5a. Leaves flat; glumes longer than flowers .... VAHLODEA p. 48
5b. Leaves folded; glumes shorter than flowers .... DESCHAMPSIA p. 48

57: *Elymus glaucus*

58: *Elymus elymoides*

59: *Elymus scribneri*

60: *Pascopyrum smithii*

Species

Danthónia .... Oatgrass
Plants tufted. Panicles rather few flowered. Spikelets rather large with bent and twisted awns protruding.

1a.   Spikelets nearly 3/4 inch long. Plants in large tufts with stout enameled bases. Leaf tips narrowed, dry and curled. Common in dry meadows of upper montane and subalpine. .... *D. párryi*, 8-24", E

1b.   Spikelets smaller. Plants less robust. Found in rather dry meadows from montane to alpine. .... *D. intermédia*, 4-20", see no. 61

Trisétum spicátum .... Spike Trisetum, 4-20", see no. 62
Plants are quite variable with several subspecies; tufted. Spike-like panicles vary from quite dense to interrupted and sparse. Awns are very delicate and bent outward giving the appearance of hairs. Spikelets green to purplish with a pearly sheen. Common throughout mountain meadows and forest openings to alpine.

Koeléria macrántha [K. cristata] .... Junegrass, 6-24", see no. 63
Panicles are green, lustrous and open during flowering. Afterwards they close up to a spike-like form and dry to a tawny color. No awns. Plants tufted. Common in meadows and forest openings foothills to subalpine.

Hierochlóe hírta [H. odorata] .... Sweetgrass, 8-24", see no. 64
Panicles diffuse and few-flowered. Spikelets are very shiny, brown and broad, without awns. Foliage has a sweet, vanilla fragrance. Plants spread by underground rootstalks, forming patches. Locally common in wet meadows from lower valleys to timberline.

Váhlodea atropurpúrea [Deschampsia] .... Mountain Hairgrass, 16-32"
Panicles open and diffuse. Spikelets are small, dark purple and shiny with short delicate awns protruding. Glumes are longer than flowers. Leaves flat. Plants loosely tufted. Subalpine meadows and open cliff areas.

Deschámpsia cespitósa .... Tufted Hairgrass, 10-40", see no. 65
Panicles open and diffuse. Spikelets are often purplish, narrow, very shiny and have short delicate awns protruding. Glumes are shorter than flowers. Leaves folded and sharp-pointed. Plants densely tufted. Abundant in moist to wet subalpine meadows.

GROUP VI - Glumes shorter than lowest flower in spikelet.

Key to Genera

1a.   Plants huge; panicles large and feathery; found in lower valley wetlands
.... **PHRAGMITES** p. 50
1b.   Plants not as above (2)

2a.   Spikelets two flowered; plants partially submerged in water
.... **CATABROSA** p. 50
2b.   Spikelets with more than two flowers; plants not submerged in water (3)

3a.   Veins of flowers parallel .... **GLYCERIA** p. 50
3b.   Veins of flowers converging at the tip (4)

61: *Danthonia intermedia*

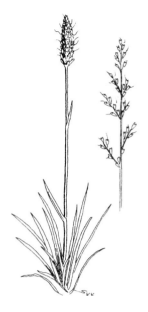

62: *Trisetum spicatum*

63: *Koeleria macrantha*

64: *Hierochloe hirta*

4a.   Spikelets 1/2 inch long or more (5)
4b.   Spikelets less than 1/2 inch long (8)

5a.   Spikelets spread all along one side of stem .... MELICA p. 50
5b.   Spikelets not so (6)

6a.   Weedy annuals with long spreading awns .... ANISANTHA p. 50
6b.   Perennials without awns or with short ones (7)

7a.   Flowers folded flat .... CERATOCHLOA p. 50
7b.   Flowers not folded flat .... BROMOPSIS p. 52

8a.   Leaf tips keeled like a boat .... POA p. 35
8b.   Leaf tips not keeled .... FESTUCA p. 54

Species

Phragmítes austrális [P. communis] .... Common Reed, 6-12'
Huge grass of lower valley wetlands and ditches. Spread by underground rootstalks, forming impenetrable thickets. Flower panicles plume-like with fuzzy hairs among the flowers.

Catabrósa aquática .... Brookgrass, 4-16"
Plants are partially submerged in slow water areas. Root along creeping slender stems. Spikelets two-flowered. Panicles with many spreading branches.

Glycéria .... Mannagrass
Plants are tufted. Flower panicles have delicate, widely spreading branches. Spikelets tiny with several to many flowers that are parallel veined.
1a.   Leaves less than 1/4 inch wide; light green. Common in wet areas and
          along streams from lower valleys to subalpine.
          .... *G. striáta*, Fowl Mannagrass, 8-40", see no. 66
1b.   Leaves 1/4 to 1/2 inch wide; dark green. Found in aspen forests and along
          pond edges of subalpine. .... *G. eláta*, Tall Mannagrass, 2-5'

Mélica pórteri .... Porter Melic, 20-40", W, see no. 67
Flower stems are delicate, the spikelets all dangling to one side. Spikelets narrow and about 1/2 inch long. Plants tufted. Locally common on steep rocky slopes and cliffs montane to subalpine.

Anisántha tectórum [Bromus] .... Cheatgrass, 6-24", see no. 68
This and species of Bromus (not included in this guide) that have spreading awns look similar. All are weedy annuals of disturbed ground in foothill and montane areas. The awns are barbed making the dried flowers a stickery nuisance. Plants emerge early in the spring, and usually complete flowering and seeding by the onset of hot, dry weather. They may also complete a life cycle late in the season with the cooler temperatures and moisture.

Ceratochlóa carináta [Bromus marginatus and B. breviaristatus] .... Rescuegrass, 20-40"
Introduced for revegetation projects. Plants tufted. Panicle branches are erect to spreading. Spikelets are about 1 inch long and have stout, straight awns. Flowers are folded flat.

65: *Deschampsia cespitosa*

66: *Glyceria striata*

67: *Melica porteri*

68: *Anisantha tectorum*

Bromópsis [Bromus] .... Perennial Brome
Spikelets about 1 inch long.
1a.   Panicle erect. Plants spread by underground rootstalks (2)
1b.   Panicle nodding. Plants tufted. Several similar species common along
     mountain roads and trails and forest openings (3)

2a.   Flowers without hairs. Introduced from Europe as a pasture grass. Used
     also for reseeding disturbed areas in the mountains.
     .... *B. inérmis*, Smooth Brome, 16-40"
2b.   Flowers with hairs. Native grass of montane to subalpine meadows and
     forest openings. .... *B. púmpelliana*, 12-40"

3a.   Stems over 24 inches tall.
     .... *B. canadénsis* [B. ciliatus and B. richardsonii], 2-4'
3b.   Stems less than 24 inches tall (4)

4a.   Lowest glume with one nerve
     .... *B. lanatípes* [B. anomalus], 12-24", see no. 69
4b.   Lowest glume with three nerves. .... *B. pórteri* [B. anomalus], 12-24"

Póa .... Bluegrass
Leaf tips keeled. Spikelets small. Panicles contracted and dense to open and diffuse.
1a.   Annual. Found on wet disturbed sites. Introduced. .... *P. ánnua*, 2-8"
1b.   Perennial (2)

2a.   Plants spreading by underground rootstalks (3)
2b.   Plants tufted (7)

3a.   Stems flat; distinctly two-edged. Common on dry slopes. Blue-green
     color. .... *P. compréssa*, Canada Bluegrass, 6-20"
3b.   Stems not two-edged (4)

4a.   Panicle nodding at the top; rather diffuse. Common in montane woods
     and meadows. .... *P. nervósa*, Wheeler Bluegrass, 12-24"
4b.   Panicle pyramid-shaped (5)

5a.   Panicle with few, broad flowers. Common on tundra and open subalpine
     areas. .... *P. árctica* [P. grayana and P. longipila],
     Arctic Bluegrass, 4-12", see no. 70
5b.   Panicle with many, narrower flowers (6)

6a.   Introduced as a pasture and lawn grass. Commonly escaped to any moist
     areas. .... *P. praténsis*, Kentucky Bluegrass, 8-24", see no. 71
6b.   Native grass; common in drier situations. .... *P. agassizénsis*, 8-20"

7a.   Flowers converting to tiny bulblets; bracts among them awn-like. Very
     base of stem swollen. Cultivated grass of dry meadows.
     .... *P. bulbósa*, 12-24", see no. 72
7b.   Flowers not converting to bulblets (8)

69: *Bromopsis lanatipes*

70: *Poa arctica*

71: *Poa pratensis*

72: *Poa bulbosa*

8a.   Plants short and stout. Abundant on tundra and upper subalpine.
           .... *P. alpína*, Alpine Bluegrass, 4-12"
8b.   Plants taller or more slender (9)

9a.   Leaves wide (more than 1/4 inch). Forest openings from montane to
           subalpine. .... *P. trácyi*, 12-20"
9b.   Leaves narrower (10)

10a.   Panicle with lower branches angled downward. Very common in wet
           areas of subalpine forests. .... *P. refléxa*, Nodding Bluegrass, 8-16"
10b.   Panicle not as above (11)

11a.   Panicle nodding at the top. Loosely tufted grass with stems decumbent
           and purplish at the base. Common in wet areas from the lower
           valleys to subalpine. .... *P. palústris*, Fowl Bluegrass, 12-32"
11b.   Panicle erect and thick. Densely tufted grasses (12)

12a.   Upper leaf on stem is short and stiffly angled away from stem. Common
           on rocky slopes. .... *P. nemorális*, Inland Bluegrass, 8-20"
12b.   Upper leaf on stem not as above. Common in open areas from dry
           foothills to subalpine. The earliest blooming grass of the foothills.
           .... *P. féndleriana*, Muttongrass, 12-20"

Festúca .... Fescue
Plants tufted. Spikelets rather narrow and many flowered; arranged in panicles; awns
lacking or very short.
1a.   Plants densely tufted; large (2)
1b.   Plants loosely tufted (3)

2a.   Leaves very narrow and bluish. Common dry, montane, forest openings
           and slopes. .... *F. arizónica*, Arizona Fescue, 10-36"
2b.   Leaves broader and green. Abundant on steep, open slopes from montane
           to lower alpine. .... *F. thúrberi*, Thurber Fescue, 20-36"

3a.   Stems tall with reddish or purplish bases. Found in montane and
           subalpine meadows. .... *F. rúbra*, Red Fescue, 12-40", see no. 73
3b.   Stems shorter; not colored at bases. Several similar species (4)

4a.   Stems two to three times as tall as leaves. Found in dry meadows and
           forest openings from upper foothills to subalpine.
           .... *F. saximontána* [F. ovina], 8-16"
4b.   Stems less than two times as tall as leaves (5)

5a.   Plants under 4 inches. Found on tundra. ...... *F. minutiflóra* [F. ovina], 2-4"
5b.   Plants over 8 inches tall. Abundant on dry tundra.
           .... *F. brachyphylla* [F. ovina], Sheep Fescue, 8-12"

TYPHACEAE (TYP)   Cat-tail Family

Týpha .... Cat-tail, 3-7', see no. 74
Plants of marshes, ditches and the shallow water of pond edges. Spread by under-

ground rootstalks forming dense stands. Leaves relatively narrow, long and flat. Flowers are in tight, cylindrical spikes; the pollen-bearing portion is above, withering early. The lower, brown portion is the seed-bearing part. Late in the season it breaks apart into wads of fuzzy cotton that the seeds are attached to. Three species are found in the area and hybridize freely making them difficult to distinquish, *T. latifólia, T. domingénsis and T. angustifólia.*

ORCHIDACEAE (ORC)   **Orchid Family**
Flowers irregular in six segments; the outer three sepal-like and the inner three of two lateral petals and one lower, lip-like petal.

Calýpso bulbósa .... Fairy Slipper, 2-8", see no. 75
Flowers single on delicate stems; pink and white. Leaves single at the base of the stem; oval. Found in shady, moist montane woods. Never disturb these plants or pick their flowers, as they can easily be exterminated.

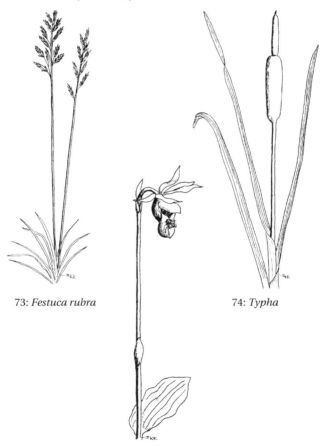

73: *Festuca rubra*   74: *Typha*

75: *Calypso bulbosa*

Corallorhíza .... Coralroot
Plants lack chlorophyll, absorbing nutrients from rotted materials in the soil. They
emerge and bloom in late spring, drying up by mid-summer.
1a.   Flowers spotted or striped (2)
1b.   Flowers plain. Whole plant yellow; rather slender. Found in moist forests
         of montane and subalpine. .... *C. trifída*, 3-10"

2a.   Flowers spotted. Whole plant usually reddish (some may be yellow);
         rather stout. Common in dry, montane forests.
         .... *C. maculáta*, Spotted Coralroot, 8-20", see no. 76
2b.   Flowers striped; purplish. Found in dry, montane forests.
         .... *C. striáta*, Striped Coralroot, 6-20"

Goodyéra oblongifólia .... Rattlesnake-Plantain, 4-16", see no. 77
Leaves thick and oblong with a white stripe down the middle. Flower stems are erect
and have numerous, tiny, whitish flowers. Found in shady, montane forests.

Limnórchis saccáta [Habernaria saccata] .... Bog Orchid, 4-24", see no. 78
Flowers are greenish, spurred and arranged in long spikes. Leaves narrow. Found in
wet areas from the lower valleys to subalpine.

CALOCHORTACEAE (CCT)   Mariposa Lily Family

Calochórtus núttallii .... Mariposa Lily, Sego Lily, 8-20", **W**, see no. 79
Leaves are few, narrow and grass-like. Stems arise from corms. Flowers have three,
cupped petals; white to rose with a brownish to purple splotch or band above the yellow
hairs inside. Plants bloom in spring and dry up by mid-summer. Seed capsule is
relatively large and three-sided. Common in meadows of foothills and montane.

AGAVACEAE (AGA)   Agave Family

Yúcca
Leaves are stiff-pointed, all in a basal rosette; evergreen. Flowers are bell-shaped,
arranged in large, terminal clusters on thick stalks. Petals and sepals appear similar;
white to cream-colored. Bloom in late spring. Fruits are capsules.
1a.   Leaves large and thickened. Flowers cream-colored. Common on rocky
         soils, rock outcrops and steep slopes of the lower foothills.
         .... *Y. baccáta*, 20-36", **W**, see no. 80
1b.   Leaves narrow and wiry. Flowers whitish. Found in rocky areas of the
         lower foothills (2)

2a.   Plants of the western slope. .... *Y. hárrimaniae*, 12-20", **W**
2b.   Plants of the eastern slope. .... *Y. glaúca*, 1-6', **E**

IRIDACEAE (IRI)   Iris Family
Leaves are sword-shaped and arranged in two rows. Petals and sepals appear similar
in color and texture.
Íris missouriénsis .... Blue Flag, 10-20", see no. 81
Plants arise from corm-like rootstalks. Flowers are large and blue-violet. Abundant in
meadows that are moist early in the season. Increase to huge patches in meadows that
are overgrazed by livestock. Found in upper foothills and montane.

76: *Corallorhiza maculata*

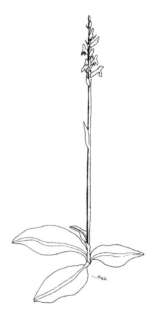

77: *Goodyera oblongifolia*

78: *Limnorchis saccata*

79: *Calochortus nuttallii*

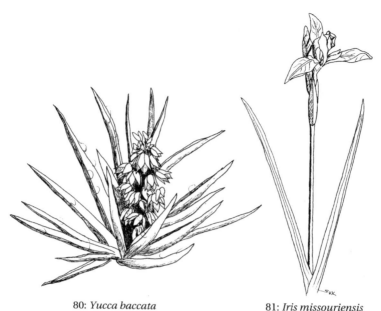

80: *Yucca baccata*   81: *Iris missouriensis*

Sisyrínchium montánum .... Blue-eyed Grass, 4-22", see no. 82
Leaves are linear and grass-like in low tufts. Flowers dark blue, small and few. Found in montane meadows.

MELANTHIACEAE (MLN)   False Hellebore Family
Plants arise from bulbs or thickened rootstalks. Flowers are arranged in racemes or panicles. Petals and sepals similar in appearance.

Verátrum tenuipétalum [V. californicum] .... Corn Husk Lily, False Hellebore, 2-7', see no. 83
Plants tall, often forming huge patches. Early in the season the large, cupped and pleated, oval leaves push up through the soil and unroll. Tall, branched, flower stalks emerge in mid-summer. Flowers are greenish-white. These plants show the first noticable signs of approaching autumn when their leaves yellow and stems collapse with the first frosts. Abundant in moist meadows of upper montane and subalpine.

Anticléa élegans [Zygadenus] .... Wand Lily, 8-24", see no. 84
Leaves narrow, grass-like and tufted. Flowers are arranged in racemes, nodding in bud and erect when open; whitish. Very poisonous. Found in subalpine, forest openings and meadows and around timberline.

Toxicoscórdion venenósum [Zygadenus] .... Death Camas, 8-14", **W**, see no. 85
Leaves narrow, grass-like and tufted. Flowers are white and arranged in racemes, these often quite dense and attractive. Very poisonous. May be confused with wild onion (Allium) before flowering, however lack an onion odor when pinched. Common among sagebrush from the lower foothills to montane meadows.

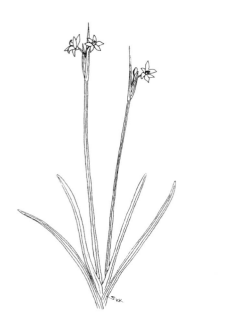

82: *Sisyrinchium montanum*

83: *Veratrum tenuipetalum*

84: *Anticlea elegans*

85: *Toxicoscordion venenosum*

ALLIACEAE (ALL)   Onion Family

Állium .... Onion
Plants have a strong onion odor when pinched. Leaves narrow, grass-like and fleshy.
Flowers are arranged in umbels with a papery bract at the base. Petals and sepals
similar in appearance.

1a.   Flowers nodding; pale pink; tips of petals rather rounded. Found in dry
       meadows of montane and subalpine.
       .... *A. cérnuum*, Nodding Onion, 8-24", see no. 86

1b.   Flowers erect (2)

2a.   Found on foothills, plateaus and dry, lower montane of the western slope (3)

2b.   Found at higher elevations (4)

3a.   Flowers bright red-purple; tips of petals very long and narrow-pointed.
       Abundant among sagebrush, oakbrush and open Ponderosa Pine
       forests. .... *A. acuminátum*, 4-18", **W**

3b.   Flowers white or very pale pink. Clay soils. .... *A. téxtile*, 4-12", **W**

4a.   Flowers are replaced with tiny bulbs that drop and root; pink. Found in
       wet areas of montane and in subalpine meadows throughout the
       range. .... *A. rúbrum*, 8-20", see no. 87

4b.   Flowers are not replaced with tiny bulbs; pink. The most common
       species. Abundant in moist meadows of montane, subalpine and
       around timberline. .... *A. géyeri*, 4-24"

LILIACEAE (LIL)   Lily Family

Plants arise from bulbs, corms or thickened rootstalks. Leaves simple and entire
without distinct petioles. Petals and sepals similar in appearance. Fruits are three-
celled capsules.

Erythrónium grandiflórum .... Glacier Lily, 4-9", see Plate 1
Flowers are large relative to the short stems; bright yellow and nodding, the petals
reflexed backward. Leaves a single pair at the base. Abundant in patches following the
melting snow-line from upper montane to timberline.

Lílium philadélphicum .... Wood Lily, 12-24"
Flowers are large on tall, leafy stems; petals orange with dark speckles. There are few
remaining isolated stands in montane woods, having been nearly exterminated by the
picking of flowers. Please do not disturb them if found.

Llóydia serótina .... Alp Lily, 2-6", see no. 88
Plants are small and slender. Leaves are narrow and about as long as the flower stems.
Flowers single; white. Common and widespread in alpine meadows, though easily
overlooked when among more showy blooms of the alpine.

Leucocrínum montánum .... Sand Lily, 1-2", **W**, see no. 89
Leaves are narrow and fleshy in lax tufts with several white flowers among them in early
spring. After blooming the plant dies back to the root until the next spring. Found in
patches among open sagebrush and grasslands of the lower foothills.

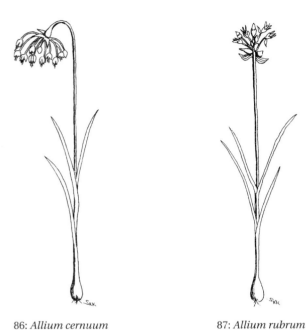

86: *Allium cernuum*

87: *Allium rubrum*

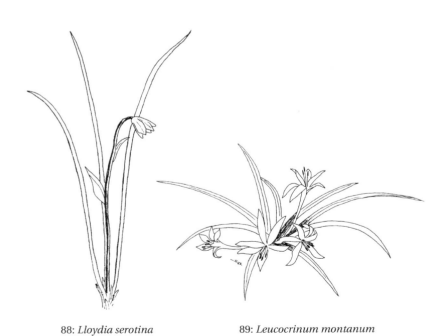

88: *Lloydia serotina*

89: *Leucocrinum montanum*

UVULARIACEAE (UVU) Bellwort Family

Plants spread by underground rootstalks forming patches. Leaves sessile or clasping the stem. Flowers are whitish; bell-shaped with reflexed petals. Petals and sepals appear similar. Fruits are berries.

Dispórum trachycárpum .... Fairybells, Bellwort, 12-24", see no. 90
Plants have arching, unbranched stems. Leaves relatively large, up to 4 inches long. Flowers terminal; single or a few together; white. Fruits are bright, red-orange, half-inch balls. Found in shaded forests of montane and subalpine.

Stréptopus fasséttii .... Twistedstalk, 12-40", see no. 91
Stems are branched and clumped several to many together. Flowers paired and axillary on the stem; white to yellowish. Fruits are paired, red berries. Found near streams in shaded montane and subalpine forests.

CONVALLARIACEAE (CVL) Mayflower Family

Maiánthemum [Smilacena] .... False Solomon's Seal
Spread by underground rootstalks. Leaves are sessile and alternate. Flowers narrow and white. Fruits are red or green berries.
1a. Flowers tiny and numerous, arranged in a panicle. Stems arching. Leaves broad elliptic. Found in shady forests of montane and subalpine.
.... *M. amplexicaúle* [S. racemosum], 10-13", see no. 92
1b. Flowers larger and fewer, arranged in a raceme. Stems erect to leaning. Leaves lanceolate. Abundant under oaks, in forests or sometimes open sites from upper foothills to alpine. Usually in patches.
.... *M. stellátum*, 8-24", see no. 93

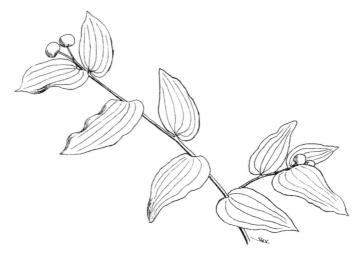

90: *Disporum trachycarpum*

91: *Streptopus fassettii*

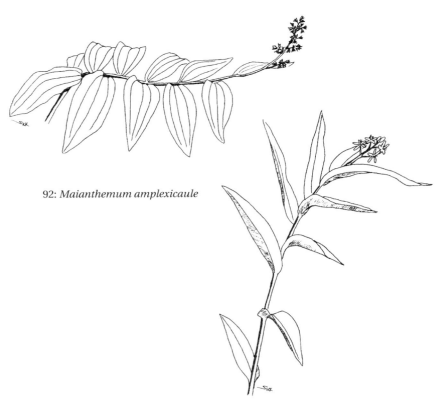

92: *Maianthemum amplexicaule*

93: *Maianthemum stellatum*

UNITED-PETAL DICOTS

Key to Families

1a.	Flowers in composite heads; either ray or disk or both types .... **AST** p. 66
1b.	Flowers not as above (2)
2a.	Flowers with a crown of hood-like appendages between the petals and stamens; plants with milky juice .... **ASC** p. 116
2b.	Not as above (3)
3a.	Flowers irregular (4)
3b.	Flowers regular (6)
4a.	Plants lack chlorophyll .... **ORO** p. 116
4b.	Plants green (5)
5a.	Stems square .... **LAM** p. 118
5b.	Stems not square or if square then flowers yellow .... **SCR** p. 118
6a.	Flowers bell-shaped (7)
6b.	Flowers not bell-shaped (14)
7a.	Plants lack chlorophyll .... **MNT** p. 129
7b.	Plants green (8)
8a.	Flowers blue or purple (9)
8b.	Flowers white, pink or yellow (10)
9a.	Stem leaves lanceolate; flowers blue .... ***Mertensia* in BOR** p. 146
9b.	Stem leaves linear; flowers blue to purple .... **CAM** p. 130
10a.	Plants woody or trailing (11)
10b.	Plants not woody nor trailing (13)
11a.	Shrubs with opposite leaves or trailing, delicate vines .... **CPR** p. 130
11b.	Shrubs with alternate leaves (12)
12a.	Low; leaves not palmately veined or lobed .... **ERI** p. 132
12b.	Taller; leaves palmately veined or lobed; stems may be prickly (actually the sepals are united —though larger than the petals, they may seem to be petals) .... **GRS** p. 156
13a.	Stems with milky juice; flowers pink to white .... **APO** p. 132
13b.	Stems without milky juice; flowers yellow; fruit surrounded by inflated papery sepals .... **SOL** p. 134
14a.	Flowers funnelform or cylindrical (15)
14b.	Flowers salverform to rotate (22)

15a.   Plants ground-trailing weeds of disturbed sites; flowers white to pale pink
.... **CNV** p. 134
15b.   Plants not as above (16)

16a.   Shrubs; flowers yellow or pink .... **CPR** p. 130
16b.   Not shrubs (17)

17a.   Flowers red-purple to rose-purple (18)
17b.   Flowers blue to violet, white or yellowish (19)

18a.   Flowers bright rose-purple, several together in a cup-like bract; stems
        swollen at joints; plants stout and sprawling or delicate and erect
.... **NYC** p. 134
18b.   Flowers deep red-purple; plants tall coarse weeds of disturbed sites; seeds
        stickery .... **Cynoglossum in BOR** p. 144

19a.   Stamens protruding far beyond petals; flowers purple or yellow-white
.... **HYD** p. 154
19b.   Stamens not protruding far beyond petals; flowers blue to violet or white (20)

20a.   Stems and leaves very rough (stick to clothing) ...... **Hackelia in BOR** p. 146
20b.   Stems and leaves smooth (21)

21a.   Leaves simple, opposite .... **GEN** p. 136
21b.   Leaves alternate, compound .... **PLM** p. 138

22a.   Shrubs; flowers tiny in dense pyramid-shaped clusters
.... **Sambucus in CPR** p. 130
22b.   Not shrubs (may be woody at the base) (23)

23a.   Plants very large and stout with flower spikes 3 feet or taller (24)
23b.   Plants not as above (25)

24a.   Leaves fuzzy, pale green; flowers in tall spikes, yellow, blooming a few at a
        time .... **Verbascum in SCR** p. 121
24b.   Leaves smooth, green; flowers in tall spikes, greenish, star-shaped,
        blooming simultaneously .... **Frasera in GEN** p. 137

25a.   Stems square (26)
25b.   Stems not square (27)

26a.   Flowers white; leaves appear whorled; smooth plants of forests and
        meadows .... **RUB** p. 142
26b.   Flowers purple to blue; rough plants of dry foothills .... **VRB** p. 142

27a.   Leaves all basal (28)
27b.   Leaves on stems (at least some) (29)

28a.   Plants miniature; alpine; form mat-like mounds; flowers blue
.... **Eritrichum in BOR** p. 146
28b.   Plants not as above .... **PRM** p. 144

29a.   Flowers some shade of purple; leaves simple; plants of moist mountain
            areas (30)
29b.   Flowers various colors, if purple then not plants of moist mountain areas (31)

30a.   Flowers tiny .... **Veronica in SCR** p. 122
30b.   Flowers larger .... **GEN** p. 136

31a.   Flowers whitish, tiny, in terminal flat-topped clusters or in widely
            branched panicles; plants erect; found in montane to subalpine
            meadows and forest openings .... **VAL** p. 144
31b.   Flowers colored or if white then plants not as above (32)

32a.   Flowers rotate and very tiny or larger, salverform and yellow; leaves
            simple .... **BOR** p. 144
32b.   Flowers salverform or rotate and rather large, not yellow; leaves simple or
            compound .... **PLM** p. 138

ASTERACEAE [COMPOSITAE] (AST)   Composite Family

Flowers are in heads which are composites of many tiny flowers. These flowers are of
two types; the inner type, seated on the center disk are tubular (disk flowers). The outer
type, seated along the edge of the disk, each have an enlarged flattened petal (rays).
Surrounding the base of each disk flower is the pappus, a ring of hairs, bristles or scales.
Those with hairs dry to fluffy balls that break apart in the wind, the hairs aiding in
dispersal of the seeds that are attached. Some species have only one type of flower while
most have both like the typical daisy and sunflower. Dandelions are examples of those
that have only ray flowers and thistles of those that have only disk flowers.

Key to Groups

1a.   Flower heads cone-type (elongated, cylindrical disks), rays present or
            absent .... **GROUP I** p. 66
1b.   Flower heads not cone-type (2)

2a.   Flower heads have both disk and ray flowers (3)
2b.   Flower heads have either all disk or all ray flowers (4)

3a.   Flowers yellow (one species has bicolored red and yellow or purple rays)
            .... **GROUP II** p. 68
3b.   Flowers not yellow .... **GROUP III** p. 82

4a.   Flower heads have only disk flowers .... **GROUP IV** p. 90
4b.   Flower heads have only ray flowers .... **GROUP V** p. 114

GROUP I - Flower heads cone-type

Key to Genera

1a.   Large plants of moist to wet places; rays yellow or absent.
            .... **RUDBECKIA** p. 67
1b.   Smaller plants of dry meadows and roadsides; rays yellow, red or mixes of
            the two. .... **RATIBIDA** p. 67

Species

Rudbéckia
Flowers have elongated disks. Rays, when present reflex downward from the disk to some degree.

1a.   Rays present; yellow (2)
1b.   Rays absent. Leaves pinnately divided into three to nine broad sections; grayish. Found in moist montane and subalpine meadows.
        .... *R. occidentális*, Rayless Coneflower, 3-7', **W**

2a.   Leaves pinnately divided into three to seven broad sections. Disks yellow to brownish. Common streamsides and moist montane forest openings. .... *R. ámpla* [R. laciniata], Golden-glow, 3-7', see no. 94
2b.   Leaves not divided; narrow. Disks dark brown. Scattered distribution in montane meadows; less common.
        .... *R. hírta*, Black-eyed Susan, 12-28"

Ratíbida columnífera .... Prairie Coneflower, 11-32", see no. 95
Rays are bright yellow, orange to deep red or sometimes bicolored; reflexed back from more or less elongated disks. Leaves pinnately divided into linear leaflets. Locally abundant in dry montane meadows.

94: *Rudbeckia ampla*   95: *Ratibida columnifera*

GROUP II - Ray and disk flowers present; yellow

Key to Genera

1a.   Pappus composed of many fine hairs (pull some disk flowers out to see) (2)
1b.   Pappus not composed of many fine hairs (may have scales or few bristles) (13)

2a.   Leaves mostly opposite ....**ARNICA** p. 70
2b.   Leaves basal or alternate (3)

3a.   Phyllaries mostly in one row (4)
3b.   Phyllaries in several overlapping rows (7)

4a.   Heads nodding in bud; crushed leaves have lemon scent
         ....**LIGULARIA** p. 70
4b.   Not as above (5)

5a.   Leaves reduced in size up the stem (compare middle ones to basal ones) (6)
5b.   Leaves about the same size up the stem ....**SENECIO** p. 72

6a.   Leaves rather small, deeply lobed or entire, teeth when present concen-
         trated near the tips or very base ....**PACKERA** p. 72
6b.   Leaves larger, barely to finely and evenly toothed throughout
         ....**SENECIO** p. 72

7a.   Flowers very small, numerous and clustered together; rays tiny and
         inconspicuous (8)
7b.   Flowers few to many, larger; rays conspicuous (9)

8a.   Leaves narrow, stiff; form thick clumps; plants of dry rocky low elevation
         hills ....**PETRADORIA** p. 74
8b.   Leaves not as above ....**SOLIDAGO** p. 74

9a.   Leaves mostly basal or at least stem leaves much smaller than basal leaves (10)
9b.   Leaves not mostly basal nor the stem leaves much smaller than basal
         leaves (12)

10a.   Plants less than 3 inches tall (11)
10b.   Plants much taller, clumped. Leaves stiff, rough, evergreen; found in
         foothills ....**STENOTUS** p. 77

11a.   Leaves very narrow (less than 1/4 inch wide); found in alpine
         ....**TONESTUS** p. 76
11b.   Leaves broader (about 1/2 inch wide), basal leaves with long petioles;
         flower heads single on a stem; found in subalpine.
         ....**PYRROCOMA** p. 77
12a.   Leaves gray-green to green, hairy, about 1/3 inch wide or less
         ....**HETEROTHECA** p. 78
12b.   Leaves bright green, about 1 inch wide ....**OREOCHRYSUM** p. 78

13a.   Phyllaries sticky (14)

13b. Phyllaries not sticky (15)

14a. Flower heads tiny, rays few and tiny, obscure; leaves tiny, narrow, spread throughout even bushy clumps; stems woody at the very base .... **GUTIERREZIA** p. 78

14b. Flower heads larger, rays obvious, showy; leaves larger, basal rosettes; flowering stems few to many .... **GRINDELIA** p. 78

15a. Leaves divided (16)
15b. Leaves not divided (18)

16a. Leaf divisions elongate, linear to thread-like (17)
16b. Leaf divisions short and somewhat rounded .... **BAHIA** p. 79

17a. Found on alpine tundra .... **RYDBERGIA** p. 78
17b. Found at lower elevations than alpine tundra .... **PICRADENIA** p. 78

18a. Rays bicolored purple and red or yellow .... **GAILLARDIA** p. 79
18b. Rays solid yellow (19)

19a. Plants low growing; leaves linear (20)
19b. Plants not as above (21)

20a. Plants of alpine tundra .... **RYDBERGIA** p. 78
20b. Plants of lower elevations than alpine tundra .... **TETRANEURIS** p. 80

21a. Plants large, robust or at least rough hairy (22)
21b. Plants not as above (25)

22a. Leaves large (basal leaves 8-16 inches long), lanceolate, mostly basal (23)
22b. Leaves smaller and spread out along stems (24)

23a. Leaves cordate, blue-gray .... **BALSAMORHIZA** p. 80
23b. Leaves lanceolate .... **WYETHIA** p. 80

24a. Seeds very flattened .... **HELIANTHELLA** p. 80
24b. Seeds rather plump .... **HELIANTHUS** p. 80

25a. Plants very smooth; flowers rather large and few; stems rather stout and little branched .... **DUGALDIA** p. 81
25b. Plants not as above (26)

26a. Flowers small and numerous; stems slender, wiry and many branched; leaves deep green, not toothed .... **HELIOMERIS** p. 81
26b. Flowers larger and fewer; stems not wiry, gray hairy; leaves grayish (especially underneath), toothed .... **XIMENESIA** p. 81

Species

Árnica
Leaves entire to toothed and opposite. Flowers with or without rays. Pappus is of fine hairs. Phyllaries are about equal in length.

1a.   Rays absent. Flower buds nodding. Open woods and meadows of
            montane and subalpine. .... *A. párryi*, 12-20"
1b.   Rays present; yellow (2)

2a.   Stems with many leaves (five or more pairs). Leaves narrow with long
            pointed tips. Flowers several to many. Found from montane to lower
            subalpine meadows. .... *A. chámissonis*, 10-36"
2b.   Stems with fewer leaves (3)

3a.   Pappus hairs are dingy yellow-brown. Flowers yellow-orange; rays blunt-
            tipped. Plants form broad clumps. Abundant in subalpine forest
            openings and lower alpine meadows. .... *A. móllis*, 8-20", see Plate 2
3b.   Pappus hairs white. Flowers bright yellow; rays with tips somewhat
            narrowed (4)

4a.   Plants form clumps. Found in moist subalpine meadows and forest
            openings. .... *A. latifólia*, 3-24"
4b.   Plants do not form clumps (5)

5a.   Leaves lanceolate; petioles shorter than the blades. Common in rocky
            areas around timberline. .... *A. rýdbergii*, 4-10"
5b.   Leaves quite variable in shape, though usually oval to cordate; at least
            some of the petioles as long as the blades. Spreads by extensive
            underground rootstalks forming whole colonies of rather widely
            spaced plants (many without flowers). Abundant in dry forests from
            upper foothills to subalpine; the most common *Arnica* throughout
            the range. .... *A. cordifólia*, 8-18", see no. 96

Ligulária [Senecio] .... Strap-flower
Flower heads are narrowed at base and nodding in bud. Rays yellow or absent. Phyllaries thick and fleshy. Pappus is of fine hairs. The leaves have a lemon odor when crushed.

1a.   Found in alpine (2)
1b.   Found at timberline or lower in elevation (4)

2a.   Leaves thick, succulent and round; reddish. Common among boulders
            and loose rock of high alpine ridges and peaks where little else
            grows. .... *L. soldanélla*, 3-6", see no. 97
2b.   Leaves not succulent; green (3)

3a.   Leaves oval to elliptic; rounded at tip. Plants without hair. Common in
            alpine meadows. .... *L. hólmii*, 4-8"
3b.   Leaves narrower; pointed at tip. Plants with patchy, cottony hairs. Form
            clumps. Scattered throughout rocky areas and slopes of high alpine.
            .... *L. taraxacoídes*, 4-8"

4a.   Rays absent. Flowers large and nodding; phyllaries dark purplish-black.
        Found in montane and subalpine forest openings and meadows.
        .... *L. bígelovii*, 12-40", see no. 98
4b.   Rays present. Leaves long and narrow-elliptic with irregular teeth. Heads
        usually tilted to nodding. Rays lemon-yellow; narrow and long
        pointed. Common in meadows and forest openings of subalpine.
        .... *L. ampléctens*, 8-24", see no. 99

96: *Arnica cordifolia*   97: *Ligularia soldanella*

98: *Ligularia bigelovii*   99: *Ligularia amplectens*

Páckera [Senecio]
Leaves are mostly basal. Stem leaves are mostly reduced in size and number. Stems under 2 feet tall. Flowers several to many on a stem; yellow to orange. Pappus is of fine hairs. The species hybridize, often making them difficult to distinguish from one another.

1a.   Flowers orange; the unopened buds red-orange. Basal leaves spatulate often with a few lobes or teeth at the base. Stem leaves auriculate, clasping the stem. Scattered in moist meadows from montane to alpine. .... *P. crocáta*, 8-24", see no. 100

1b.   Flowers yellow (2)

2a.   Leaves deeply and irregularly divided and toothed. Dry lower foothill woodlands or clay hills. Blooms in spring.
        .... *P. multilobáta*, 6-12", **W**, see no. 101

2b.   Leaves not deeply divided (3)

3a.   Stem leaves tiny and bract-like. Form low mat-like mounds with erect flowering stems. Common on rocky ridges of subalpine and alpine.
        .... *P. werneriifólia*, 2-8"

3b.   Stem leaves larger; not bract-like (4)

4a.   Stem leaves with enlarged, triangular bases clasping the stem. Found in dry, montane and subalpine meadows. .... *P. dimorphophylla*, 4-12"

4b.   Stem leaves not as above (5)

5a.   Leaves without teeth; gray with hair; narrow-elliptic. Plants form low mat-like mounds. Found on gravelly areas from lower elevation mesas to alpine. .... *P. cána*, 5-20"

5b.   Leaves toothed (6)

6a.   Leaves with three teeth at apex; smooth. Found on open, gravelly areas of montane. .... *P. tridenticuláta*, 4-20"

6b.   Leaves with many teeth concentrated toward tip; may have some degree of hairiness. A quite variable widespread and common species of foothills and dry montane woodlands and meadows.
        .... *P. neomexicána*, 6-20", see no. 102

Senécio
Plants are quite variable in appearance. Many are late-season bloomers. Flowers yellow and generally small in relation to the size of the plants. Pappus is of fine hairs. Phyllaries are mostly equal in length.

1a.   Leaves reduced in size up the stem; gray, blue-green to green (2)

1b.   Leaves similar in size throughout; green (5)

2a.   Plants large; usually in thick, robust clumps. Leaves gray; edges with small, dark, thickened teeth. Flowers in dense, terminal clusters. Abundant and widespread throughout rocky areas and roadsides of subalpine and lower alpine. .... *S. atrátus*, 8-32", see Plate 3

2b.   Plants more slender (3)

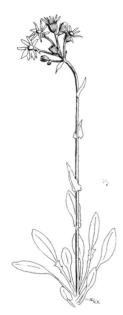

100: *Packera crocata*

101: *Packera multilobata*

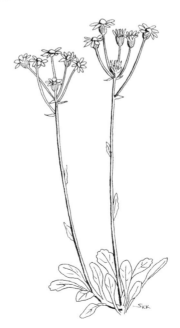

102: *Packera neomexicana*

3a.   Stems and leaves with patchy, cottony hairs; quite variable in leaf size and amount of hair. Leaves elliptic. Flowers grouped rather closely together. Very common and widespread among sagebrush and oakbrush in the foothills to moist meadows of montane and subalpine. .... *S. integérrimus*, 12-28", see no. 103

3b.   Stems and leaves without such hairs (4)

4a.   Leaves pale blue-green; oblanceolate with rather rounded tips; teeth small when present; petioles slightly winged; mostly basal. Open areas of drier montane. .... *S. woótonii*, 8-20"

4b.   Leaves green; elliptic with pointed tips; coarsely toothed; winged petioles; spread along stems. Flowers yellow-orange. Plants form clumps. Common dry slopes and meadows of montane and subalpine.
.... *S. crássulus*, 8-20", see no. 104

5a.   Plants in bushy clumps with many-branched stems. Leaves linear to nearly thread-like. Stems and leaves pale-green. Flower heads narrow (twice or more tall as wide); few rays. Found in dry, gravelly, open, montane parks; common in certain areas such as near Lake City. .... *S. spartioídes*, 8-24"

5b.   Plants not as above (6)

6a.   Plants less than 20 inches tall. Leaves small and succulent; sessile; coarsely toothed with rounded tips; bright green. Form loose mounds. Common, scattered in rocky areas or on bare slopes near timberline (sometimes lower).
.... *S. frémontii* [S. carthamoides], 4-20", see no. 105

6b.   Plants more than 20 inches tall (7)

7a.   Leaves deeply divided; pinnate or more irregular. Common disturbed sites such as along roads and trails of montane and subalpine.
.... *S. eremophílus*, 12-24", see no. 106

7b.   Leaves not divided, only toothed (8)

8a.   Leaves triangular; coarsely toothed. Abundant along subalpine streams.
.... *S. trianguláris*, 20-60", see no. 107

8b.   Leaves linear-lanceolate with small even teeth. Common along subalpine streams. .... *S. sérra*, 24-48", **W**, see no. 108

Petradória púmila [Solidago petradoria] .... Rock Goldenrod, 4-8", **W**, see Plate 4
Plants form thick, low clumps. Leaves narrow, stiff and rough. In spring leaves are bright green, darkening in summmmer. Blooms in mid-summer with numerous, small, yellow flowers. Rays very few and tiny on each small flower head. Abundant on rocky, dry hillsides of the far, western foothills.

Solidágo .... Goldenrod
Flowers are yellow and very small. Phyllaries arranged in several rows. Pappus is of fine hairs. The large species are quite showy in early autumn.

1a.   Flower heads all to one side of the stem; very numerous; showy (2)

103: *Senecio integerrimus*

104: *Senecio crassulus*

105: *Senecio fremontii*

106: *Senecio eremophilus*

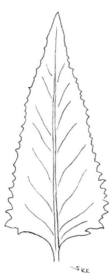

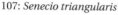

107: *Senecio triangularis*   108: *Senecio serra*

1b.	Flower heads not all to one side of the stem; rather few. Form loose, mat-like clumps. Leaves mostly basal; obovate to oblanceolate. Stem leaves narrower (5)
2a.	Leaves fewer and smaller up the stems; mostly narrow oblanceolate to elliptic. Rather low plants. Common on dry slopes and embankments of upper foothills and lower montane.
	.... *S. velútina* [S. sparsiflora], 12-24"
2b.	Leaves similar throughout; narrow-lanceolate; variously toothed. Mostly tall plants. Found in moist areas. Three very similar species (3)
3a.	Found from lower valleys to higher elevation meadows (4)
3b.	Found only in lower valleys. Usually very tall.
	.... *S. serotinoídes* [S. gigantea], 1-7'
4a.	Flower heads about 1/8 inch tall. .... *S. canadénsis*, 1-4', see Plate 5
4b.	Flower heads about 1/4 inch tall .... *S. altíssima*, 2-4'
5a.	Rays thirteen or more. Common in open areas of subalpine.
	.... *S. multiradiáta* [S. ciliosa], 4-28", see no. 109
5b.	Rays about eight. Common in meadows from montane to alpine. The alpine form is very small. .... *S. spathuláta*, 1-18"

Tonéstus pygmaéus [Haplopappus], 1-3", see no. 110
Leaves mostly basal, forming small low mounds. Flowers with yellow rays are on short stems among the leaves. Found on gravelly ground of alpine.

Pyrrocóma uniflóra [Haplopappus], 4-16", **E**, see no. 111
Leaves are narrow with long petioles, arranged mostly in a basal rosette. Flower heads are relatively large and single or a few together on stems. Rays deep yellow. Stems and phyllaries have fuzzy, white hairs. Commonly scattered in dry, subalpine meadows.

Stenótus armerioídes [Haplopappus], 5-10", **W**, see no. 112
Basal leaves are evergreen, stiff, somewhat shiny and narrow- oblanceolate. Form thick clumps. Bloom in late spring with many, bright, yellow flowers on nearly leafless stems. Phyllaries are broad and rounded. Found in sandy loam soils of steep, wooded foothills on the far western slope.

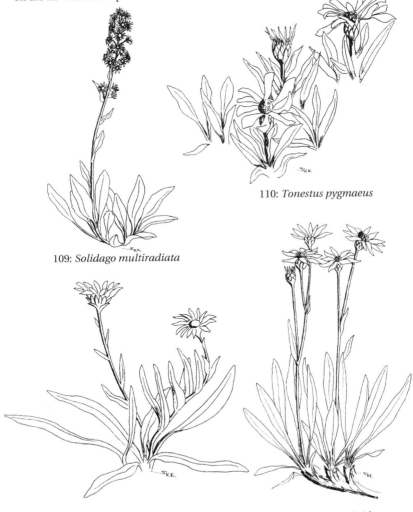

110: *Tonestus pygmaeus*

109: *Solidago multiradiata*

111: *Pyrrocoma uniflora*

112: *Stenotus armerioides*

Heterothéca [Chrysopsis] .... Golden Aster
Low bushy plants with numerous leafy stems. Leaves mostly oblanceolate, 1/3 inch wide or less. Flowers are yellow and numerous. Phyllaries arranged in several rows. Pappus is of fine hairs.

1a.   Leaves grayish. Flower heads relatively small. Abundant, weedy plant of open, dry sites from foothills to montane; especially disturbed sites.
        .... *H. villósa*, 4-20", see no. 113
1b.   Leaves green (2)

2a   Flower heads mostly one per stem. Form perfect even clumps. Found on rocky to gravelly ground of subalpine and alpine. .... *H. púmila*, 6-15"
2b.   Flower heads mostly more than one per stem (3)

3a.   Flower heads closely surrounded by leaves. Found in open areas of upper montane and subalpine. .... *H. fulcráta*, 8-24"
3b.   Flower heads quite separate from and above leaves. Found in open gravelly areas of montane. .... *H. hórrida* [C. hispida], 8-24"

Oreochrýsum párryi [Haplopappus], 6-20", see no. 114
Leaves rather wide and bright green. Several flower heads are tightly bunched together. Rays are yellow and short, relative to the size of the head. Phyllaries are rather broad (tan with green tips or at least the edges are tan). Bloom in late summer. Stems rough and purple-brown. Plants spread by underground rootstalks forming loose patches. Common in upper montane and subalpine forests.

Gutierrézia saróthrae .... Broom Snakeweed, 4-28"
Stems are densely tufted, broom-like and only woody at the very base. Leaves tiny, linear and bright green. Flowers are small with a few tiny rays, bright yellow and arranged in terminal clusters. Phyllaries are rather sticky. Common in lower foothill meadows.

Grindélia .... Gumweed
Weedy plants of lower elevations. Leaves toothed. Flowers bright yellow. Phyllaries are very sticky.

1a.   Perennial with large, basal leaf rosettes present during bloom. Phyllaries erect. Common in clay soils of lower foothills and valleys.
        .... *G. arizónica*, 6-18", **W**
1b.   Biennial or annual lacking basal leaf rosettes during bloom. Phyllaries reflexed backwards. Abundant in lower valleys. ..... *G. squarrósa*, 6-24"

Rýdbergia [Hymenoxys] .... Old-Man-Of-The-Mountain
Flowers very large relative to the short stems; yellow. Leaves are linear or divided into linear segments. Locally abundant to commonly scattered on alpine tundra.

1a.   Plants not wooly. Basal leaves undivided or only divided near the tip.
        .... *R. brándegei*, 2-8", **E**
1b.   Plants wooly. Basal leaves divided into three or more linear lobes.
        .... *R. grandiflóra*, 1-12", **W**, see Plate 6

Picradénia ríchardsonii [Hymenoxys], 3-18", see Plate 7
Plants form clumps with the bases of stems thickened and knarled. Leaves and stems pale green. Leaves are divided into linear or thread-like divisions. Flowers yellow, small

and numerous. Bloom in late summer. Abundant in dry gravelly meadows and mountain parks from montane to subalpine.

Báhia dissécta, 10-40", see no. 115
Annual. Stems are rough, slender and branched above. Leaves alternate and two to three times ternately divided; mostly in basal rosettes. Flowers deep yellow; rays short and blunt. Bloom in late summer. Found on dry, gravelly, open sites of montane.

Gaillárdia aristáta .... Blanketflower, 10-24", see no. 116
Plants are tufted, often forming thick clumps. Rays are bicolored to some degree; red and purple, sometimes yellow. Leaves variously shaped, and with a rough, hairy surface. Local on slopes and road embankments of foothills and montane.

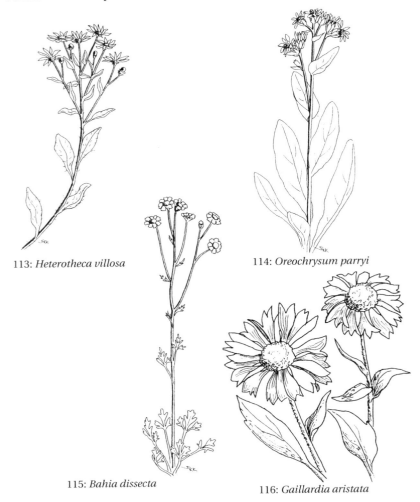

113: *Heterotheca villosa*

114: *Oreochrysum parryi*

115: *Bahia dissecta*

116: *Gaillardia aristata*

Tetraneúris [Hymenoxys]
Plants have primarily basal leaves in dense tufts on thickened and gnarled root-crowns. Flowers on naked or few-leaved stems. Rays yellow, rather blunt and toothed. Spring blooming.

1a.   Leaves mostly basal; long-linear; green. Leaf bases often among long, wooly hairs. Common to abundant in rocky soil of open, lower foothills. .... *T. ívesiana,* 7-14", **W**, see no. 117

1b.   Leaves entirely basal; small, linear-oblanceolate. Leaf bases not among wooly hairs. Leaves and stems with short, silky hair making them appear grayish. Locally common on the eastern slope's grassy, foothill ridges and among sagebrush on the northwestern side of the range. .... *T. acaúlis,* 2-6"

Balsamorhíza sagittáta .... Balsam-Root, 10-20", **W**
Plants showy. Leaves are large, blue-gray and tufted. Flowers large and bright yellow. Bloom in late spring. Abundant in the sandy-loam soils of the far western plateaus.

Wyéthia .... Mule's Ears
Plants are coarse and deeply rooted, allowing them to bloom in the driest years when little else can. Flowers are large with bright yellow rays. Bloom in spring. Found in meadows, among oaks and in forest openings from upper foothill to dry, lower montane.

1a.   Upper stem leaves have distinct petioles. Stems mostly with one flower head. Plants rather sparse; evenly sized and spaced; form continous stands among brush on far western plateaus. .... *W. arizónica,* 6-12", **W**

1b.   Upper stem leaves more or less lacking petioles. Stems with several flower heads. Plants large, in robust clumps. These are a hybrid of the above and a more northern species, *W. amplexicaúlis.* Common in often dense stands under Ponderosa Pines and in meadows of upper foothills and lower montane. .... *W. x mágna,* 12-24", **W**, see no. 118

Helianthélla .... Little Sunflower
Plants are rough and hairy. Stems several to many together. Flowers have yellow rays and dark disks. Seeds are flattened.

1a.   Flowers with large disks (1 1/2 to 2 inches). Leaves have five prominent veins. Abundant in open areas of upper montane; sometimes also lower subalpine where the plants are smaller.
        .... *H. quinquenérvis,* 2-5', see Plate 8

1b.   Flowers with smaller disks (3/4 inch). Leaves not prominently veined. Found in dry montane meadows. .... *H. párryi,* 8-20"

Heliánthus .... Sunflower
Plants are rough and hairy. Flowers have yellow rays and dark disks. Seeds are plump.

1a.   Leaves primarily opposite; narrow diamond-shaped. Plants perennial spreading by underground rootstalks forming patches. Uncommon in dry open forests of lower montane. .... *H. rígidus,* 12-32", **W**

1b.   Leaves alternate; broader. Plants annual. Abundant along roads and disturbed ground. Quite variable through hybridization of the following two species and varying site conditions (2)

2a.   Phyllaries broad with stiff hairs along the edges. .... *H. ánnuus,* 1-7'
2b.   Phyllaries narrower without stiff hairs along the edges. .... *H. petioláris,* 1-7'

Dugáldia hoópesii [Helenium] .... Orange Sneezeweed, 12-40", see no. 119
Flowers are large with yellow-orange rays that often droop downward to some degree.
Leaves bright green and smooth. Abundant in moist meadows from montane to alpine.

Helioméris multiflóra [Viguiera] .... Showy Goldeneye, 10-40", see Plate 9
Plants many branched with wiry, leafy stems. Leaves are elliptic. Flowers yellow,
long blooming late in the season. Abundant roadsides and meadows from upper
foothills to subalpine.

Ximenesia encelioides [Verbesina] .... Cowpen Daisy, 10-24"
Annual plants. Stems and leaves gray with hair. Leaves opposite to alternate; toothed.
Flowers have yellow to yellow-orange rays. Common on disturbed ground of fields and
roadsides in the lower valleys.

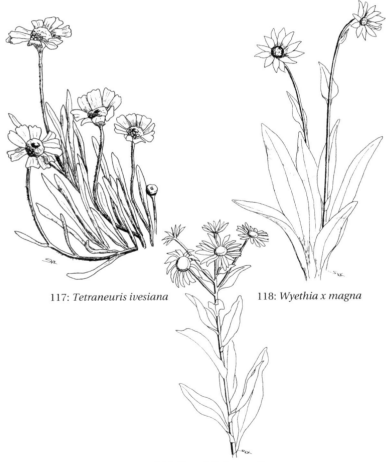

117: *Tetraneuris ivesiana*   118: *Wyethia x magna*

119: *Dugaldia hoopesii*

GROUP III - Ray and disk flowers present; not yellow

Key to Genera

1a.   Plants very low growing; found in dry foothills (2)
1b.   Plants taller, inhabiting various sites or if low-growing then found only at higher elevations (3)

2a.   Leaves less than 3/8 inch long on numerous tufted stems; flowers relatively small .... **LEUCELENE** p. 82
2b.   Leaves over 3/8 inch long; appears stemless; flowers rather large .... **TOWNSENDIA** p. 83

3a.   Pappus of many fine hairs (pull some disk flowers out to see); rays purple, pink or white (4)
3b.   Pappus not of many fine hairs; rays white (9)

4a.   Rays narrow and numerous (except in one species); phyllaries nearly equal in length in one row, erect .... **ERIGERON** p. 83
4b.   Rays broader and fewer; phyllaries definitely of different lengths in several rows, erect to reflexed (5)

5a.   Leaves divided or toothed to some degree .... **MACHAERANTHERA** p. 86
5b.   Leaves not divided or toothed (6)

6a.   Pappus hairs brown-tinged; leaves and flowers pale .... **EUCEPHALUS** p. 86
6b.   Pappus hairs white; leaves and flowers not both pale (7)

7a.   Rays white; flower heads many, small; leaves short, linear .... **VIRGULUS** p. 86
7b.   Rays purple; flower heads fewer; leaves broader (8)

8a.   Plants form dense patches .... **VIRGULASTER** p. 88
8b.   Plants single, few together or forming loose spread out patches .... **ASTER** p. 88

9a.   Leaves dissected (10)
9b.   Leaves lobed, not dissected .... **LEUCANTHEMUM** p. 88

10a.   Flowers small, numerous in tight flat-topped clusters; leaves soft, finely dissected; plants have pungent odor .... **ACHILLEA** p. 88
10b.   Flowers larger and fewer, not in such clusters (11)

11a.   Leaf divisions thread-like .... **MATRICARIA** p. 88
11b.   Leaf divisions linear but not thread-like .... **HYMENOPAPPUS** p. 88

Species

Leuceléne ericoídes [Aster arenosus] .... Sand Aster, 3-4", see no. 120
Plants are low-tufted with many stems of tiny, linear leaves. Rays are white, narrow and pointed with very small, yellow disks. Common to abundant on dry, gravelly or clay soil of the lower foothills.

Townséndia .... Easter Daisy
Leaves in low mat-like mounds with flowers among them. Rays whitish and disks yellow.

1a.   Phyllaries linear or rather narrow, arranged in five to seven rows. Plants few-stemmed in tight clusters against the ground. One of the earliest blooming plants. Found on rocky hillsides of the lower foothills.
        .... *T. exscápa*, 1-2"

1b.   Phyllaries broader, arranged in two to five rows. Stems several, branched; form compact mounds (2)

2a.   Leaves hairy; gray-green. Stems rather slender. Locally abundant. Found in dry, lower foothills where sandstone outcrops on the surface.
        .... *T. incána*, 1-8", **W**, see Plate 10

2b.   Leaves smooth and fleshy. Stems thick and knarled. Found in alpine areas that hold snow late or gravelly ridge-tops and bare hills of lower montane. .... *T. róthrockii*, 1-4", **W**

Erígeron .... Daisy
Flowers have white, pink to purple rays with yellow disks. Most species have numerous, narrow rays. Phyllaries are nearly the same length and in one row. Pappus is of many fine hairs.

1a.   Leaves lobed or divided (2)
1b.   Leaves not lobed or divided (4)

2a.   Leaves lobed; fan-shaped with three, short, broad, round lobes. Rays whitish to pink. Found on rocky, alpine tundra.
        .... *E. vágus*, 1/2-2 1/2", **W**, see no. 121

2b.   Leaves divided (3)

120: *Leucelene ericoides*

121: *Erigeron vagus*

3a.   Leaves ternately divided one to three times. Rays white to purple or
        lacking. Found on rocky ground and rock outcrops of montane and
        subalpine. .... *E. compósitus*, 2-6", see no. 122

3b.   Leaves pinnately divided; segments linear. Rays purple. Found on rocky
        alpine ridges or upper subalpine rock outcrops.
        .... *E. pinnatiséctus*, 1 1/2-5"

4a.   Plants annual or biennial; base rather slender (5)
4b.   Plants perennial; base stout (7)

5a.   Plants small with runners spreading over the ground. Flowers single on a
        stem. Rays white to pinkish (6)

5b.   Plants larger without runners. Rays purplish; very narrow. Leaves
        oblanceolate; rather fuzzy soft. Flower stems branched; leafy. Found
        on dry, disturbed ground of the foothills. .... *E. divérgens*, 4-28"

6a.   Runners rooting to form new plants. Abundant in dry open sites of
        montane and subalpine, especially roadsides and other disturbed
        sites. .... *E. flagelláris*, Whiplash Daisy, 2-12", see no. 123

6b.   Runners not rooting, only elongating and spreading outward later in the
        season. During blooming time in spring the previous year's runners
        still evident as dried sticks. Found on dry, gravelly areas of foothills
        and montane. .... *E. colo-mexicánus*, 4-12"

7a.   Plants tall and erect or at least with well developed stem leaves; lanceolate
        or broader. Generally in forested areas (8)

7b.   Plants shorter or at least with stem leaves linear or greatly reduced in size
        and number (14)

8a.   Flower heads wooly; large; nodding in bud. Rays purple. Found in upper
        montane and subalpine. .... *E. elátior*, 8-24"

8b.   Flower heads not wooly (may be hairy) (9)

9a.   Rays white. Found in upper montane and subalpine. .... *E. coúlteri*, 4-24"
9b.   Rays some shade of purple (10)

10a.   Rays deep violet to purple; about 1/8 inch wide or more. Heads large.
        Found in subalpine meadows. .... *E. peregrínus*, 4-28"

10b.   Rays lighter purple to bluish; less than 1/8 inch wide. The following
        species hybridize, often making species identification difficult (11)

11a.   Leaves reduced in size and number up the stem (12)
11b.   Leaves rather uniform up the stem (13)

12a.   Stems curved at the base. Common upper montane and subalpine
        meadows. .... *E. formosíssimus*, 4-16"

12b.   Stems straight. Found in upper montane and subalpine meadows.
        .... *E. glabéllus*, 4-28"

13a.   Leaves without hair. Often forming large clumps. Stems reddish.
       Abundant in montane and subalpine meadows and forest openings.
       .... *E. speciósus*, Showy Daisy, 6-32"
13b.   Leaves with hair. Otherwise similar to the above. .... *E. subtrinérvis*, 6-36"

14a.   Found in alpine or rocky open areas of subalpine (15)
14b.   Found at lower elevations. Leaves narrow (18)

15a.   Phyllaries with wooly hairs (16)
15b.   Phyllaries not wooly (17)

16a.   Hairs on phyllaries black. Rays whitish to pink. Common near timberline.
       .... *E. melanocéphalus*, 2-6"
16b.   Hairs on phyllaries light-colored. Rays purplish to pink or whitish.
       Common to abundant in alpine meadows. .... *E. símplex*, 1 1/2-8"

17a.   Found in dry alpine meadows. Leaves mostly wide and rounded at the tip.
       Rays purple. Spread by underground rootstalks forming small, mat-
       like patches. .... *E. úrsinus*, 2-10"
17b.   Found on rocky to gravelly bare slopes of subalpine and alpine. Leaves
       mostly narrow and acute. Rays purple or sometimes white. Form
       mat-like mounds. .... *E. leiomérus*, Rockslide Daisy, 2-6"

122: *Erigeron compositus*   123: *Erigeron flagellaris*

18a.   Stems curve out widely from the base. Leaves long linear (reaching over
        half way up the flowering stems). Petals white. Common in sage-
        brush. .... *E. eátoni,* 2-10", **W**, see no. 124
18b.   Not as above (19)

19a.   Stems in tight low clumps; delicate; many. Leaves nearly all basal. Rays
        lilac to whitish. Blooms early in the foothills and later at higher
        elevations. Locally common on the eastern slope's dry gravelly hills
        and rock outcrops; foothills to montane. Also common at the
        northern end of the range in mountain parks.
        .... *E. veténsis,* 2-9", see Plate 11
19b.   Stems in thick, taller clumps; many; hairy and rather leafy. Rays white to
        purple-tinged. Abundant among oakbrush and sagebrush on
        western plateaus. .... *E. púmilus,* 2-12", see no. 125

Machaeránthera [Aster] .... Tansy Aster
Leaves toothed. Phyllaries are in many rows with the tips bent backwards. Pappus is of
fine hairs. Rays yellow or purple with yellow disks.
1a.   Flowers yellow; late blooming. Leaves tiny; basal leaves toothed with the
        tip tapering to a bristle; stem leaves short and linear. Form low tufts.
        Annual plants. Common dry foothill woodlands and lower montane.
        .... *M. grácilis* [Haplopappus], 2-12", **W**
1b.   Flowers purple (2)

2a.   Plants tall and branched. Annual to short-lived perennial (3)
2b.   Plants low and mat-forming or sometimes just a few stems together.
        Perennial. Found on open gravelly ground of subalpine and alpine.
        Flowers relatively large on short stems; rays red-purple to pink-
        purple. .... *M. coloradoénsis,* 1 1/2-4", see Plate 12

3a.   Leaves linear. Stems many; rough but not sticky. Flower heads very
        numerous; rays lilac-purple. Abundant along roads and fields of
        foothills and montane. .... *M. canéscens,* 4-16"
3b.   Leaves broader. Stems fewer; rather sticky. Flowers several to many; rays
        deep violet. Common along roads and disturbed meadows of upper
        montane. .... *M. páttersonii* [A. bigelovii], 8-40"

Eucéphalus glaúcus [Aster glaucodes], 12-20"
Plants form dense patches. Leaves are pale blue-green. Blooms midsummer, the
flowers with pale lilac rays. Common along roads and in open rocky areas of montane.

Vírgulus falcátus [Aster], 8-16"
Spread by underground rootstalks forming patches. Flowers have white rays and
yellow disks. They are small and densely clustered along the ends of stems. Blooms late
summer. Stems rough with hair. Leaves are short, linear, and gray-green, with tips
sharp-pointed. Leaves are concentrated on upper part of stem. Abundant roadsides,
fields, dry meadows and forest-openings of foothills and lower montane.

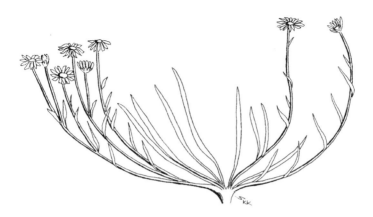

124: *Erigeron eatoni*

125: *Erigeron pumilus*

Virguláster ascéndens [Aster], 10-30"
Plants are quite variable in height. Spread by underground rootstalks, forming large continuous patches. Stems hairy. Flowers have lilac rays. Blooms late summer. Found in gravelly soils and roadsides of upper montane and subalpine.

Áster
Flowers have rather small, yellow disks and few, purple rays. Blooms in late summer. Pappus is of fine hairs.

1a.   Leaves blue-green. Stems dark; smooth. Rays purple. Often numerous in an area, usually with plants spaced out. Common dry montane roadsides. .... *A. laévis*, 12-48", see no. 126

1b.   Leaves green. Stems light or darker near the top; hairy to some degree (2)

2a.   Flower heads numerous. Common in wet areas and along ditches of foothills and montane valleys. Leaves linear to broader. Rays pale purple-blue to white or pink. Stems green with hairs concentrated in vertical lines. .... *A. hésperius*, 12-40"

2b.   Flower heads few. Common in gravelly meadows and open areas of montane and subalpine. Stem leaves oblong; lower leaves obovate. Rays violet to whitish. Upper stems dark red-purple with gray hairs. Quite variable in size. Spread by underground rootstalks, forming patches. .... *A. foliáceus*, 2-40"

Achilléa lanulósa .... Yarrow, 4-24", see no. 127
Flowers are white and arranged in tight, terminal corymbs. Old tawny-colored flower heads persist from the previous year. Leaves are very finely dissected and soft. Often just a few of the leaves of young plants are seen among grass. Plants have a strong pungent odor. Abundant throughout the mountains in meadows and forest openings.

Matricária perforáta [M. inodora] .... Wild Chamomile, 8-20", see no. 128
Leaves are two to three-times pinnately divided, the divisions thread-like. Flowers have white rays and yellow disks. Introduced and escaped to moist disturbed sites from lower valleys to montane. Locally abundant.

Hymenopáppus
Leaves are once or twice pinnately divided; mostly basal. Flowers with rays present or absent.

1a.   Flowers lack rays; disks yellowish to bright yellow. Stems white cottony, especially at the base. Leaf divisions thread-like. Quite variable with several subspecies. Common in dry foothills. .... *H. filifólius*, 10-20"

1b.   Flowers have white rays; disks yellow. Blooms in late summer. Leaf divisions linear. Found in open areas of montane. Abundant in some areas such as the dry, montane hills northeast of Lake City. .... *H. néwberryi* [Leucampyx], Wild Cosmos, 8-24", **W**, see no. 129

Leucánthemum vulgáre [Chrysanthemum leucanthemum] .... Ox-eye Daisy, 10-28", see no. 130
Flowers have white rays and yellow disks. Leaves small and lobed. Plants are introduced and have escaped cultivation, often spreading through whole meadows along roads of moist montane and subalpine (used in so-called regional wildflower mixes).

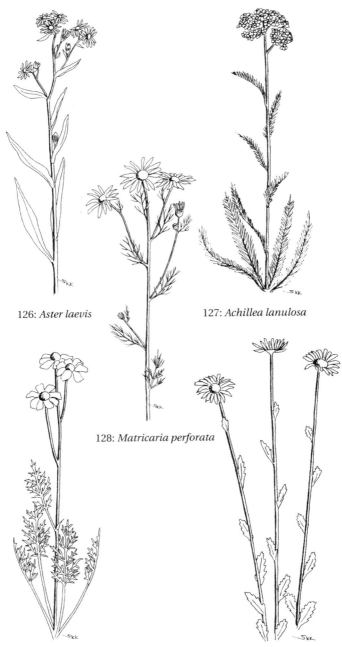

126: *Aster laevis*

127: *Achillea lanulosa*

128: *Matricaria perforata*

129: *Hymenopappus newberryi*

130: *Leucanthemum vulgare*

GROUP IV - Disk flowers only

Key to Genera

1a.	Shrubs or at least stems woody at the very base (2)
1b.	Not shrubs or if appearing so, then stems not woody at the base (5)

2a.	Stems woody only at the very base; leaves linear, bright green; flowers yellow .... **GUTIERREZIA** p. 78
2b.	Stems woody throughout (3)

3a.	Leaves silvery-gray (4)
3b.	Leaves green; flowers bright yellow .... **CHRYSOTHAMNUS** p. 91

4a.	Plants with strong sage odor; flowers about the same color as leaves .... **SERIPHIDIUM** p. 91
4b.	Plants not with sage odor; flowers yellow .... **TETRADYMIA** p. 91

5a.	Plants with strong pungent sage odor; leaves most often silvery-gray .... **ARTEMISIA** p. 92
5b.	Plants not as above (6)

6a.	Leaves divided (7)
6b.	Leaves not divided (may be lobed or toothed) (9)

7a.	Plants with strong pineapple odor .... **LEPIDOTHECA** p. 94
7b.	Plants not as above (8)

8a.	Leaf divisions elongate linear to thread-like .... **HYMENOPAPPUS** p. 88
8b.	Leaf divisions short and broad .... **CHAENACTIS** p. 94

9a.	Leaves triangular (10)
9b.	Leaves otherwise (12)

10a.	Flowers whitish to cream-colored (11)
10b.	Flowers yellow .... **PERICOME** p. 94

11a.	Leaves opposite .... **AGERATINA** p. 94
11b.	Leaves alternate .... **BRICKELLIA** p. 94

12a.	Leaves mostly basal; often mat-like .... **ANTENNARIA** p. 94
12b.	Leaves on stem (though may be near the base) (13)

13a.	Leaves opposite .... **ARNICA** p. 70
13b.	Leaves alternate (14)

14a.	Plants bristly .... **CIRSIUM** p. 96
14b.	Plants not bristly (15)

15a.	Leaves linear (16)
15b.	Leaves broader or if linear then much lighter underneath (17)

16a.	Flowers greenish; leaves along tall stems .... **OLIGOSPORUS** p. 113
16b.	Flowers yellow; leaves in low thick clumps .... **PETRADORIA** p. 74

17a. Flowers whitish; phyllaries with a pearly sheen (18)
17b. Flowers not white (19)

18a. Plants form patches of unbranched stems; found in subalpine
.... **ANAPHALIS** p. 113
18b. Plants form clumps of branched stems; found in montane
.... **PSEUDOGNAPHALIUM** p. 113

19a. Flowers yellow (20)
19b. Flowers pink to purple; phyllaries bur-like; leaves huge .. **ARCTIUM** p. 113

20a. Flowers very small and numerous, grouped together in large clusters
.... **SOLIDAGO** p. 74
20b. Flowers larger and fewer, single or several together, nodding
.... **LIGULARIA** p. 70

Species

Seriphídium [Artemisia] .... Sagebrush
Shrubs. Flowers lack rays and are small and greenish-gray. They are numerous and arranged in often large panicles late in the season. Plants have a pungent odor.
1a. Plants over 12 inches tall (2)
1b. Plants less than 12 inches tall. Leaves small; overall form is stunted and darker in color than the other species. Found on lower elevation foothills and plateaus. .... *S. nóvum,* Black Sagebrush, 4-12", **W**

2a. Leaves wedge-shaped with three teeth at the apex (3)
2b. Leaves mostly long, linear and lacking teeth. Scattered distribution from foothills to lower montane. Usually found in more moist sites than the other species. .... *S. cánum,* 1-7'

3a. Found in rocky shallow soil of foothills; abundant. Medium height shrubs.
.... *S. vaseyánum,* Mountain Sagebrush, 12-36"
3b. Found in deep soil of dry, lower valleys. Tall shrubs. .... *S. tridentátum,* 3-10'

Tetradýmia canéscens .... Horsebrush, 8-40"
Low, stiff shrubs. Leaves gray. Flowers are dull yellow and lack rays. They are arranged in terminal clusters. Phyllaries mostly in one row, equal in length and four-angled. Common in sagebrush meadows, open areas and embankments of the foothills and dry lower montane.

Chrysothámnus .... Rabbitbrush
Shrubs. Leaves small and narrow. Flowers are small and yellow and lack rays. They are arranged in terminal and often showy, large clusters.
1a. Stems with a whitish velvet or film coating (2)
1b. Stems without a whitish velvet or film coating (3)

2a.   Flowers numerous and small, in broad clusters. Showy display of bright
          yellow blooms late in the season. Form dense even shrubs. Abundant
          in open foothill areas especially sites with additional moisture such
          as roadsides and arroyos. Many subspecies account for a wide
          variation in size, shape and color. .... *C. nauseósus*, 1-7'
2b.   Flowers among leaves on the upper stems; rather large and few. Leaves
          often spiraled. Form dense ragged-looking shrubs. Common in
          upper montane meadows. .... *C. párryi*, 8-24", see Plate 13

3a.   Phyllaries strongly keeled like a boat; in five distinct vertical rows. Flower
          heads around 1/2 inch tall. Leaves flat. Found in dry open areas of
          the lower foothills. .... *C. depréssus*, 4-12", W
3b.   Phyllaries not as above. Flower heads around 1/4 inch tall. Leaves spiraled
          or flat (4)

4a.   Seeds densely hairy. Abundant and widely distributed in dry meadows
          from foothills to montane. Flowers numerous; sticky. Form dense
          evenly rounded clumps. .... *C. viscidiflórus*, 1-4'
4b.   Seeds not hairy. Flowers in small clusters. Leaves vary from narrow
          needle-like to wider. Plants with a sweet evergreen tree odor. Dry
          foothills. .... *C. váseyi*, 4-12"

Artemísia .... Sagewort, Mugwort
Flowers are small, lacking rays and about the same color and texture as the leaves
and stems. Flowers usually numerous in panicles or racemes. Plants have a strong
pungent odor.
1a.   Leaves divided into tiny segments that are clumped tightly together.
          Leaves and flowers silvery. Forms low mounds. Abundant on dry
          plains, stony meadows and slopes from foothills to subalpine.
          .... *A. frígida*, Fringed Sage, 4-16", see no. 131
1b.   Leaves not as above (2)

2a.   Leaves green and narrow; pale underneath. Stem leaves not reduced
          upwards. Basal leaves withered by flowering time. Found on moist,
          disturbed sites of upper foothills and montane. ...... *A. biénnis*, 12-40"
2b.   Leaves gray-green to silvery or if green then broader or at least white fuzzy
          underneath. Spread by underground rootstalks (3)

3a.   Leaves densely white fuzzy underneath (4)
3b.   Leaves pale underneath but not fuzzy-white (6)

4a.   Leaves gray-green on top. Flowers dark purplish. Leaves deeply divided
          and lobed; tips pointed. Form large, dense patches in rocky open
          areas of montane and subalpine. .... *A. michaúxiana*, 8-14", W
4b.   Leaves silvery-gray or otherwise not as above (5)

5a.   Form loose patches of stems, differing in height and mostly more than 12
          inches tall. Leaves entire to toothed or divided; acute; linear to
          narrow-elliptic. Quite variable with many subspecies recognized.
          Most abundant in meadows and forest openings from upper
          foothills to subalpine. .... *A. ludoviciána*, 12-40", see no. 132

5b.   Plants evenly spaced over a large area. Stems of nearly equal heights less than 12 inches. Leaves divided linearly; acute. Found on dry, rocky ground of foothills and montane. .... *A. carrúthii*, 8-12"

6a.   Leaf segments fairly broad, elliptic to lanceolate; tips rather rounded. Flowers all on one side of the stem. Stems reddish near the base. Common in rocky openings of montane and subalpine woods. .... *A. franserioídes*, 12-40", see no. 133

6b.   Leaf segments linear; gray-green. Flowers dark or bicolored dark and light. Common in meadows and on ridges of subalpine and alpine. .... *A. scopulórum*, 2-4", see no. 134

131: *Artemisia frigida*

132: *Artemisia ludoviciana*

133: *Artemisia franserioides*

134: *Artemisia scopulorum*

Lepidothéca suaveólens [Matricaria matricarioides] ....Pineapple Weed, 4-28"
Most noticed by the strong, pineapple odor when stepped upon. Leaves are finely divided. Flowers lack rays and disks are rounded to somewhat pointed. Common on disturbed sites of lower montane.

Chaenáctis .... Pincushion
Leaves are thick and one to three times pinnate, arranged in tight basal clumps. Disk flowers are yellowish to cream-colored; lack rays. Plants have cottony hair.
1a.   Found in dry woods of foothills; common. Leaves two to three times
          pinnate; tight, low, basal clumps. Flower stems tall.
          .... *C. doúglasii*, 8-14", see no. 135
1b.   Found on rocky alpine slopes. Leaves once pinnate. Form low mat-like
          mounds. Flower stems short, hardly above the leaves.
          .... *C. alpína*, 2-8", see Plate 14

Ageratína herbácea [Eupatorium], 12-32", **W**, see no. 136
Plants are bushy and have triangular-ovate, toothed, opposite leaves. Disk flowers are white to cream-colored or slightly rose-tinged; lack rays. They are small and arranged in dense terminal clusters. Found in rocky areas of the foothills and montane.

Brickéllia .... Bricklebush
Stems are rather woody at the base, forming thick clumps. Leaves are triangular, toothed and alternate. Flowers white to cream-colored, lacking rays. They are arranged clusters; erect to nodding. Found in open, dry, rocky areas of the forested zones.
1a.   Flower heads less than 1/2 inch tall; erect. Found in foothills and
          montane. .... *B. califórnica*, 10-40"
1b.   Flower heads more than 1/2 inch tall; nodding. Found from foothills to
          subalpine. .... *B. grandiflóra*, 12-40", see no. 137

Pericóme caudáta ....Taperleaf, 3-5'
Plants form very large, thick clumps. Leaves are opposite and triangular with the points very narrow and elongated. Flowers in dense clusters; yellow. Lack rays. Blooms in late summer. Found on rock outcrop areas in canyons of the foothills and montane. Mostly on the eastern slope of the range.

Antennária .... Pussytoes
Leaves are low in tight mats to loose clumps. Flowers lack rays and pappus hairs are more evident than the disk flowers. These make the tightly-bunched flowers appear fuzzy, resembling the toes of a cat (hence the common name). When mature they loosen and spread; the cottony pappus hairs remain attached to seeds to aid in dispersal. The species are often difficult to distinguish due hybridization and differences in appearances of male and female plants.
1a.   Flowers among the leaves; only noticed when mature and cottony pappus
          is dispersing; one flower head per stem. Tiny leaves form tight silvery
          mats in spring among sagebrush of lower foothills. As summer
          approaches the mats dry up and disappear until cool, moist weather
          again in autumn (2)
1b.   Flowers on stems well above the leaves; more than one per stem (3)

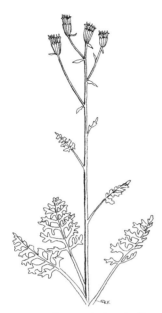

135: *Chaenactis douglasii*

136: *Ageratina herbacea*

137: *Brickellia grandiflora*

2a.   Phyllaries brownish; those on female heads very long and pointed.
          .... *A. dimórpha,* under 1", **W**, see Plate 15
2b.   Phyllaries white; all similar. .... *A. rosuláta,* under 1"

3a.   Not mat-forming. Found in dry forest openings and meadows of
          montane. .... *A. pulchérrima,* 6-16"
3b.   Mat-forming (4)

4a.   Leaves green on top with a fine white edge. Found in dry pine forests from
          foothills to montane. .... *A. margináta,* 2-6"
4b.   Leaves not as above (5)

5a.   Phyllaries dingy or blackish (6)
5b.   Phyllaries white to pink (7)

6a.   Phyllaries dingy yellow. Found in dry subalpine meadows.
          .... *A. umbrinélla,* 3-6"
6b.   Phyllaries green-black. Stems and leaves fuzzy white. Common alpine.
          .... *A. média,* 1-3"

7a.   Phyllaries with a brown spot at the base. Leaves narrow and thin; pale
          green; sparsely hairy. Common in moist subalpine meadows.
          .... *A. corymbósa,* 6-12"
7b.   Phyllaries without a brown spot at the base (8)

8a.   Heads 1/4 inch or less tall. Abundant throughout the mountains.
          .... *A. rósea,* 4-6"
8b.   Heads 1/3 inch or more tall. Abundant in open montane woods.
          .... *A. parvifólia,* 2-6"

Círsium .... Thistle
Plants are spiny and most very large. Flowers lack rays. There are additional introduced, weedy thistles found in disturbed areas at low elevations that have not been
included in this guide.
1a.   Flowers bright purple (2)
1b.   Flowers white to pale purple or yellowish (3)

2a.   Flower heads small (less than 1 1/4 inch). Introduced from Europe.
          Perennial, spreading by deep underground rootstalks forming
          extensive patches to the exclusion of all else. Found mainly in the
          lower valleys along ditches and in fields.
          .... *C. arvénse,* Canada Thistle, 12-40"
2b.   Flower heads large (more than 1 1/4 inch). Stout with branched stems.
          Leaves spiny on the upper surface. Introduced weed. Biennial. Often
          numerous in an area but not spreading by roots. Found mainly in the
          lower valleys on disturbed or overgrazed sites.
          .... *C. vulgáre,* Bull Thistle, 1-6'

3a.   Bracts or their spines curved or bent outward (4)
3b.   Bracts and their spines straight (5)

4a.   Flower heads with long cobweb-like hairs. Leaf bases continue along stem
        below the point of attachment. Found in canyons of lower eleva-
        tions. .... *C. neomexicánum,* 12-48", **W**
4b.   Flower heads without long hairs. Leaf bases do not continue along stem.
        Common, scattered throughout foothills and montane.
        .... *C. trácyi* [C. undulatum], 12-32", **W**

5a.   Inner phyllaries with a spine tip (6)
5b.   Inner phyllaries lack a spine tip, instead rather fringed. Flowers white to
        yellowish. Common subalpine forests. .... *C. centaúreae,* 24-40"

6a.   Plants wooly (7)
6b.   Plants not wooly. Flowers purple to white. Abundant in montane
        meadows. .... *C. coloradénse* [C. drummondii], 4-16"

7a.   Stems bent over nodding. Flowers yellowish to pale purplish. Found
        scattered in upper subalpine and alpine meadows.
        .... *C. scopulórum,* 8-24"
7b.   Stems erect (8)

8a.   Flower yellow. Common in moist montane and subalpine meadows.
        .... *C. párryi,* 12-40", **W**
8b.   Flower purple. Common in alpine and subalpine meadows.
        .... *C. hésperium,* 12-24"

Oligospórus dracúnculus [Artemisia] .... Wild Tarragon, 12-30"
Plants tall and tufted; tarragon odor. Leaves linear and green. Basal rosettes are lacking
during bloom. Flowers minute and numerous among the leaves of the upper stem; rays
lacking. Found along rock outcrops, rocky soil and roadsides of foothills and montane.
Widespread and common.

Anáphalis margaritácea .... Pearly Everlasting, 10-24", see no. 138
Stems unbranched and white with fuzzy hair. Spread by underground rootstalks,
forming patches. Leaves are green on top and white underneath. Flowers are white and
lack rays. Phyllaries white with a pearly sheen, even when dry. Bloom in late summer.
Common gravelly to rocky, open sites of subalpine.

Pseudognaphálium vicósum [Gnaphalium macounii] .... False Cudweed, 10-24"
Plants are clumped. Stems branched above; white with fuzzy hair. Leaves are green on
top and lighter underneath. Bloom late in the season with abundant whitish flowers
that lack rays. Phyllaries are white and have a pearly sheen, even upon drying. Scattered
throughout montane, disturbed forest openings.

Árctium mínus .... Burdock, 2-6', see no. 139
Biennial. Leaves are very large, oblong-ovate arranged in basal rosettes. Flower
stalks tall and branched. Disk flowers purple; lack rays. Phyllaries have hooked
bristles making the heads appear bur-like. Common on disturbed sites of foothill
and montane.

GROUP V - Rays only

Key to Genera

1a.   Flowers blue ....**CICHORIUM** p. 114
1b.   Flowers yellow to orange or purple (2)

2a.   Flowers on leafy stems, yellow or purple; leaves narrow; plants with milky
        juice ....**TRAGOPOGON** p. 114
2b.   Flowers on naked stems (or nearly so); leaves mostly basal (3)

3a.   Flower stems unbranched; one head per stem (4)
3b.   Flower stems branched; several heads per stem .... **PSILOCHENIA** p. 116

4a.   Phyllaries reflexed backward; flowers yellow ....**TARAXACUM** p. 114
4b.   Phyllaries erect; flowers yellow or burnt-orange ....**AGOSERIS** p. 116

Species

Cichórium íntybus ....Chicory, 12-36"
Rather weedy plants with branched, wiry and persistent stems. Leaves mostly basal;
pinnately lobed. Stem leaves few and small. Flowers open in the morning and close
during the heat of the day. Rays bright blue; disks lacking. Bloom throughout most of
the summer with the peak in July. Locally abundant along roads and fields of the lower
valleys and foothills.

Tragopógon
Stems with milky juice; leafy. Leaves are narrow and pointed. Flowers lack disks.
Pappus hairs form white, fluffy, spherical heads at seed maturity. They break apart and
are carried on the wind, dispersing the seeds that are attached.
1a.   Flowers purple. Escaped from cultivation to fields and roadsides.
                .... *T. porrifólius*, Oyster-plant, 20-40"
1b.   Flowers yellow. Common to abundant in moist meadows and disturbed
        sites from lower valleys to montane.
                .... *T. praténsis*, Salsify, 12-32", see no. 140

Taráxacum ....Dandelion
Leaves are all basal, toothed or pinnately lobed to some degree. Stems have milky juice.
Rays are yellow and disks lacking. White, pappus hairs persist and aid in seed dispersal
by wind.

1a.   Phyllaries reflexed backward. Introduced and now widespread and
        abundant from moist areas of the lower valleys to alpine. Often
        carpeting overgrazed meadows. By far the most common and
        widespread species of the family throughout the mountains and
        valleys. .... *T. officinále*, 2-12"
1b.   Phyllaries erect (2)

2a.   Plants miniature (less than 2 inches tall). Outer phyllaries dark. Found in
        rocky, high alpine areas. .... *T. scopulórum* [T. lyratum], 1-2"

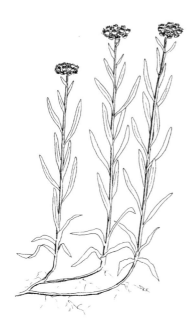

138: *Anaphalis margaritacea*

139: *Arctium minus*

140: *Tragopogon pratensis*

2b.   Larger (more than 2 inches tall). Outer phyllaries green. Common on
           alpine tundra. .... *T. ovínum* [T. ceratophorum], 2 1/2-10"

Agoséris
Leaves are all basal and linear to linear-elliptic, may also be pinnately lobed. Stems
have cottony hairs below the flower head. Flowers lack disks. Fluffy, white seed heads
follow blooming.
1a.   Flowers burnt-orange to pink-orange. Scattered in meadows from
           montane to alpine. ....*A. aurantiáca*, 4-24"
1b.   Flowers yellow. Common in brushland of upper foothills to montane.
           ....*A. glaúca*, 4-20", see no. 141

Psilochénia occidentális [Crepis] ....American Hawksbeard, 6-16", see no. 142
Plants have basal rosettes of deeply pinnately lobed leaves (resembling a dandelion).
Leaves and stems grayish with short, fuzzy hairs. Flower stems are branched near the
top with several flower heads. Rays yellow and disks lacking. Fluffy, white seed heads
follow bloom. Common among sagebrush and oakbrush of the foothills.

ASCLEPIADACEAE (ASC)   Milkweed Family

Asclépias ....Milkweed
Flowers have an odd crown of hood-like appendages in the middle. Leaves rather thick
and leathery. Plants have milky juice. Fruits are follicles that split open at maturity
releasing silky tufts of hair with the seeds attached.
1a.   Stems low, sprawling and clumped. Leaves narrow and erect; yellow-
           green; resembling very coarse grass. Flowers whitish with a purplish
           center crown. Found on dry slopes of the foothills.
           ....*A. aspérula* [A. capricornu], 10-12", **W**, see Plate 16
1b.   Stems erect (2)

2a.   Stems many, forming a bushy clump. Leaves narrow-lanceolate. Flowers
           yellow-orange to red-orange; numerous and small. Uncommon near
           springs and seeps. ....*A. tuberósa*, Butterfly Milkweed, 12-32", **W**
2b.   Stems few (3)

3a.   Stems stout. Leaves broad. Flowers in ball-like clusters; pink to whitish.
           Common in moist areas along roads, ditches and valley bottoms.
           ....*A. speciósa*, Showy Milkweed, 24-48", see Plate 17
3b.   Stems slender. Leaves linear; whorled. Flowers greenish to white. Found
           along roads and in fields at lower altitudes.
           ....*A. subverticilláta*, Whorled Milkweed, 6-40", see no. 143

OROBANCHACEAE (ORO)   Broom-Rape Family
Plants lack chlorophyll; pink to yellow-colored. Parasitic on the roots of sagebrush and
seen only during bloom in spring. Stems fleshy with scale-like leaves. Flowers persist
long after withering. Plants dry-up after blooming. Fruits are capsules.

Orobánche multiflóra ....Broom-Rape, 2-12", **W**
Flowers are deep rose-purple on the inside and paler on the outside. Flower pedicels
short. Found in sandy soil of the lower foothills.

141: *Agoseris glauca*

142: *Psilochenia occidentalis*

143: *Asclepias subverticillata*

Aphýllon fasiculátum [Orobanche fasiculata] 1-6", see no. 144
Flowers yellow to pinkish-orange. Flower pedicels are long and slender. Common foothills to montane.

LAMIACEAE (LAM) [LABIATAE]   **Mint Family**
Leaves opposite and simple. Stems square in cross section. Flowers are irregular, usually with the upper three sepals united and the lower two separate. Many are aromatic herbs. Fruits are nutlets.

Agastáche pallidiflóra ....Giant Hyssop, 16-24", see no. 145
Flowers in dense, terminal or axillary clusters; white to pink. Bracts below the individual flowers are also somewhat pink. Leaves more or less cordate and evenly toothed. Uncommon in rocky areas of montane.

Prunélla vulgáris ....Self-Heal, 2-12", see no. 146
Flowers are deep, dusky violet to bright purple in tight to interrupted terminal clusters. Leaves oblong-elliptic. Common in moist sites from meadows in the lower valleys to aspen groves.

Monárda fistulósa ....Bee Balm, Horse Mint, 12-30", see no. 147
Flowers are in broad, terminal clusters that are encircled by bracts; lilac. The individual flowers are long, slender and arching; splitting into an upper and lower lip at the tip. Leaves nearly triangular and barely toothed. Locally common in moist montane meadows and forest openings.

Monardélla odoratíssima ....Cloverhead Horse Mint, 8-12", **W**, see no. 148
Flowers pale lilac and arranged in small terminal clusters, encircled by bracts. Leaves elliptic and small. Stems are many, twisted and rather woody with splitting bark at the base. Found in rocky areas of montane and subalpine.

Marrúbium vulgáre ....Horehound, 8-40"
Flowers are in dense axillary clusters; individual flowers rather inconspicuous. Leaves grayish and crinkly. Stems white and fuzzy. Form dense, low clumps. Fruits have stickers. Introduced from Europe. Found on dry disturbed sites of the lower foothills.

Méntha arvénsis ....Fieldmint, 4-16", see no. 149
Flowers are tiny, in axillary clusters; pink-purple. Plants are most noticed by a mint odor when stepped on or brushed against since they are often obscured by the dense vegetation of the areas they inhabit. Common along ditches, streams and in wet meadows of the lower valleys.

SCROPHULARIACEAE (SCR)   **Figwort Family**
Leaves mostly opposite, simple and either entire or pinnately lobed. Flowers are irregular with the stamens attached to the flower tube. Fruits are two-parted capsules, first splitting apart at the top.

Key to Genera

1a.   Flowers rather inconspicuous, greenish to brown or red-orange on tips
        ....**SCROPHULARIA** p. 121
1b.   Flowers conspicuous or at least colored throughout (2)

144: *Aphyllon fasiculatum*

145: *Agastache pallidiflora*

146: *Prunella vulgaris*

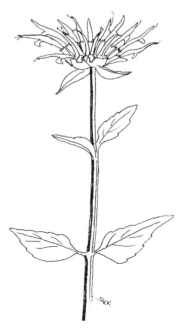

147: *Monarda fistulosa*

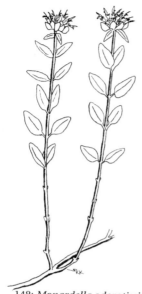

148: *Monardella odoratissima*   149: *Mentha arvensis*

2a.	Flowers regular or nearly so (3)
2b.	Flowers irregular (4)
3a.	Plants large; flowers yellow .... **VERBASCUM** p. 121
3b.	Plants small; flowers blue .... **VERONICA** p. 122
4a.	Flowers spurred .... **LINARIA** p. 122
4b.	Flowers not spurred (5)
5a.	Flowers club-shaped, yellow or bicolored purple and white
	.... **ORTHOCARPUS** p. 122
5b.	Flowers not as above (6)
6a.	Flowers with an upper lip narrowed and extended outward, downward or
	sideways; leaves toothed or dissected .... **PEDICULARIS** p. 122
6b.	Flowers not as above (7)
7a.	Flowers tiny, in dense spikes; leaves finely toothed .... **BESSEYA** p. 124
7b.	Flowers rather large or otherwise not as above (8)
8a.	Flowers in terminal brush-like clusters .... **CASTILLEJA** p. 124
	Flowers not as above (9)
9a.	Flowers yellow .... **MIMULUS** p. 126
9b.	Flowers some shade of purple, blue or red .... **PENSTEMON** p. 126

Species

Scrophulária lanceoláta .... Figwort, 2-7', see no. 150
Flowers small and numerous in open panicles. They are inconspicuously colored, yellow-green to brown or red-orange-tipped. Leaves opposite, triangular and coarsely toothed. Stems dark. Found along montane roads and trails.

Verbáscum thápsus .... Mullein, 1-7', see no. 151
Biennial. The first year plants have a large basal rosette of pale green, soft, fuzzy leaves. The second year they send up a tall, dense, flower spike. A few yellow flowers bloom at a time on the spike. Introduced from Europe. Abundant along roads and in fields from lower valleys to montane.

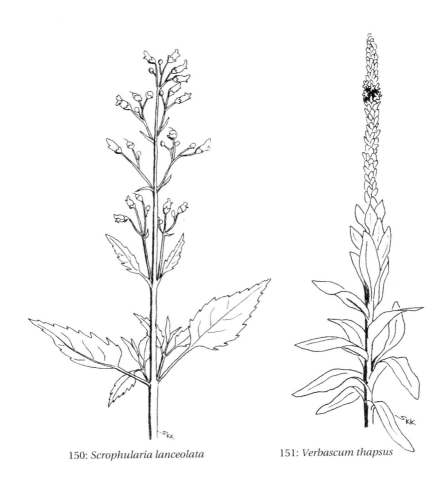

150: *Scrophularia lanceolata*   151: *Verbascum thapsus*

Verónica .... Speedwell
Flowers are tiny and blue. Leaves opposite. Plants quite variable in size according to site conditions.
1a.   Stems erect. Found in subalpine and alpine meadows.
                    .... *V. nútans*, Alpine Speedwell, 4-16", see no. 152
1b.   Stems decumbent, weak and sprawling. Found in muddy areas from the
            lower valleys to subalpine.
                    .... *V. americána*, American Speedwell, 4-24", see no. 153

Linária .... Butter-and-Eggs, Toadflax
Flowers are spurred and arranged in terminal racemes. Leaves entire and sessile. Plants spread by underground rootstalks forming dense patches. Introduced and escaped from cultivation.
1a.   Leaves linear. Flowers yellow and orange. Locally common in open areas
            of foothills and montane. .... *L. vulgáris*, 8-32", see no. 154
1b.   Leaves cordate; thick; clasping stout stems. Flowers yellow. Aggressive
            weed. Hybridizes with *L. vulgaris* creating plants with mixed
            characteristics. Found in foothills and lower montane.
                    .... *L. genistifólia* [L. dalmatica], 3-4'

Orthocárpus .... Owl-clover
Slender annuals with small, alternate, sessile leaves; linear and entire or cleft. Flowers club-shaped and arranged in terminal spikes. Bloom mid-summer.
1a.   Flowers yellowish. Found in montane and subalpine meadows.
                    .... *O. lúteus*, 4-12", see no. 155
1b.   Flowers purple and white. Found in dry foothills. *O. purpureoálbus*, 4-16"

Pediculáris .... Lousewort, Woodbetony
Flowers are bilabiate, the upper lip usually elongated into a narrow beak that arches sideways, downward or outward and upward. Leaves deeply lobed, divided or toothed to some degree. Some appear fern-like. Found in moist areas or forests.
1a.   Flowers pink to purple (2)
1b.   Flowers white to yellowish (4)

2a.   Found in bogs of subalpine and lower alpine (3)
2b.   Found in woodlands of dry lower foothills; locally common in sandy-loam
            soils of the southwestern edge of the range. Leaves deeply lobed; in
            low clumps forming loose mats. Bloom in early spring. Flowers dull
            purple; rather hidden among the leaves.
                    .... *P. centránthera*, 4-6", **W**, see no. 156

3a.   Flower beak very slender and s-curved (resembling an elephant's trunk).
            Leaves deeply dissected. Abundant, often in continuous stands
            across a bog. .... *P. groenlándica*, Elephanthead, 6-24", see Plate 18
3b.   Flower beak not as above. Leaves deeply and pinnately lobed. Uncom-
            mon. .... *P. scopulórum*, 4-8"

4a.   Leaves simple; narrow; evenly and finely toothed; often dark reddish
            tinged. Flowers white. Abundant in subalpine forests.
                    .... *P. racemósa*, Sickletop Lousewort, 8-20", see no. 157
4b.   Leaves compound or dissected (5)

152: *Veronica nutans*

153: *Veronica americana*

154: *Linaria vulgaris*

155: *Orthocarpus luteus*

5a.   Leaves dissected. Flowers cream to yellowish. Found in dry areas of
          subalpine and alpine. ....*P. párryi*, 4-16", see no. 158
5b.   Leaves compound; fern-like. Plants very large (6)

6a.   Flowers yellowish streaked with dull red. Found in shady, moist subalpine
          and montane forests.
          ....*P. procéra* [P. grayi], Fern-leaf Lousewort, 12-36"
6b.   Flowers not streaked; yellowish. Found in dry subalpine woods.
          ....*P. bracteósa*, 12-24," see Plate 19

Bésseya ....Kittentails
Flowers are small and arranged in dense terminal spikes. Leaves are mostly basal,
cordate-ovate to oblong and finely toothed.
1a.   Flowers purple. Common in alpine meadows or sometimes found at
          lower elevations. ....*B. alpína*, 2-6"
1b.   Flowers yellow. Found in rocky alpine and upper subalpine meadows.
          ....*B. rítteriana*, 8-12", **W**, see no. 159

Castilléja ....Paintbrush
Flowers are quite showy, acquiring the common name from their bright array of colors
and their large brush-like form. The colored portion of the flowers are actually the
sepals and bracts surrounding them. Petals are much less conspicuous, slender tubes
within. Leaves mostly narrow and few.
1a.   Found in alpine (2)
1b.   Found from foothills to upper subalpine meadows (3)

2a.   Flowers rose to lilac. Common on alpine ridges.
          ....*C. háydenii*, 4-6", see Plate 20
2b.   Flowers yellow. Common in alpine meadows. ....*C. occidentális*, 2-8"

3a.   Flowers yellow. Plants rather tall. Common upper montane and subal-
          pine. ....*C. sulphúrea*, 12-20"
3b.   Flowers not yellow (4)

4a.   Flowers rose; the colored bracts entire to shallowly lobed. Abundant in
          subalpine meadows. This species and *C. sulphurea* hybridize
          creating various colors and sizes. ....*C. rhexifólia*, 8-12"
4b.   Flowers orange to bright red or scarlet (5)

5a.   Plants with stems tall and branched. Leaves quite narrow. Flowers orange.
          Common in dry meadows of foothill and montane.
          ....*C. linariifólia*, 12-32"
5b.   Plants not as above (6)

6a.   Found in montane and subalpine. Most common in montane woodlands
          and openings. Flowers red-orange to red. Stems few or single;
          usually unbranched or may be branched near the top.
          ....*C. miniáta*, 12-24"
6b.   Found among sagebrush or in grasslands of the lower foothills (7)

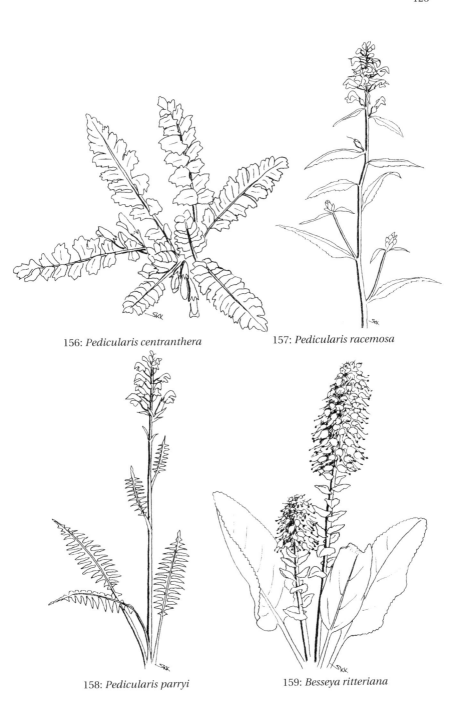

156: *Pedicularis centranthera*

157: *Pedicularis racemosa*

158: *Pedicularis parryi*

159: *Besseya ritteriana*

7a.   Flowers scarlet; colored bracts deeply divided into linear segments. Stems
           several to many; tufted. Blooms in spring and often again later in the
           season. Common among sagebrush.
           .... *C. chromósa,* 4-16", **W,** see Plate 15
7b.   Flowers red-orange to orange; colored bracts not deeply divided.
           Common on the eastern slope's foothill grasslands and the western
           slope's lower foothill sagebrush. .... *C. intégra,* 4-16," see cover

Mímulus .... Monkeyflower
Flowers rather bilabiate, the lips lobed. Flowers yellow, most with some red speckles
inside. Stems are square and leaves are opposite. Grow in very moist ground or in small
streams and seeps.
1a.   Sepals unequal, the upper one definitely longer than the others. Annual or
           perennial (2)
1b.   Sepals approximately equal. Annual. Leaves broad and toothed. Found in
           montane. .... *M. floribúndus,* 1-12"

2a.   Stems creeping. Flower tube open. Flowers less than 3/4 inch long. Found
           in muddy areas of foothills and montane. .... *M. glabrátus,* 4-20"
2b.   Stems erect. Flower tube at least partially closed (3)

3a.   Flowers over 3/4 inch long; few. Stems less than 8 inches tall. Found in
           upper subalpine and alpine. .... *M. tílingii,* 2-7"
3b.   Flowers less than 3/4 inch long; more than five. Stems over 8 inches tall.
           The most common species from montane to alpine.
           .... *M. guttátus,* 8-22", see no. 160

Penstémon
Flowers salverform to bilabiate. The flower tube is narrow or inflated. Flowers have
five stamens, one of which is larger and often hairy. Leaves are entire, simple and
opposite, though mostly basal.
1a.   Found in foothills and montane (2)
1b.   Found in subalpine and alpine (10)

2a.   Flowers red (3)
2b.   Flowers some shade of purple (4)

3a.   Stems in clumps; woody at the base. Flowers few, scattered. Leaves linear.
           Common on rocky, lower foothill slopes of the far western plateaus.
           .... *P. brídgesii,* 12-24", **W**
3b.   Stems single or few together; not woody at the base. Flowers many. Stem
           leaves narrow; basal leaves oval. Common on open slopes and road
           embankments of upper foothills and montane and among trees of
           the lower foothills.
           .... *P. barbátus,* Scarlet Bugler, 16-50", see Plate 21

4a.   Plants low (5)
4b.   Plants tall (7)

5a.   Leaves elliptic; basal, in mat-like clumps. Flower stems few and very
        slender. Flowers narrow (longer than wide); blue-purple; deeply
        grooved on the bottom side. Found in dry meadows and parks of
        montane and subalpine.
        .... *P. gríffinii* [P. oliganthus], 4-20", E, see no.161
5b.   Leaves linear (6)

6a.   Flowers dark blue-purple to lilac; flattened and ridged on the bottom side.
        Bloom in spring. Leaves dark green to gray-green; short to up to 1 1/2
        inches long. Stems low and mat-forming to erect in loose tufts.
        Varies considerably in appearance from one area to another.
        Common in dry rocky soil or grassy slopes of foothills and montane.
        .... *P. caespitósus* , Mat Penstemon, 1-12", see Plate 22

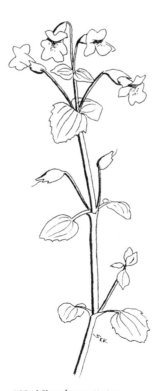

160: *Mimulus guttatus*   161: *Penstemon griffinii*

6b.   Flowers lilac; rounded on the bottom side. Bloom in spring. Leaves pale
           blue-green; short. Stems low and mat-forming. Common in dry
           rocky soil of the foothills, primarily of the western slope.
           .... *P. linarioídes*, 6-10"

7a.   Leaves dark green; basal leaves oblanceolate, stem leaves narrower.
           Flowers bright purple-blue; the lower ones on short pedicels. Blooms
           early to mid-summer. Common and widespread and in meadows
           and roadsides of foothills and montane.
           .... *P. stríctus*, Rocky Mountain Penstemon, 8-28", see Plate 23
7b.   Leaves blue-green (8)

8a.   Flowers lilac; the lower ones on long pedicels. Leaves narrow. Blooms in
           early summer. Found scattered in rocky soil of the foothills.
           .... *P. comarrhénus*, 16-40", **W**
8b.   Flowers bright pink-purple. Leaves pale; oblanceolate to obovate (9)

9a.   Found on clay knolls and rocky hillsides of the lower foothills; local.
           Blooms in late spring. .... *P. ósterhoutii*, 6-12", **W**, see no. 162
9b.   Found in meadows of dry montane; mostly eastern slope, coming over
           the continental divide around Cochetopa Pass. Blooms in early
           summer. Flowers mostly leaning to one side of the stem.
           .... *P. secundiflórus*, 4-16", see Plate 24

10a.   Plants low and mat-forming (11)
10b.   Plants taller (12)

11a.   Flowers on short stems among the leaves; red-purple to lilac. Leaves
           elliptic and blue-green. Form low mat-like mounds. Found on rocky
           ground of high alpine or rock slides.
           .... *P. hárbourii*, 2-6", see Plate 25
11b.   Flowers on stems above the leaves; bright pink-purple; relatively large (1
           inch long); numerous all leaning to one side of the stem. Leaves
           narrow, oblanceolate and dark-green. Form low thick clumps on
           rocky slopes and cliffs of subalpine and alpine.
           .... *P. hállii*, 4-8", see Plate 26

12a.   Flowers dark wine-red to purple; 1 inch long; not tightly clustered. Basal
           leaves oval. Common in moist, gravelly, open areas such as old roads
           and trail-sides of upper subalpine and lower alpine.
           .... *P. whíppleanus*, Dusky Penstemon, 4-20", see Plate 27
12b.   Flowers blue-purple; 1/2 inch long; tightly clustered (13)

13a.   Flowers reflexed downward to some degree. Sepals without distinct,
           papery edges. Found in moist montane and subalpine meadows.
           .... *P. confértus* [P. procerus], 4-12", see no. 163
13b.   Flowers pointing out horizontally from the stem. Sepals with distinct,
           papery edges. Common in wet meadows of montane and subalpine.
           .... *P. rýdbergii*, 6-24"

MONOTROPACEAE (MNT)   **Pinesap Family**

Pterospóra andromedéa ....Pinedrops, 8-32", see no. 164
Plants lack chlorophyll. They are parasitic on the roots of conifers. Flower stems stout,
pinkish and short when first emerging in early summer, elongating and turning to
brown or chestnut later in the season. Flowers are pendulous bells with inconspicuous
petals. Leaves reduced to small scales. Fruits are persistent spherical capsules. Found
in dry montane forests.

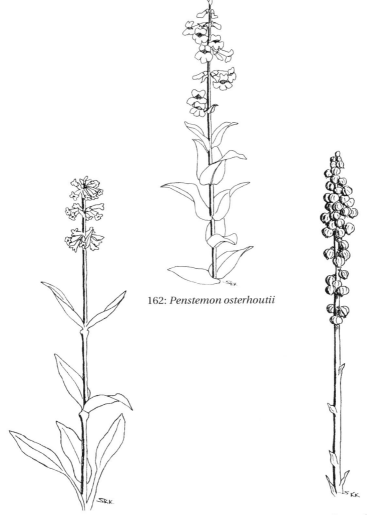

162: *Penstemon osterhoutii*

163: *Penstemon confertus*   164: *Pterospora andromedea*

CAMPANULACEAE (CAM)   Bellflower Family

Campánula .... Harebell
Flowers are bell-shaped; erect or pendulous. Flower parts in fives. Sepals usually partially united. Leaves alternate and simple. Stem leaves are often different in size and shape than basal leaves. Fruits are capsules within the sepals, opening by pores to release the seed.

1a.   Flowers narrow and erect; single; blue. Found on alpine tundra.
           .... *C. uniflóra*, 2-4", see no. 165
1b.   Flowers bell-shaped (2)

2a.   Flowers erect; bright purple; usually single on a stem. Seed capsule erect.
           Found in montane and subalpine meadows. .... *C. párryi*, 4-12"
2b.   Flowers mostly pendulous; blue-lilac; usually several together on a stem.
           Seed capsules pendulous. Found on rocky sites from montane to
           alpine.
           .... *C. rotundifólia*, 4-16", see no. 166

CAPRIFOLIACEAE (CPR)   Honeysuckle Family
Shrubs or trailing plants. Leaves are opposite and simple or pinnately compound. Flowers are small. Calyx three to five-lobed or toothed and corolla four to five-lobed. Stamens five, except *Linnaea* with four. Fruits are various.

Linnaéa boreális .... Twinflower, up to 40", see no. 167
Stems are delicate and trail over the ground, rooting along their length. Leaves small, roundish and paired; dark evergreen. Flowers are paired, pink bells on slender, erect stems. Found in moist shaded montane and subalpine woods scattered throughout the range.

Distégia involucráta [Lonicera] .... Twinberry, 3-9', see no. 168
Shrub with large elliptic leaves. Flowers are pale yellow, funnelform, paired and encircled by a saucer-like bract. When the flowers mature into paired black berries the bract is colored deep red. Common in upper montane and subalpine forest openings, sometimes also among boulders of lower alpine.

Sambúcus microbótrys [S. racemosa] .... Elderberry, 3-9', see no. 169
Shrubs with large, pinnate leaves. Flowers are tiny and numerous and arrranged in terminal, pyramid-shaped clusters; white. Stems are pithy canes. Fruits are numerous tiny berries, either red or nearly black. Common in moist forest openings, meadows and old clearcuts of montane and subalpine.

Lonícera sp. .... Honeysuckle, 3-6'
Several species of cultivated honeysuckle shrubs have established along the Animas River in Durango and may be expected in the vicinity of other towns. Leaves are rather small, oblong-ovate. Flowers white or deep pink; narrow and erect; paired. Fruits are red berries.

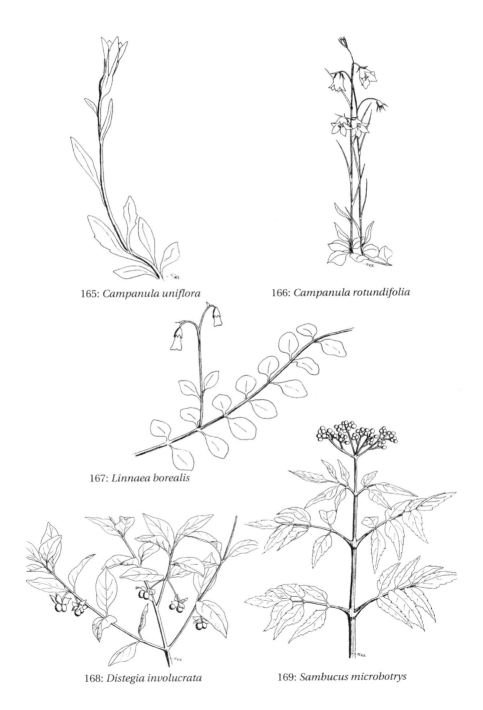

165: *Campanula uniflora*

166: *Campanula rotundifolia*

167: *Linnaea borealis*

168: *Distegia involucrata*

169: *Sambucus microbotrys*

Symphoricárpos rotundifólius .... Snowberry, 2-4', see no. 170
Densely branched shrub with the older bark shredding. Leaves quite variable in size
and shape though generally small and elliptic. Flowers are small, pendulous, narrow
bells; pale pink; few clustered together. Abundant upper foothills and montane, fewer
at higher altitudes.

ERICACEAE (ERI)   Heath Family
Shrubs that are very low or prostrate. Leaves alternate, simple and entire or toothed.
Flowers have united petals and sepals. Fruits are berries.

Arctostáphylos úva-úrsi .... Kinniknnick, Bearberry, 5-8", see no. 171
Plants usually prostrate. Often forming mats by stems trailing across the ground and
rooting along their length. Leaves leathery, waxy and dark evergreen; vary from round
to oblong. Flowers are white to pink bells in few-flowered racemes. Fruits are bright, red
berries that mature late in the season. Common to abundant in open, dry, rocky forests
of upper foothills and montane.

Vaccínium
Shrubs very low and delicately branched. Leaves bright green and thin. Flowers are tiny
white to pink bells hanging on the undersides of branches.
1a.   Leaves broadest above the middle. Branches are not strongly angled in
           cross-section. Twigs orangish. Found from montane forests to
           alpine. Berry blue. .... *V. cespitósum*, Dwarf Bilberry, 2-12"
1b.   Leaves broadest below the middle. Branches strongly angled (2)

2a.   Leaves very small. Berry red. Branches crowded. Usually found in alpine. .
           .... *V. scopárium*, Broom Huckleberry, 2-8"
2b.   Leaves larger (about an inch long). Berry blue. Common under spruce
           from montane to subalpine throughout the range.
           .... *V. myrtíllus*, Blueberry, 4-12", see no. 172

APOCYNACEAE (APO)   Dogbane Family

Apocýnum .... Dogbane
Plants spread by underground rootstalks often forming continuous patches along
roads. Leaves are opposite or alternate, simple and entire. In autumn they turn bright
yellow. Stems have milky juice. Flowers have five, partly-united petals. Fruits are
follicles, the seeds with tufted hair.
1a.   Leaves drooping. Branches alternate. Flowers pink; petals three times the
           length of the sepals. Found in rocky, open areas of montane and
           subalpine; more common on the western slope.
           .... *A. androsaemifólium*, Spreading Dogbane, 8-20", see no. 173
1b.   Leaves erect or spreading. Branches opposite. Flowers white; petals less
           than three times the length of the sepals. Common along roads at
           lower elevations. .... *A. cannábinum*, Indian Hemp, 12-36"

The two species hybridize forming plants with combinations of characteristics. These
plants are referred to as *A. x médium.*

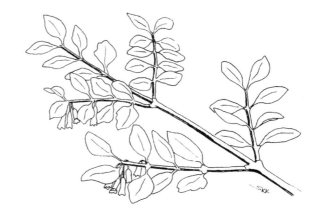

170: *Symphoricarpos rotundifolius*

171: *Arctostaphylos uva-ursi*

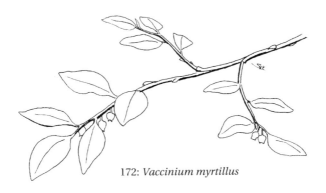

172: *Vaccinium myrtillus*

SOLANACEAE (SOL)   **Nightshade Family**

Phýsalis hederifólia .... Ground-cherry, 8-12", see no. 174
Plants are low and branched. Leaves alternate and variously shaped. Flowers have petals that are somewhat united and five-lobed; yellow with dark centers. Sepals inflate, resembling paper lanterns that surround the berry in late summer. Found in dry foothills.

CONVOLVULACEAE (CNV)   **Morning-Glory Family**

Convólvulus arvénsis .... Bindweed, 1-4' or more
Plants are tenacious, introduced, ground-trailing weeds of disturbed ground. Plants spread by deep, creeping, underground rootstalks, often forming extensive patches. Leaves simple and oblong-sagitate. Flowers are numerous, either solitary along stems or in clusters of a few; pale pink to white, funnelform. Fruits are capsules. Found from lower elevations to montane.

NYCTAGINACEAE (NYC)   **Four O'Clock Family**
Leaves usually opposite; simple and entire. Stems have swollen nodes. Flowers are in terminal or axillary clusters encircled at the base by bracts. Petals and sepals not differentiated. Fruits are achenes.

Mirábilis .... Four O'Clock
Plants with sprawling stems, often forming large masses. Leaves are thick, large and somewhat cordate. Flowers showy, large, funnel-shaped; bright rose-purple. There are several together within a fused-bracted cup.
1a.   Leaves pale green to bluish. Found on dry, lower foothill slopes and
            embankments. .... *M. multiflóra*, 10-14", see Plate 28
1b.   Leaves dark green. Found under trees on dry slopes of sandy soil in the far
            western foothills. .... *M. glandulósa*, 10-14", **W**

Oxybáphus [Mirabilis] .... Umbrella-wort
Stems slender and erect to leaning. Few leaves. Plants are easily overlooked until the few, small, bright purple flowers open. Found along roads and trails and in fields from lower valleys to montane.
1a.   Leaves linear; small. Stems white. .... *O. lineáris*, 8-40", see no. 175
1b.   Leaves broad cordate. .... *O. nyctaginéus*, 12-40"

HYDROPHYLLACEAE (HYD)   **Waterleaf Family**
Leaves alternate and simple or pinnately compound. Flowers are usually densely clumped, often to one side of the stem. Flower-parts in fives. Stamens protrude far beyond the petals. Sepals more or less united. Plants often sticky or hairy. Fruits are capsules.

Hydrophyllum .... Waterleaf
Flowers are arranged in ball-like clusters.
1a.   Leaves hairy; pinnately lobed with the end lobe much larger; not toothed.
            Flower clusters tight; petals blue and inconspicuous. Common in
            woods from lower montane to subalpine.
            .... *H. capitátum*, 4-18", see no. 176

173: *Apocynum androsaemifolium*   174: *Physalis hederifolia*

175: *Oxybaphus linearis*   176: *Hydrophyllum capitatum*

1b. Leaves smooth; pinnately lobed with the lobes about equal in size; coarsely toothed. Flower clusters loose; petals pale yellowish and conspicuous. Common in moist montane and subalpine forests and meadows. .... *H. féndleri*, 8-36", see no. 177

Phacélia
Flowers are more or less arranged in clusters that are coiled to one side of the stem.
1a. Found in foothills and montane. Flowers arranged in clusters that are distinctly coiled to one side (2)
1b. Found in alpine and subalpine. Flowers arranged in dense racemes, not distinctly coiled; purple. Plants grayish with short fuzzy hairs. Leaves pinnately divided with many linear divisions. Locally common in gravelly areas. .... *P. serícea*, Purple Fringe, 4-12", see Plate 29

2a. Flowers whitish. Plants coarsely hairy. Perennial. Leaves pinnately lobed with the end lobe much larger. Common disturbed areas and bare ground. .... *P. heterophýlla*, Scorpionweed, 4-32", see no. 178
2b. Flowers purple to violet. Plants sticky. Annual or biennial. Leaves pinnately divided; the divisions lobed. Form loose clumps. Locally common on gravelly ground in canyon bottoms such as near Lake City. .... *P. glandulósa*, 4-12", see no. 179

GENTIANACEAE (GEN)   **Gentian Family**
Leaves smooth and opposite or whorled. Stem leaves are sessile and the basal ones sometimes petioled. Flowers of many of the species are few and large relative to the short stems. They have four to five united petals. Fruits are two-parted capsules.

Key to Genera

1a. Flowers rotate or more open (2)
1b. Flowers tubular (3)

2a. Plants huge; flower spikes up to 6 feet tall; leaves in a basal rosette, large; flowers greenish; plants of meadows .... **FRASERA** p. 137
2b. Plants small and slender; flowers dusky purple; plants of wet subalpine .... **SWERTIA** p. 137

3a. Plants miniature; inhabit alpine; flowers blue .. **CHONDROPHYLLA** p. 137
3b. Plants not miniature; may inhabit alpine; flowers purple to blue-violet or white (4)

4a. Flower tube flares into an open star-shape .... **GENTIANELLA** p.138
4b. Flower tube cup-like with the top open or twisted shut (5)

5a. Flowers white with dark purple streaks; inhabit high alpine .... **GENTIANODES** p. 138
5b. Flowers some shade of blue or purple; inhabit montane to lower alpine (6)

6a. Petals fringed .... **GENTIANOPSIS** p. 138
6b. Petals not fringed, only teeth present between the petal lobes .... **PNEUMONANTHE** p. 138

177: *Hydrophyllum fendleri*

178: *Phacelia heterophylla*

Species

Frásera speciósa .... Green Gentian, Monument Plant, 1-6', see Plate 30
Leaves bright green and smooth, arranged in large, basal rosettes. Produce a massive flower stalk in 20 to 60 years and die after blooming. Flowers are open star-shaped with four petals, each are speckled and have a band of stiff hairs in the middle; greenish. Common in meadows and forest openings from upper foothills to subalpine.

Swértia perénnis .... Star Gentian, 4-12", see no. 180
Flowers are few on slender, erect stems. They are dusky, dark purple and open star-shaped. Leaves few, narrow and mostly basal. Uncommon in boggy areas of subalpine.

Chondrophýlla [Gentiana] .... Siberian Gentian
Miniature plants. Stems several. Leaves tiny. Flowers are erect, narrow tubes that open into four points. They close shut when shaded from the sun.
1a.   Flowers dark blue. Found in alpine. .... *C. prostráta*, 1/2-4", see no. 181
1b.   Flowers pale blue. Common in wet subalpine meadows.
            .... *C. aquática*, 1/2-4"

Gentianélla acúta [Gentiana amarella] .... Little Gentian, 8-14", see no. 182
Flowers are paired along the stems and several clustered at the top. Flower tubes flare
into an open star shape, fringed at the opening; lilac to pale blue (sometimes whitish).
Leaves elliptic-oblong. Plants are quite variable in form and size according to site
conditions. Common in moist meadows from upper foothills to subalpine.

Gentianódes álgida [Gentiana romanzovii] .... Arctic Gentian, 2-8"
Flowers are large, cylindrical cups; whitish with purple streaks. Bloom late in the
season, often during the first snows. Leaves are narrow, thick and waxy. Locally
common in upper alpine meadows.

Gentianópsis thérmalis [Gentiana] .... Fringed Gentian, 8-12", see Plate 31
Plants are annual, putting on a magnificent show of bloom in late summer. Flowers are
relatively large and narrow-cylindrical. Petals are fringed, deep violet and twisted
together at the top. Locally common to abundant in very wet meadows from upper
montane to lower alpine.

Pneumonánthe [Gentiana] .... Bottle Gentian
Showy plants with relatively large, cylindrical flowers that have teeth between the
petal lobes.
1a.   Flowers spread along upper part of stem; lowest ones have long pedicels;
         violet. Common in large, rather dry, montane meadows.
         .... *P. affinis*, 4-12", see no. 183
1b.   Flowers in tight terminal clusters; none have pedicels; blue-violet; barrel-
         shaped. Bloom in late summer. The most common large gentian of
         upper montane and subalpine meadows. .... *P. párryi*, 4-16"

POLEMONIACEAE (PLM)   **Phlox Family**
Leaves various. Flowers have parts usually in fives. Petals united and sepals partly
united. Fruits are three-celled capsules.

Gília
Leaves are mostly in basal rosettes. Flower stems have a few reduced leaves. Flowers
salverform.
1a.   Leaves pinnately dissected into narrow segments. Flowers numerous.
         Petals tiny; blue to lavender or whitish, the base of the tube may be
         yellowish. Stamens protrude. Biennial or perennial. Plants quite
         variable in size according to site conditions. Found in rocky or
         gravelly open areas from foothills to subalpine, scattered throughout
         the range. .... *G. pinnatifida* [G. calcarea], 4-20", see no.184
1b.   Leaves toothed, not dissected; thick-textured. Flowers rose-purple; larger.
         Stamens not protruding. Found on barren clay slopes such as the
         gray hills west of Durango. .... *G. subnúda*, 8-12", **W** see Plate 32

Ipomópsis
Flowers salverform.
1a.   Flowers tiny, in ball-like clusters; white. Perennial with rather woody
         stems. Leaves appear to be palmately divided into three to five linear
         segments. Found in foothills.
         .... *I. congésta*, Ball-Head Gilia, 4-12", see no. 185

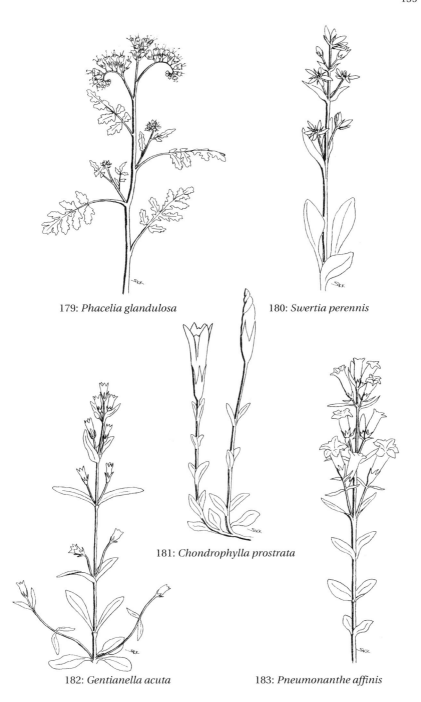

179: *Phacelia glandulosa*

180: *Swertia perennis*

181: *Chondrophylla prostrata*

182: *Gentianella acuta*

183: *Pneumonanthe affinis*

1b.   Flowers much larger and more spread out along stem. Biennial. Leaves
           pinnate, the divisions linear and sharp-pointed (2)

2a.   Flowers red to coral-pink, often speckled with yellow or white. Plants
           quite variable; separated into a number of subspecies. Abundant in
           meadows and along roads of montane.
           ....*I. aggregáta*, Scarlet Gilia, 6-24", see no. 186
2b.   Flowers pink with purple speckles or whitish

3a.   Uncommon in upper montane meadows. ....*I. tenuitúba*, 10-24", **W**
3b   Local in shale soils around Pagosa Springs...............*I. polyantha*, 12-24", **W**

Leptodáctylon púngens...Spiny Gilia, 6-12", see no. 187
Plants woody at the base. Stems have numerous gray-green, prickly, needle-like leaves.
Flowers white and showy, salverform. Bloom in spring. Common throughout lower
foothill grasslands, woodlands and among sagebrush.

Linanthástrum núttallii ....Nuttall's Gilia, 5-10", see no. 188
Plants have a low, loose, clumped form. Flowers are salverform; white. Leaves numerous, appearing whorled though actually palmately three to seven-parted into linear
segments. Found on open, gravelly ground of subalpine ridges.

Phlóx
Plants with opposite, linear or needle-like leaves. Profuse bloomers of pink-purple to
white, salverform flowers.
1a.   Plants in low, tight cushions. Leaves short and needle-like (2)
1b.   Plants with erect stems; few to several. Leaves narrow and sparse. Plants
           dry up after blooming in spring. Flowers vary from nearly white to
           deep pink-purple; numerous and showy. Abundant throughout
           sagebrush of the foothills. ....*P. longifólia*, 4-12", **W**, see Plate 33

2a.   Found at high altitudes; common on tundra and sometimes in open
           gravelly areas of subalpine. Form tight, dense, almost moss-like
           mats. Flowers white. When not blooming looks similar to *Silene
           acaulis* though leaves are more grayish.
           ....*P. condensáta*, Alpine Phlox, under 1", see Plate 34
2b.   Found in lower foothills; locally common among sagebrush, sometimes
           carpeting the ground. Flowers pale purple to white. Blooms early in
           spring. ....*P. hoódii*, 1-4"

Polemónium ....Jacob's Ladder
Flowers very showy; violet to white. Leaves compound, the leaflets simply pinnate or
pinnately-whorled. Plants are usually somewhat sticky.
1a.   Leaves mostly basal; compound with the leaflets very small, thick, elliptic
           and whorled. Alpine tundra or sometimes found on gravelly soil in
           high mountain parks. Flowers bright violet to white; funnelform. The
           following species hybridize creating mixed characteristics (2)
1b.   Leaves along stems; pinnate, not whorled. Found in montane and
           subalpine. Flowers violet to purple (4)

141

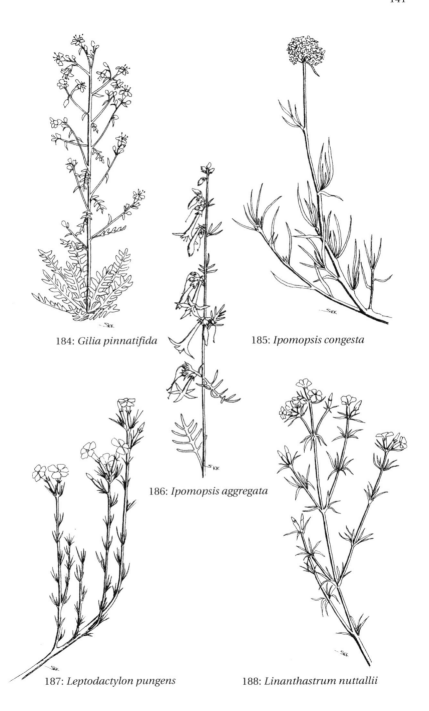

184: *Gilia pinnatifida*

185: *Ipomopsis congesta*

186: *Ipomopsis aggregata*

187: *Leptodactylon pungens*

188: *Linanthastrum nuttallii*

Flora of the San Juans ~

2a.   Flowers some shade of violet (3)
2b.   Flowers white to slightly bluish. Form thick leafy clumps with many old
        stems persisting. Strong skunk-like odor. Found in subalpine and
        alpine scree. .... *P. brándegei*, 6-12", see no. 189

3a.   Flowers twice as long as sepals; pale blue-violet. Leaves sticky; strong
        skunk-like odor. Found in alpine scree.
        .... *P. confértum* [P. grayanum], 3-8"
3b.   Flowers about as long as sepals; deep blue-violet. Leaves not sticky nor
        with a strong odor. Found on alpine tundra or sometimes dry, upper,
        subalpine meadows. .... *P. viscósum*, 2-12", see Plate 35

4a.   Plants less than 12 inches tall. Flowers pale violet; few. Stems delicate and
        weak. Common in dry areas of rather open subalpine forests
        throughout the range. .... *P. pulchérrimum*, 2-8", see no. 190
4b.   Plants over 12 inches tall; flowers violet to bright purple (5)

5a.   Panicles longer than broad. Uncommon in subalpine willow bogs.
        .... *P. caerúleum* [P. occidentale], 12-36", see no. 191
5b.   Panicles shorter than broad. Common in meadows and along streams
        and roads of moist montane and subalpine throughout the range.
        .... *P. foliosíssimum*, 12-36", see Plate 36

RUBIACEAE (RUB)   Madder Family

Gálium .... Bedstraw
Leaves are entire and opposite though they appear whorled (actually the stipules are
large and leaf-like giving the appearance of extra leaves). Stems mostly square in cross-
section. Flowers have three to five, united petals. Seeds often bristly.
1a.   Leaves appear as four per node. Stems erect. Flowers fragrant; white;
        arranged loosely when in shady situations and more tightly in
        pyramid-shaped clusters when in sunny situations. Common in
        moist forests and meadows of montane and subalpine throughout
        the range. .... *G. septentrionále* [G. boreale], Northern Bedstraw,
        8-28", see no. 192
1b.   Leaves appear as six or more per node. Stems are weak and leaning.
        Flowers inconspicuous; white to greenish; arranged in sparse axillary
        clusters. Leaves fragrant. Found in moist, shady areas of upper
        foothills and montane. .... *G. triflórum*, Fragrant Bedstraw,
        8-32", see no. 193

VERBENACEAE (VRB)   Vervain Family
Leaves are opposite or whorled, simple and entire to dissected. Stems square in cross-
section. Flowers are slightly irregular with united petals. They are arranged in elongated or condensed spikes. Blooming follows a progression up the spike, so that seeds
are maturing at the bottom while the top buds are first opening. Fruits are nutlets.

Glandulária bipinnatifída [Verbena] .... Showy Vervain, 8-14", see Plate 37
Flowers are small and brilliant lilac to rose-purple, arranged in condensed spikes.
Stems few to many tufted. Leaves are deeply divided and rough. Bloom in late spring
and often again later in the season. Found in lower foothill meadows and on slopes.

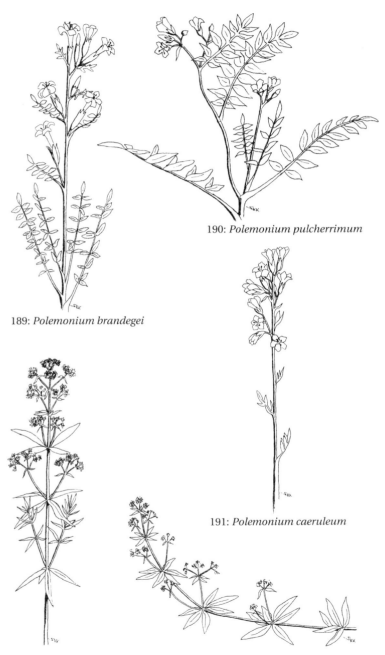

189: *Polemonium brandegei*

190: *Polemonium pulcherrimum*

191: *Polemonium caeruleum*

192: *Galium septentrionale*

193: *Galium triflorum*

Verbéna bracteáta .... Bracted Vervain, 4-8"
Weed of disturbed sites. Stiff bracts overshadow the flowers on elongated, sprawling spikes. Flowers themselves are tiny and inconspicuous; pale blue to purple. Stems sprawling. Leaves are pinnately lobed. Found in lower foothills.

PRIMULACEAE (PRM)   **Primrose Family**
Leaves simple and entire or toothed. Flowers parts in fives; petals and sepals are both united. Fruits are capsules.

Andrósace septentrionális .... Rock Jasmine, 1/2-12", see no. 194
Flowers are tiny, white stars in a diffuse, delicate, umbrella-like panicle. Leaves are arranged in a basal rosette. Plants vary in stature according to site conditions; often miniature. Common and widespread throughout the mountains.

Dodecátheon pulchéllum .... Shooting Star, 4-16", see no. 195
Flowers are few and nodding with bright pink petals that are reflexed backward, exposing the yellow bases and black stamens. Found along streams and boggy areas of subalpine.

Prímula párryi .... Parry's Primrose, 3-16", see Plate 38
Flowers are arranged in showy, terminal clusters; bright rose-purple. Leaves mostly basal, smooth and bright green. Plants have a strong grape gelatin-like odor. Common in bogs and along streams of subalpine and lower alpine.

VALERIANACEAE (VAL)   **Valerian Family**

Valeriána .... Valerian
Leaves opposite. The united petals are five-lobed. Sepals become plumes at seed maturity, aiding in seed dispersal.
1a.   Flowers rather inconspicuous and sparsely arranged on large, branched
           stems; yellow-white. Leaves with lateral veins parallel to midvein;
           leaf edges white. Stem leaves sessile or nearly so; pinnately parted
           into three to seven narrow segments. Common in gravelly meadows
           and forest openings from montane to lower alpine.
           .... *V. édulis*, 12-24", see no. 196
1b.   Flowers conspicuous; arranged in rather tight terminal clusters; pinkish to
           white. Leaves with lateral veins not parallel to midvein. Stem leaves
           in several pairs; sessile; lobed at the base or throughout. Basal leaves
           spatulate. Found in subalpine and alpine meadows or forest
           openings. .... *V. capitáta*, 6-16", see no. 197

BORAGINACEAE (BOR)   **Borage Family**
Plants are often bristly hairy. Leaves mostly alternate and simple. Flowers have five united petals. Many species have flowers arranged in one-sided racemes. Fruits are nutlets, often stickery, attaching to clothing or fur.

Cynoglóssum officinále .... Hound's Tongue, 16-32", see no. 198
Tall, weedy annual or biennial plant of open disturbed areas. Flowers are relatively small, deep red-purple and arranged in one-sided racemes. Leaves large, soft and hairy; oblong to lanceolate. Seeds disc-shaped and stickery. Introduced from Europe. Found in foothills and montane.

194: *Androsace septentrionalis*

195: *Dodecatheon pulchellum*

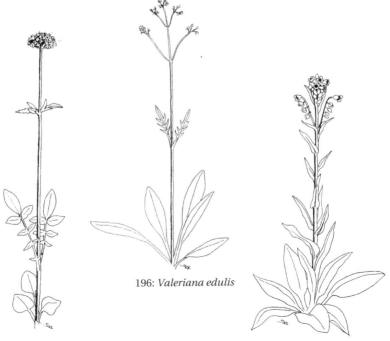

196: *Valeriana edulis*

197: *Valeriana capitata*

198: *Cynoglossum officinale*

Hackélia floribúnda .... Stickseed, 12-48", see no. 199
Plants rather weedy. Stems and leaves are hairy. Flowers are tiny and inconspicuous; blue to white in one-sided racemes. Seeds very stickery. Common disturbed dry open ground of foothills and montane.

Lithospérmum .... Puccoon
Flowers tubular with the end flaring into five lobes. Leaves are narrow.
1a.   Flowers pale green-yellow; differ in size between plants. Stems stout; many in a tall clump. Common among oakbrush on the far western, foothill plateaus. .... *L. ruderále*, 8-24", **W**
1b.   Flowers bright yellow. Stems narrower (2)

2a.   Flower tube twice as long as the sepals. Petals wavy-margined. Found in forest openings of montane and subalpine. .... *L. multiflórum*, 12-24"
2b.   Flower tube three to four times as long as the sepals. Petals fringed. Form varies from a few tufted stems to thick low clumps. Common among sagebrush and dry, foothill woodlands on the western slope. Abundant in the foothill grasslands on the eastern slope.
        .... *L. incísum*, 4-20", see Plate 39

Merténsia .... Bluebells
Flowers small, pendulous bells arranged in terminal clusters that hang to one side of the stem. Leaves vary from oblong to ovate.
1a.   Flowers deep blue. Stems less than 16 inches tall. Stem leaves without obvious side veins. Plants scattered (2)
1b.   Flowers pale blue to pink. Stems over 16 inches tall. Stem leaves with obvious side veins. Often in large patches (3)

2a.   Hairs on upper leaf surface all point away from the center. Stems single or a few together. One of the earliest bloomers in dry sagebrush areas; dies back to a tuberous root before summer. Common throughout the foothills and montane among sagebrush and oakbrush.
        .... *M. fusifórmis*, 4-10", **W**
2b.   Hairs on the upper leaf surface not oriented away from the center. Quite variable in width of leaves, heights and the amount of hairs on the leaves. Form varies from numerous tufted, leafy, arching stems to low, few-leaved tufts. Found in open areas of foothills, montane and alpine throughout the range.
        .... *M. lanceol</ata* [includes M. bakeri and M. viridis], 4-18", see no. 200

3a.   Leaves pale blue-green; very smooth. Common along streams of subalpine and lower alpine. .... *M. ciliáta*, 16-40", see Plate 40
3b.   Leaves green; slightly textured. Common along streams of montane and subalpine. .... *M. franciscána*, 16-40"

Eritríchum aretioídes [E. elongatum] .... Alpine Forget-me-not, under 2"
Flowers are miniature and bright blue with white center eyes. Plants form low, mound-like clumps of tiny rosettes of silky-hairy leaves. Found on dry, gravelly alpine tundra and upper subalpine.

Oreocárya [Cryptantha]
Plants are gray with dense hairs, prickly when dry. Flowers are tiny, white with yellow center eyes and arranged in hairy clusters. There are several species that are distinquished on technical characteristics not visible with the naked eye. The most common species on the western slope of the range in dry lower foothill woodlands is *O. bákeri* (5-12") and on rocky foothill ridges is *O. nitída* [C. flavocanescens] (3-8") see no. 201. On the eastern slope a taller species with flowers more loosely arranged and found in the upper foothill meadows is *O. thrysiflóra* (8-16"). Found around Cochetopa Pass is *O. wéberi* (4-8").

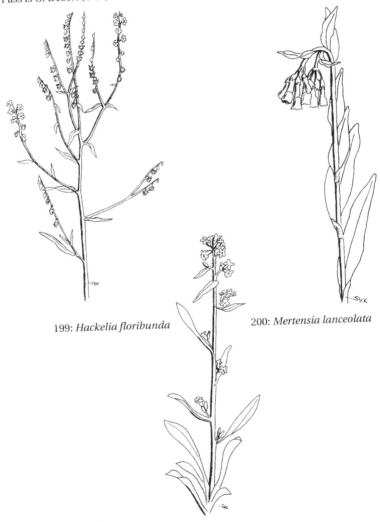

199: *Hackelia floribunda*

200: *Mertensia lanceolata*

201: *Oreocarya nitida*

FREE-PETAL DICOTS

Key to Families

1a.	Leaves are large pads floating on the surface of ponds .... **NYM** p. 150
1b.	Leaves not as above (2)
2a.	Plants succulent to fleshy (note: some MONOCOTS also fleshy) (3)
2b.	Plants not succulent or fleshy (5)
3a.	Stems enlarged, succulent and spiny; no leaves (stems may be flattened pads that appear to be leaves) .... **CAC** p. 151
3b.	Not as above; leaves succulent to fleshy (4)
4a.	Leaves fleshy, in basal rosettes; flowers among them .... **POR** p. 152
4b.	Leaves succulent, in tiny basal rosettes or fleshy and larger along stems; flowers on stems .... **CRS** p. 152
5a.	Plants woody, not vines (6)
5b.	Plants herbs or vines (12)
6a.	Plants small trees; leaves minute and overlapping; flowers in feathery clusters at the ends of branches, pink to whitish .... **TAM** p. 152
6b.	Plants shrubs (7)
7a.	Leaves opposite (8)
7b.	Leaves alternate or fascicled (9)
8a.	Leaves narrow; found in dry foothills .... **HDR** p. 154
8b.	Leaves broad; found in moist drainages .... **COR** p. 154
9a.	Flowers either tiny, yellow-green and axillary or small, white and in terminal clusters on thorny branches of low shrubs .... **RHM** p. 154
9b.	Not as above (10)
10a.	Plants low with large, spine-tipped, pinnate leaves or tall and spiny-stemmed with elliptic, simple leaves; flowers tiny, yellow, bell-shaped .... **BER** p. 154
10b.	Plants not with spine-tipped leaves; if stems spiny then leaves broader palmately veined, lobed or parted and flowers not bell-shaped; white, pink, coral or yellow (11)
11a.	Flowers several together on twigs, petals usually smaller than the united sepals; stems with or without spines or thorns .... **GRS** p. 156
11b.	Flowers single or if clustered then densely so on tall shrubs or small trees; petals larger than sepals; stems may have spines or thorns ..... **ROS** p. 156
12a.	Plants with flowers arranged in umbels and leaves compound with enlarged petiole bases .... **API** p. 169
12b.	Plants not as above (13)

13a. Flowers irregular (14)
13b. Flowers regular (17)

14a. Sepals and petals distinctly different in appearance (15)
14b. Sepals and petals look similar .... **HEL** p. 190

15a. Sepals two, small, bract-like .... **FUM** p. 177
15b. Sepals more than two, larger (16)

16a. Lower petal with a spur, flowers with open face .... **VIO** p. 177
16b. Lower two petals join into a boat-shaped keel; flowers without an open
      face .... **FAB** p. 178
17a. Plants either vines or clumped to sprawling with flowers dark, leathery,
      inverted urn-shaped .... **RAN** p. 192
17b. Plants not as above (18)

18a. Plants with leaves trifoliate and flowers purple (19)
18b. Plants not as above (20)

19a. Leaves all basal or nearly so, squared at tips; plants low .... **OXL** p. 194
19b. Leaves on stems, pointed at tips; plants tall and branched .... **CPP** p. 196

20a. Petals and sepals distinctly different in appearance or absent (21)
20b. Petals and sepals look the same (36)

21a. Plants with leaves evergreen and mostly basal; round, elliptic to oblong;
      low plants of shady montane forests .... **PYR** p. 196
21b. Plants not as above (22)

22a. Flowers with an obvious united column of parts in the middle (23)
22b. Flowers not as above (24)

23a. Leaves opposite or basal .... **GER** p. 198
23b. Leaves alternate .... **MLV** pp. 199

24a. Stamens more than ten (25)
24b. Stamens less than or equal to ten (28)

25a. Stamens far-protruding (26)
25b. Stamens not far-protruding (27)

26a. Found in wet places; flowers yellow; leaves small, elliptic, entire ..... **HYP** p. 200
26b. Found on dry foothills slopes; leaves pinnately lobed .... **LOA** p. 200

27a. Sepals united, at least at base .... **ROS** p. 156
27b. Sepals not united or absent .... **RAN** p. 194

28a. Petals four or five; stamens four to ten; flowers white or pink; sepals two;
      leaves basal or absent .... **Claytonia in POR** p. 152
28b. Not as above (29

29a.   Petals four (30)
29b.   Petals five (32)

30a.   Stems swollen at nodes; stamens ten .... ASN p. 212
30b.   Stems not swollen at nodes (31)

31a.   Stamens four or eight .... ONA p. 200
31b.   Stamens six (two short and four long ones) .... BRA p. 204

32a.   Flowers very pale to dark blue, petals drop early .... LIN p. 210
32b.   Flowers white or pink (33)

33a.   Stems with swollen nodes, stamens five or ten (34)
33b.   Stems without swollen nodes (35)

34a.   Sepals united; petals narrowed at base like a pan handle, white or pink
         .... CRY p. 210
34b.   Sepals separate; petals not as above, white .... ASN p. 212

35a.   Stamens alternate with five yellow fringed stalks; petals white .. PAR p. 214
35b.   Not as above .... SAX p. 214

36a.   Leaves divided or compound (37)
36b.   Leaves simple and entire (38)

37a.   Leaves palmately divided and stem leaves opposite or whorled .... RAN p. 192
37b.   Leaves variously divided, if palmate then stem leaves alternate .... HEL p. 190

38a.   Flowers relatively large; found in high altitude bogs
         .... **Psychrophila in HEL** p. 190
38b.   Flowers small to tiny (39)

39a.   Flowers encircled by united bracts .... **Eriogonum in PLG** p. 219
39b.   Flowers not as above (40)

40a.   Flowers in corymbs; leaves smooth, pale green; low plants of dry foothills
         .... SAN p. 222
40b.   Flowers in spikes or racemes; papery stipules sheath stems; white or
         greenish flowers .... PLG p. 218

NYMPHAEACEAE (NYM)   Water-Lily Family

Núphar lúteum .... Pond Lily
Plants have stems rooted in the bottom of ponds and leaves floating on the surface.
Leaves are large and oval-cordate. Flowers occur just below the water's surface or
floating. Petals are inconspicuous and sepals are petal-like and yellow. Found in cold
montane and subalpine ponds.

CACTACEAE (CAC)   Cactus Family
Plants lack leaves. Stems are succulent, spiny and jointed or single. Flowers and spines arise from tiny pads (areoles) on the stem. Bloom in late spring.

Coryphántha vivípara .... Beehive, 2-4"
Stems are round to barrel-shaped and deeply tubercled. Tubercles have a groove on the upper surface. Flowers pink, single or a few together. Common among sagebrush of the lower foothills.

Pediocáctus símpsonii .... Ball Cactus, 1-3"
Stems are barrel-shaped and deeply tubercled. Tubercles lack a groove on the upper surface. Flowers are pinkish on eastern slope plants and more yellowish on western slope plants. Locally common on the far western plateaus and the eastern slope foothills.

Echinocéreus
Stems are barrel-shaped, ribbed and bumpy but not deeply tubercled. Flowers arise from short, side branches. The digging of these species has seriously threatened their future. Every effort should be made to rescue them from construction sites and leave those in wildland areas alone.

1a.   Stems many bunched together; sometimes forming a huge mass several feet across. Flowers scarlet. Found among sagebrush or open woods of the lower foothills.
                .... *E. triglochidiátus*, Claret Cup Hedge-Hog, 4-8"
1b.   Stems single or a few together (2)

2a.   Flowers bright rose-purple. Uncommon on rocky knolls of the lower foothills. .... *E. féndleri*, Sitting Cactus, 2-4", **W**
2b.   Flowers green-yellow. Stems usually reddish. Locally common on foothill grasslands. .... *E. viridiflórus*, Hen-and-Chickens, 1-2 1/2", **E**

Cylindropúntia whípplei .... Rat-tail, Plateau Cholla, 3-7", **W**
Stems are in a chain-like form with cylindrical segments. These spread along ground, forming large thickets. Flowers pale yellow to chartreuse. Common in open woods of the lower foothills.

Opúntia .... Prickly Pear
Stems are flattened pads. Pads can be rather plump when moisture is plentiful and wrinkled when dry. The species hybridize creating an array of colors and pad-shapes and variation in the amount of spines.

1a.   Pads oval and plump; easily breaking off. Flowers yellow. Abundant lower foothills. .... *O. frágilis*, Potato Cactus, 3-5", **W**
1b.   Pads roundish and flat; not easily breaking off (2)

2a.   Pads large; gray-green. Spines spaced 1 to 1 1/2 inches apart; brown-tipped. Fruits fleshy, red-purple at maturity. Flowers yellow with reddish bases. Found on lowest foothill canyonsides and slopes.
                .... *O. phaeacántha*, New Mexican Prickly Pear, 8-12", **W**
2b.   Pads smaller; green. Spines close together. Fruits dry at maturity. Flowers red, yellow to apricot. Abundant on canyonsides and at lower elevations. .... *O. polyacántha*, Starvation Prickly Pear, 4-8"

PORTULACACEAE (POR)   **Purslane Family**
Plants arise from corms or thickened rootstalks. Leaves are mostly succulent to fleshy, simple and entire. Flowers have four to five overlapping petals. Stamens are of the same number and arranged opposite the petals. Sepals two (except Oreobroma has six to eight). Fruits are capsules.

Claytónia .... Spring Beauty
1a.   Found on alpine scree of the higher peaks. Leaves round, fleshy and often
             reddish; arranged in tight rosettes with whitish flowers among them.
             .... *C. megarhíza*, 1-3"
1b.   Found in montane forest openings and meadows. Leaves lanceolate; a
             basal pair (may be absent entirely). Flowers several on rather long
             pedicels that hang down from stems; light pink to white with darker
             veins. Bloom in early spring. .... *C. lanceoláta*, 2-8", **W**, see no. 202

Oreobróma [Lewesia] .... Bitteroot
Leaves are narrow and fleshy in a basal rosette with white to pink flowers among them. Found in rocky soils or gravelly open sites; often in the center of little-used, two-track roads.
1a.   Inhabit subalpine and lower alpine throughout the range. Petals about 1/
             4 inch long. Leaves linear. .... *O. pygmaéa*, 1-2"
1b.   Inhabit montane. Petals about 1/2 inch long. Leaves narrow-oblanceolate.
             .... *O. nevadénsis*, 1-2", **W**, see no. 203

CRASSULACEAE (CRS)   **Stonecrop Family**
Leaves are fleshy to succulent, simple and usually entire. Flowers have the same number of petals as sepals. Flowers persistent. Fruits are follicles.

Amerosédum lanceolátum [Sedum] .... Yellow Stonecrop, 2-8", see no. 204
Plants have basal rosettes of tiny, plump, succulent leaves; often reddish. Usually occur in loose patches. Flowers are yellow and star-shaped; few on delicate, wiry stems. Common on gravelly open ground from foothill grasslands to alpine tundra.

Cleméntsia rhodántha [Sedum] .... Rose Crown, 4-14", see Plate 41
Plants are attractive during bloom in late summer. Flowers are pale pink-rose and crowded into dense, terminal racemes. Plants have fleshy leaves; alternate and sessile; oblong to oblanceolate. Common in wet areas of upper subalpine and lower alpine.

Rhodióla integrifólia [Sedum] .... Kings Crown, 2-12", see Plate 42
Flowers are deep red, drying to red-brown and persisting. Bloom mid-season. Plants fleshy. Leaves alternate, sessile and obovate. Occassionally form large patches. Common to abundant in alpine meadows.

TAMARICACEAE (TAM)   **Tamarisk Family**

Támarix ramosíssima .... Tamarisk, 5-25', **W**
Weedy, introduced, large shrub or small tree that has taken over whole areas of the lower river valleys to the exclusion of everything else. Occasionally found scattered in moist areas of the foothills. Branches have a feathery appearance with tiny overlapping leaves. Flowers are pink to whitish, arranged in plumes at the ends of branches. Bloom in early summer.

202: *Claytonia lanceolata*

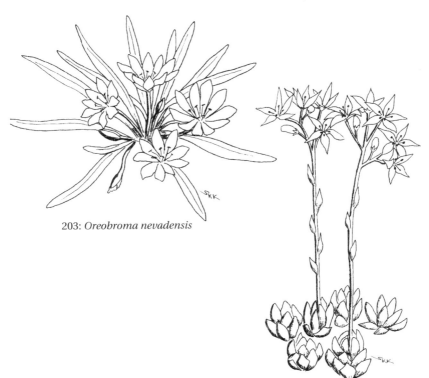

203: *Oreobroma nevadensis*

204: *Amerosedum lanceolatum*

HYDRANGEACEAE (HDR)   Hydrangea Family

Féndlera rupicóla .... Fendlerbush, 4-6', **W**, see no. 205
Tall wiry shrubs. Leaves are opposite, linear to oblong; thick and dark green. Flowers are large with four, white, somewhat triangular petals. One of the showy, spring-blooming shrubs. Fruits are long-persisting capsules. Locally abundant on rocky hillsides of upper foothills.

CORNACEAE (COR)   Dogwood Family

Swída serícea [Cornus stolonifera] .... Dogwood, 3-5' or more, see no. 206
Shrubs, densely branched with red twigs. Leaves opposite, entire and elliptic; side-veins long. Flowers have four to five, small, white petals. Sepals tiny. Fruits are white drupes. Found in cool, deep drainages of montane.

RHAMNACEAE (RHM)   Buckthorn Family
Shrubs. Leaves are simple and variously arranged. Flowers are small with four to five petals and sepals. Fruits are capsules or berries.

Ceanóthus féndleri .... Buckbrush, 12-24", see no. 207
Low, spiny shrub with small, elliptic leaves that are whitish underneath. Flowers are tiny and numerous in tight, umbel-like clusters; white. Common in dry, open, montane forests.

Rhámnus smíthii .... Smith's Buckthorn, 4-6', **W**, see no. 208
Large, dense shrub with shiny, olive leaves; elliptic to lanceolate. Flowers are yellow-green and rather inconspicuous; axillary. Berries black. Uncommon on wooded or brushy slopes of the upper foothills and montane.

BERBERIDACEAE (BER)   Barberry Family
Shrubs. Leaves are alternate and simple or compound. Flowers are composed of six sepals and six petals, arranged in racemes; yellow. Inner bark and wood are yellow. Fruits are berries.

Bérberis féndleri .... Fendler's Barberry, 2-6', see no. 209
Erect shrubs. Branches are prickly-stemmed with three-parted spines. Often form large thickets. Flowers are in axillary clusters; yellow. Late in the season the oblong berries ripen to bright red and the leaves turn orange. Found mostly under Ponderosa Pines in valley bottoms of montane.

Mahónia répens [Berberis] .... Oregon-Grape, 3-10", see no. 210
Leaves holly-like, pinnate with spine-tipped edges and semi-evergreen (turning red when exposed to cold weather). Flowers yellow, in showy dense clusters. Bloom in spring. Bluish berrries ripen in late summer. Spread by underground rootstalks forming rather loose patches. Abundant and widespread throughout dry, pine forests and oakbrush of foothills and montane.

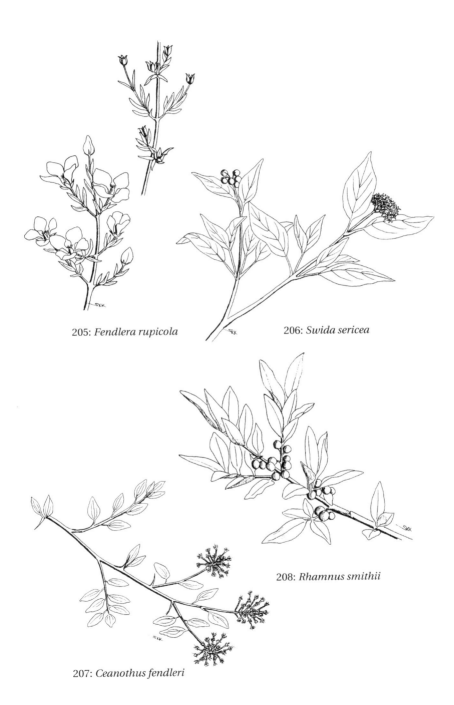

205: *Fendlera rupicola*

206: *Swida sericea*

208: *Rhamnus smithii*

207: *Ceanothus fendleri*

GROSSULARIACEAE (GRS)   Gooseberry Family

Ríbes
Shrubs. Stems often spiny. Leaves alternate, simple and palmately veined, lobed or parted. Flowers are usually arranged in small terminal or axillary racemes and have five petals and five united sepals. Fruits are berries.

1a.	Spines or thorns absent (2)
1b.	Spines or thorns present (5)

2a.   Leaves smooth and shiny; three-lobed and not serrated. Flowers bright yellow; long tubular. Berries black or red. Found on moist sites in lower valleys. .... *R. aúreum*, Golden Currant, 3-9', see no. 211

2b.   Not as above (3)

3a.   Leaves small; reniform with shallow lobes; rough and serrated. Flowers pink. Berries orange-red. Found on dry sites from foothills to subalpine ridges. The dominant shrub of the eastern slope.
.... *R. céreum*, Squaw Currant, 2-6', see no. 212

3b.   Leaves large; palmately lobed and cordate at the base (4)

4a.   Flowers arise from the tips of new twigs; white. Stems erect. Berries black. Common in subalpine forests; occasionally in moist montane forests. .... *R. wólfii*, 3-5', see no. 213

4b.   Flowers arise from the sides of older twigs; pink. Stems sprawling on the ground or over logs and rocks. Berries black. Common in subalpine forests near the continental divide. .... *R. coloradénse*, 12-24"

5a.   Stems with both thorns and spines (6)

5b.   Stems with few thorns singly or in threes at the nodes (mostly on new twigs) and usually without spines. Leaves smooth; lobed and toothed (no teeth across the bottom edge). Flowers pink or white. Berries wine red. Common in shaded montane. .... *R. inérme*, Mountain Gooseberry, 24-36"

6a.   Stems very thorny and with few spines. Low-growing. Leaves hairy; parted and many toothed. Flowers pink to orangish or coral. Berries deep red. Common in dry montane and subalpine forests.
.... *R. montigénum*, Red Prickly Currant, 12-24", see no. 214

6b.   Stems with thorns single at nodes and spiny in between. Stems long; erect to arching; unbranched. Taller. Leaves smooth; rather deeply lobed and toothed. Flowers green or purplish. Berries purple-black. Found in wet areas of montane and subalpine. .... *R. lacústre*, 36-48"

ROSACEAE (ROS)   Rose Family
Leaves are alternate and simple or compound. Flowers have four or five separate petals. Sepals are partly united; four or five. Five stamens and the petals are seated on a tube formed by the sepals or on a disk that lines it. Fruits various.

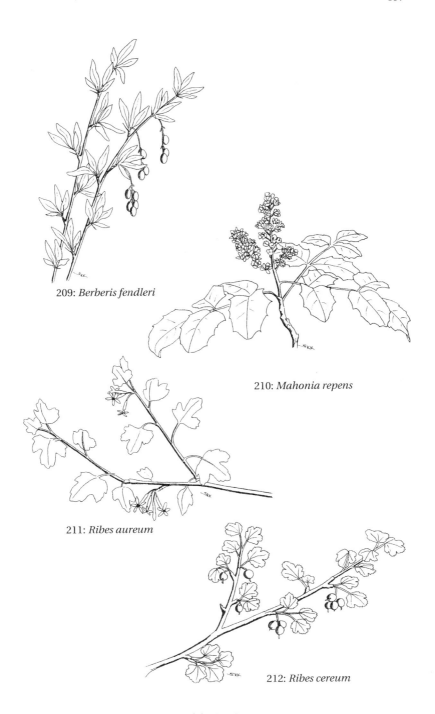

209: *Berberis fendleri*

210: *Mahonia repens*

211: *Ribes aureum*

212: *Ribes cereum*

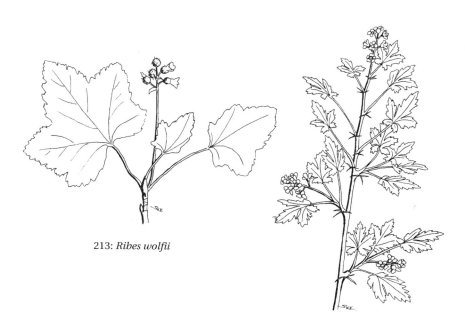

213: *Ribes wolfii*

214: *Ribes montigenum*

Key to Genera

1a.	Shrubs or small trees (2)
1b.	Herbs (14)

2a.	Leaves compound (3)
2b.	Leaves simple (6)

3a.	Stems with thorns or spines (4)
3b.	Stems without thorns or spines (5)

4a.   Flowers pink; fruit round, red, mealy; leaves nearly the same color top and bottom .... **ROSA** p. 160

4b.   Flowers white; fruit a dark red juicy berry; leaves dark green on top and very light underneath .... **RUBUS** p. 160

5a.   Leaves very small, pinnately divided into three to seven segments all crowded together; low shrubs of dry mountain meadows .... **PENTAPHYLLOIDES** p. 160

5b.   Leaves large; pinnate. Tall shrubs or small trees of shaded moist woods .... **SORBUS** p. 160

6a.	Leaves very finely serrated or entire (7)
6b.	Leaves more coarsely toothed (8)

7a. Shrubs; leaves small and narrow, mostly entire or barely serrated; flowers white, solitary or a few together; fruits yellow to orange.
.... **PERAPHYLLUM** p. 160
7b. Tall shrubs or small trees; leaves larger and broader, regularly serrated; bark with small scattered white marks; flowers white, in elongated clusters; fruits red .... **PADUS** p. 160

8a. Leaves very large (nearly the size of your hand) .... **RUBACER** p. 160
8b. Leaves smaller (9)

9a. Branches with thorns (may be very few) .... **CRATAEGUS** p. 160
9b. Branches without thorns (10)

10a. Leaves lobed (11)
10b. Leaves not lobed, only toothed (12)

11a. Leaves palmately lobed .... **PHYSOCARPUS** p. 162
11b. Leaves wedge-shaped, three-lobed at apex .... **PURSHIA** p. 162

12a. Leaves elliptic, gray-green (13)
12b. Leaves oval to round, dark green, thin .... **AMELANCHIER** p. 164

13a. Flowers tiny, arranged in large conspicuous terminal plumes
.... **HOLODISCUS** p. 162
13b. Flowers inconspicuous, scattered along twigs .... **CERCOCARPUS** p. 162

14a. Leaves trifoliate (15)
14b. Leaves pinnate or palmate (16)

15a. Spread by above-ground runners; flowers white .... **FRAGARIA** p. 164
15b. Spread by underground rootstalks; flowers yellow, tiny .... **SIBBALDIA** p. 164

16a. Leaves pinnate, tip leaflet the largest (17)
16b. Leaves pinnate or palmate, tip leaflet much the same size as the others (19)

17a. Plants with leaves greatly reduced on the flower stems (18)
17b. Plants with leaves rather uniform throughout .... **GEUM** p. 166

18a. Plants found on open dry ground of montane and subalpine meadows and open forests; leaves grayish; flowers nodding, pink, urn-shaped
.... **ERYTHROCOMA** p. 164
18b. Plants abundant throughout alpine meadows; leaves dark green; flowers yellow, erect .... **ACOMASTYLIS** p. 164

19a. Leaflets nearly round .... **DRYMOCALLIS** p. 166
19b. Leaflets narrow (20)

20a. Plants with stolons .... **ARGENTINA** p. 166
20b. Plants without stolons .... **POTENTILLA** p. 166

Species

Rósa woódsii .... Woods Rose, 3-6', see no. 215
Shrubs with thorny and spiny stems. Leaves pinnately compound and toothed. Flowers are large and clustered several together; pink. Fruits red and mealy (hips). Often form thickets. Common in open areas from lower valleys to subalpine.

Rúbus idaéus [R. strigosus] .... Red Raspberry, 24-48", see no. 216
Plants have spiny stems. Leaves are pinnate with three to five leaflets. Flowers large and white. Dark red berrries composed of several sections ripen in late summer. Most often form thickets along roads and rockslide areas. Common rocky, moist areas of upper montane and subalpine.

Pentaphylloídes floribúnda [Potentilla fruticosa]
.... Shrubby Cinquefoil, 12-40", see Plate 43
Low, stiffly-branched shrub with shredding bark. Leaves are tiny and pinnate with leaflets so crowded as to appear palmate. Flowers bright yellow. Common to locally abundant in dry montane and subalpine meadows.

Sórbus scopulína .... Mountain-ash, 12-15'
Small trees of moist, shaded areas of montane. Often clumped. Leaves are large and pinnate with eleven to fifteen, toothed leaflets. Leaves turn pink-orange in autumn. Flowers in terminal corymbs; white. Berries orange.

Peraphýllum ramosíssimum .... Squaw Apple, 4-6' W, see no. 217
One of the showy blooming shrubs of the foothills in the springtime. Densely branched. Leaves are narrow-oblanceolate; smooth. Flowers solitary or a few together; white and fragrant. Yellow fruits ripen to orangish in mid-summer. Locally abundant on rocky, lower foothill slopes.

Pádus virginiána [Prunus] .... Chokecherry, 12-30', see no. 218
Tall shrub or small tree. Leaves are finely serrated on the edges. Bloom in spring; a showy display of tiny white flowers in dense cylindrical racemes. Red fruits darken by August in some years the branches bending under the weight. Leaves turn orange in autumn. Abundant in moist areas from foothill riverbottoms to montane.

Rubácer parviflórum [Rubus] .... Thimbleberry, 3-6', see no. 219
Shrubs with large, palmately five-lobed leaves. Flowers large and white. Berries composed of many tiny segments ripen red in late summer. Found in shady, moist woods of upper montane and subalpine; more common on the western slope.

Crataégus .... Hawthorn
Tall shrubs to small trees; often thorny. Leaves are elliptic to ovate; toothed. Bloom in spring with white flowers arranged in corymbs. Fruits are pomes.
1a.   Thorns mostly 1 1/2 inch or longer. Fruits bright red. Leaves lobed and toothed; hairy throughout season. Uncommon near streams in the southern part of the range. .... *C. macracántha*, 10-20', W
1b.   Thorns mostly less than 1 1/2 inches or absent (2)

2a.   Leaves lobed and toothed; hairy only early in the season. Fruits dark. Found on dry slopes of the foothills. .... *C. erythropóda*, 6-15'

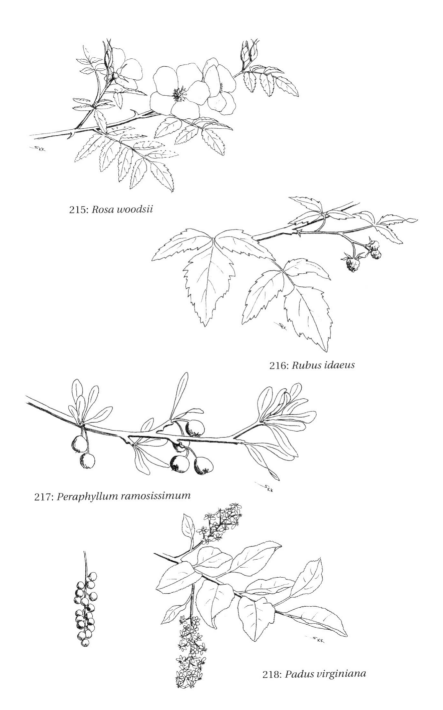

215: *Rosa woodsii*

216: *Rubus idaeus*

217: *Peraphyllum ramosissimum*

218: *Padus virginiana*

2b.   Leaves not distinctly lobed, only toothed. Fruits red, darkening with age. Most common hawthorn along rivers and streams.
.... *C. riváláris*, 9-18', see no. 220

Physocárpus monogýnus .... Ninebark, 2-7', see no. 221
Many branched shrub. Leaves are ovate and palmately three to five-lobed and also toothed. May be confused with *Ribes* except the bark is peeling and the white flowers are in tight clusters. Found on steep rocky slopes or talus.

Púrshia tridentáta .... Bitterbrush, 3-9', **W**, see no. 222
Shrub often with arching branches. Leaves are small, wedge-shaped and three-lobed at the apex. Flowers pale yellow in abundance. Bloom in spring. Fruits are dry and cone-shaped with a curled tip. Common in rocky ground of the foothills.

Holodíscus dumósus .... Rock Spiraea, 2-9'
Shrubs with the older stems having gray, peeling bark. Leaves are small and grayish, elliptic and toothed. Flowers tiny and arranged in loose, dense, plume-like panicles; cream-colored. Fruits are achenes. Common and scattered on dry, rocky, bare ground and cliffs. More prevalent east of the Continental Divide.

Cercocárpus montánus .... Mountain-Mahogany, 5-9', see no. 223
Shrubs with small, obovate leaves toothed mostly above the middle. Flowers are inconspicuous. Seeds have whitish, spiraled bristles attached. In some years these make the whole shrub look fuzzy in early summer. Common in rocky lower foothills.

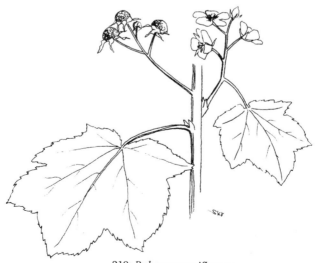

219: *Rubacer parviflorum*

220: *Crataegus rivularis*

221: *Physocarpus monogynus*

222: *Purshia tridentata*

223: *Cercocarpus montanus*

224: *Amelanchier alnifolia*

Amelánchier .... Serviceberry
Shrubs with oval to obovate leaves toothed mostly above the middle; thin and dark green. Flowers several together in terminal clusters; white. Bloom in spring. Berries ripen to blue-purple in mid-summer.

1a.   Leaves hairy only early in the season. Common upper foothills and
            montane. .... *A. alnifólia*, 4-9' or more, see no. 224
1b.   Leaves hairy throughout the season. Common in rocky areas of lower
            foothills. .... *A. utahénsis*, 4-9' or more

Fragária .... Strawberry
Low growing plants that spread by above-ground runners. Leaves are trifoliate, the leaflets toothed. Flowers white. Berries are tiny, ripening bright red.

1a.   Leaf surface grooved by veins; bright green. Common in moist montane
            and subalpine forests. .... *F. vésca* [F. americana], 1-3"
1b.   Leaf surface smooth; blue-green. Common in drier forests of montane
            and subalpine. .... *F. virginiána* [F. ovalis], 1-3", see no. 225

Sibbáldia procúmbens, 1-5", see no. 226
Low growing plants with trifoliate leaves, toothed at the tips. Spread by underground rootstalks forming patches. Flowers tiny and yellow. Abundant on bare, gravelly areas of subalpine and alpine.

Erythrocóma triflóra [Geum] .... Prairie Smoke, 8-20", see no. 227
Flowers nod. Pink sepals overshadow the tiny, whitish petals. Leaves are pinnate with the leaflets toward the apex larger than the lower ones; hairy. Seeds have feathery, pinkish plumes. Locally abundant in open, dry, gravelly ground of montane and subalpine scattered throughout the range.

Acomastýlis róssii [Geum] .... Alpine Avens, 2-12", see Plate 44
Flowers are bright yellow, contrasting the deep green, tufted basal foliage. Leaves pinnate, the tip leaflet largest; turn dark red in autumn. Extremely abundant and widespread in alpine meadows.

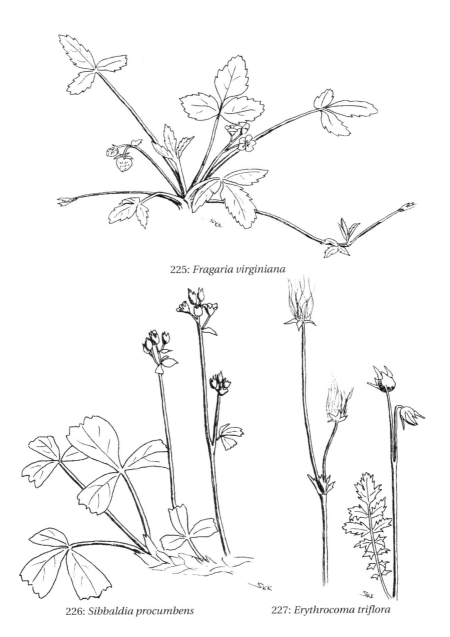

225: *Fragaria virginiana*

226: *Sibbaldia procumbens*

227: *Erythrocoma triflora*

Géum .... Avens
Leaves are pinnate with the uppermost leaflets much larger than the lower ones.
Flowers relatively small and few on tall branched stems; yellow.
1a.   Uppermost leaflet greatly enlarged and lobed, but not divided. Found in
             moist meadows and along streams of montane and subalpine.
             .... *G. macrophýllum*, 12-40", see no. 228
1a.   Uppermost leaflet not greatly enlarged; further divided. Found in moist
             montane areas. .... *G. aléppicum*, 12-30", see no. 229

Drymocállis [Potentilla]
Leaves are long pinnate with the leaflets rounded and coarsely toothed; yellow-green.
Stems hairy. Flowers small.
1a.   Flowers whitish; crowded together. Petals barely longer than the sepals.
             Found in montane meadows. .... *D. argúta*, 12-40", see no. 230
1b.   Flowers yellow; not crowded together. Petals longer than sepals. Found in
             foothill and montane meadows. .... *D. físsa*, 8-12"

Argentína anserína [Potentilla], 3-8", see no. 231
Leaves long pinnate with the leaflets oblong to elliptic and toothed; white underneath
and dark green on top. Flowers are single on stems; yellow. Plants spread by red stolons.
Found in moist, montane meadows.

Potentílla .... Cinquefoil
Leaves pinnately or palmately compound and toothed; lighter on the underside.
Flowers among the species are nearly identical having five small, yellow petals
often with an orange spot at the base. Flowers are clustered, several together on
branched stems.
1a.   Plants large (over 16 inches tall); form thick robust clumps; silky hairy.
             Leaves long; pinnate. Bloom mid to late summer. Found locally
             around Wagon Wheel Gap. .... *P. ámbigens*, 16-28", E
1b.   Plants smaller (or if over 16 inches tall, then with slender sparse stems,
             not in thick robust clumps) (2)

2a.   Weedy annuals. Basal leaves dried by blooming time; palmate. Petals
             shorter than sepals. .... *P. norvégica*, 10-20"
2b.   Perennials. Basal leaves functional during blooming. Petals longer than
             sepals (3)

3a.   Leaves pinnate (4)
3b.   Leaves palmate or nearly so (5)

4a.   Leaves small; gray-green and fuzzy. Plants in dense, erect tufts. Flowers
             barely top the leaves. Found in moist valleys to rocky areas of
             subalpine and alpine. .... *P. pensylvánica*, 4-15", see no. 232
4b.   Leaves larger; silvery-hairy (more so on underside). Plants not densely
             tufted. Flowers well above leaves. Abundant on dry slopes through-
             out the mountains. .... *P. hippiána*, 4-20", see no. 233

5a.   Leaves fully mature by blooming time (6)

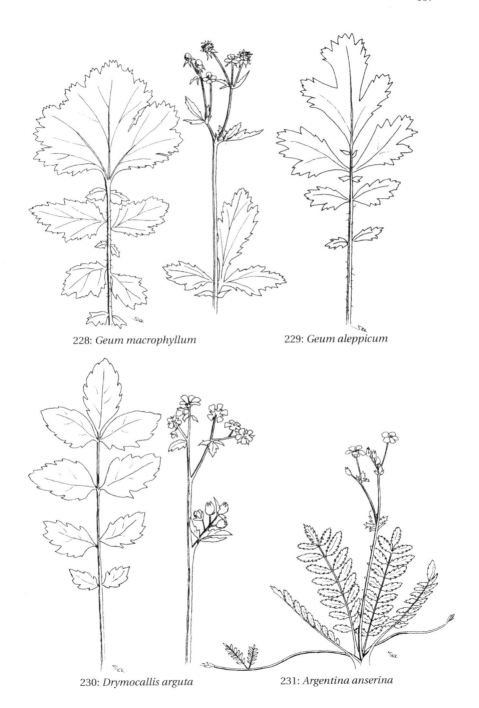

228: *Geum macrophyllum*

229: *Geum aleppicum*

230: *Drymocallis arguta*

231: *Argentina anserina*

5b.   Leaves still emerging while blooming in spring. Leaves white underneath
        and green above. Found in meadows and forest openings from
        montane to alpine. .... *P. concínna,* 2-8"

6a.   Leaves nearly palmate (the two lowest leaflets are slightly lower on the
        petiole than the others). Leaves small with narrow teeth; gray with
        hair underneath and green on top. Found in upper subalpine and
        alpine. .... *P. subjúga,* 4-12"
6b.   Leaves definitely palmate (7)

7a.   Teeth on leaves concentrated near the tip end. Leaves smooth or sparsely
        hairy. Abundant in meadows of subalpine and alpine.
        .... *P. diversifólia,* 4-16"
7b.   Teeth on leaves spread all along edges. Leaves light underneath and green
        on top. Found in meadows from upper montane to lower alpine.
        .... *P. pulchérrima,* 8-24", see no. 234

Note: *P. hippiana* hybridizes with *P. pulcherrima* producing plants with mixed
characteristics.

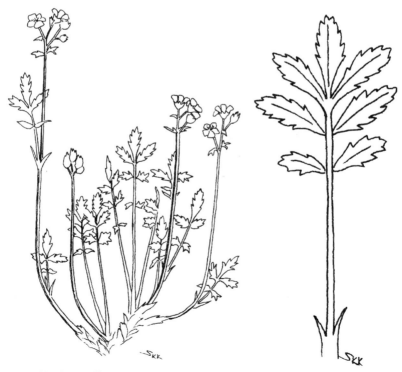

232: *Potentilla pensylvanica*   233: *Potentilla hippiana*

234: *Potentilla pulcherrima*

APIACEAE [Umbelliferae] (API)   **Carrot Family**
Leaves are compound with petioles enlarged at the base and clasping the stem. Flowers are very small and arranged in compound or simple umbels. This family contains such members as dill, carrot, celery and other edibles but also the deadly poisonous species, Poison Hemlock and Water Hemlock.

Key to Genera

1a.	Leaves ternate (2)
1b.	Leaves pinnate (6)

2a.	Flowers bright yellow (3)
2b.	Flowers white or tinged (4)

3a.	Inhabit alpine .... **PSEUDOCYMOPTERIS** p. 177
3b.	Inhabit dry foothills .... **LOMATIUM** p. 174

4a.	Plants rather sparse or at least not robust; flower umbels diffuse .... **OSMORHIZA** p. 171
4b.	Plants large and robust; flower umbels large and dense (5)

5a.	Flowers white, umbels flat-topped; leaves not further subdivided (may be lobed) .... **HERACLEUM** p. 172
5b.	Flowers tinged green to purple-brown, umbels rounded; leaves further subdivided twice pinnate .... **ANGELICA** p. 172

6a.   Leaves not further subdivided (may be lobed) (7)
6b.   Leaves further subdivided (9)

7a.   Flowers white or tinged; inhabit high elevations (8)
7b.   Flowers yellow; inhabit low elevations on eastern side of the range; plants in low dense clumps .... **ALETES** p. 172

8a.   Plants slender; found along streams in subalpine forests .... **OXYPOLIS** p. 172
8b.   Plants stout .... **ANGELICA** p. 172

9a.   Inhabit high elevations or moist areas in lower valleys (10)
9b.   Inhabit dry foothills (18)

10a.   Plants low to the ground; flowers yellow (11)
10b.   Plants with erect stems (12)

11a.   Leaflets fan-shaped; found in rocky open subalpine .... **PODISTERA** p. 172
11b.   Leaflets more elongated; found on alpine tundra .... **OREOXIS** p. 172

12a.   Flowers yellow .... **PSEUDOCYMOPTERIS** p. 171
12b.   Flowers white to greenish (13)

13a.   Flower umbels sparse and diffuse .... **OSMORHIZA** p. 171
13b.   Flower umbels condensed, conspicuous (14)

14a.   Stems stout relative to height; flowers white to greenish; found in rocky upper subalpine and alpine or moist montane woodlands .... **ANGELICA** p. 172
14b.   Stems slender relative to height (15)

15a.   Found in montane and subalpine, undisturbed sites (16)
15b.   Found from lower valleys to montane, wet disturbed sites (17)

16a.   Leaves large, fern-like, several to many; stems tall; flowers white; inhabit moist montane and meadows of subalpine .... **LIGUSTICUM** p. 172
16b.   Leaves smaller, one or two; stems shorter and slender; flowers white; inhabit wet subalpine meadows .... **CONIOSELINUM** p. 174

17a.   Leaves with many divisions, fern-like; stems purple-spotted .... **CONIUM** p. 174
17b.   Leaves less divided with elongate leaflets .... **CICUTA** p. 174

18a.   Plants low growing; found in open areas (19)
18b.   Plants taller; found under oakbrush .... **LOMATIUM** p. 174

19a.   Leaves lacy with very fine thread-like or simple, linear leaflets .... **LOMATIUM** p. 174
19b.   Leaves coarser .... **CYMOPTERIS** p. 176

Species

Pseudocymoptéris montánus .... Mountain Parsley, 6-32", see no. 235
The most common yellow-flowered species of the family from upper foothills to lower
alpine; widespread throughout the range. In alpine areas its form is dwarfed, hardly
resembling the larger, lower elevation individuals. Leaves are quite variable in shape
and the amount of dissection.

Osmorhíza .... Sweet Cicely
Flowers are tiny and usually go unnoticed. The few, umbel rays elongate as fruits
mature, becoming more noticable. Fruits are narrow and cylindrical; some with tails.
Usually found among the lush vegetation of moist forests and meadows.

1a.   Leaves divided into several pairs of three, these pinnately arranged.
         Mature fruit lacks tails. Plants rather large and leafy. Rays of umbel
         erect; flowers yellowish. Found in montane and subalpine meadows
         and under aspens and oak. ...... *O. occidentális*, 12-40", **W**, see no. 236
1b.   Leaves ternately divided. Mature fruit with conspicuous tails. Plants more
         delicate with fewer leaves. Flowers white to greenish (2)

235: *Pseudocymopteris montanus*   236: *Osmorhiza occidentalis*

2a.   Rays of umbel diverging at right angles; fruit widest at apex. Common in
        montane forests. .... *O. depauperáta* [O. obtusa], 6-28", see no. 237
2b.   Rays of umbel not diverging at right angles; fruit an even width through-
        out. Less common. Found in montane streambottoms.
        .... *O. chilénsis*, 12-40"

Heracléum sphondýlium [H. lanatum] .... Cow Parsnip, 3-6', see Plate 45
Large plants with stout stalks. Leaves large with broad divisions. Flowers in broad
umbels; white. Fruits are flat discs. Common in moist montane meadows,
streambottoms and aspen forests and subalpine meadows.

Oxypólis féndleri .... Cowbane, 20-40", see no. 238
Slender plants. Leaves once-pinnate, the leaflets oval and toothed. Flowers white
to slightly purplish, arranged in small umbels. Common to abundant along subalpine streams. Also found along deep, moist, montane stream courses.

Alétes lithophílus, 2-8", E, see Plate 46
Plants low and densely clumped (some up to 12 inches across). Old stems persist in the
clumps. Leaves pinnate with linear leaflets. Flowers are yellow, arranged in many small
umbels. Bloom in spring. Common on gravelly, volcanic hilltops and rock outcrops of
the foothills.

Podístera eástwoodiae, 3-5"
Dwarfed plants of gravelly soils in subalpine meadows and forest openings throughout
the range. In some areas nearly carpeting the ground. Leaves are dark green and
pinnate, the leaflets fan-shaped. Flower umbels tiny and yellow.

Oreóxis bákeri .... Alpine Parsley, 1/2-5", see no. 239
Dwarfed plants of alpine tundra. Leaves are dark green and somewhat bipinnate,
arranged in basal tufts. Flower umbels tiny and pale to bright yellow.

Angélica
Plants are large. Fruits flat and disc-like. Leaf petioles conspicuously enlarged at the
base.
1a.   Found scattered near and above timberline. Plants stout especially in
        contrast to the dwarfed plants of some of the rocky areas they
        inhabit. Leaves one to three-times pinnate. Flowers white to
        greenish. .... *A. gráyi*, 8-24", see no. 240
1b.   Found under aspens or along montane streams. Rather uncommon (2)

2a.   Plants huge and robust. Leaves ternate with the divisions further twice-
        pinnately divided. Flowers tinged green to purple-brown. Sporadi-
        cally distributed in moist montane meadows. .... *A. ámpla*, over 4'
2b.   Plants smaller. Leaves pinnate; some of the leaflets somewhat lobed to
        ternately divided. Leaflets lanceolate-ovate with long, pointed tips.
        Flowers white to pinkish. .... *A. pinnáta*, 10-36", W, see no. 241

Ligústicum pórteri .... Porter's Lovage, Osha, 20-40", see no. 242
Leaves are large and fern-like, ternately pinnate one to three times. Flowers white in
relatively small umbels on often tall, slender stems. Fruits small and pellet-shaped.

237: *Osmorhiza depauperata*

238: *Oxypolis fendleri*

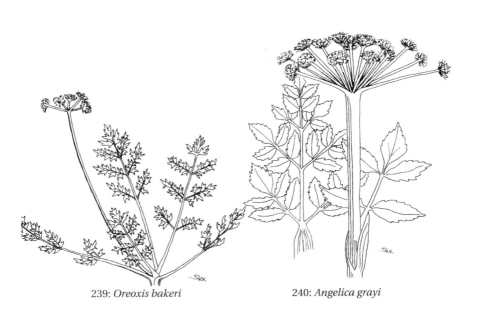

239: *Oreoxis bakeri*

240: *Angelica grayi*

Plants have a noticable celery fragrance especially after frost in the fall. Similar in appearance to Poison Hemlock (see below). Common in moist meadows, aspen groves and along streams from montane to subalpine.

Conioselínum scopulórum .... Hemlock-Parsley, 12-36", see no. 243
Plants are often hidden among the tall sedges and grasses and only noticed when blooming. Stems are single and slender with one or two leaves. Leaves three-times pinnate. Flowers white. Common in wet, subalpine meadows.

Conium maculátum .... Poison Hemlock, 2-9', see no. 244
Extremely poisonous. Leaves are large and several-times pinnate, appearing fern-like. Stems have noticable purplish spots. White flowers are produced on stout stems the second year. Abundant in moist areas in and around towns and cultivated areas from the lower valleys to montane.

Cicúta doúglasii .... Water Hemlock, 2-4', see no. 245
Extremely poisionous. Leaves are once to three times pinnate with long, finger-like leaflets. Veins of the leaflets terminate in the notches between the teeth. The thick root cut longitudinally reveals cross partitions separating air spaces. Found in wet areas of valleys.

Lomátium .... Indian Balsam
Flowers are yellow, blooming in early spring. Fruits are flattened and narrowly winged on the margins. Plants turn yellow and wither after the fruits mature in early summer.
1a.   Plants low (2)
1b.   Plants taller. Leaves ternate, the leaflets further subdivided and lobed;
            fern-like appearance. Abundant under oakbrush.
                .... *L. disséctum*, 12-36", **W**, see no. 246

241: *Angelica pinnata*   242: *Ligusticum porteri*

243: *Conioselinum scopulorum*

244: *Conium maculatum*

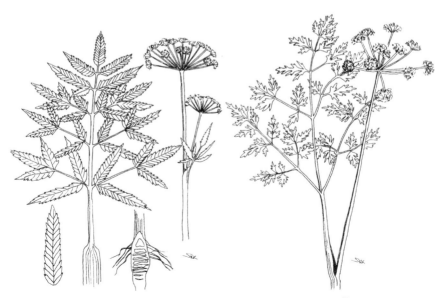

245: *Cicuta douglasii*

246: *Lomatium dissectum*

2a.   Leaves very finely divided numerous times into thread-like divisions.
                Found on bare clay soils of foothills. .... *L. gráyi*, 8-12", **W**
2b.   Leaves with only a few elongated divisions. Common to abundant among
                sagebrush and oakbrush on the far western plateaus.
                .... *L. triternátum* [L. simplex], 6-12", **W,** see no. 247

Cymoptéris .... Biscuit Root
Plants are low with leaves pinnate one to three times. Flower umbels are on naked stems among or surpassing the leaves. Fruits have obvious winged margins. Found in clay soils of lower foothills.
1a.   Leaves gray to pale blue-green. White papery bracts surround the tiny
                clusters of purple-pink flowers in the umbel (2)
1b.   Leaves green (3)

2a.   Found on western slope; common. .... *C. bulbósus*, 2-12", **W**
2b.   Found on eastern slope. .... *C. montánus*, 2-12", **E**

3a.   Flowers bright yellow. Flower umbels compact.
                .... *C. féndleri*, 2-12", **W**, see no. 248
3b.   Flowers dirty yellow to purplish. Flower umbels rather open and diffuse.
                Leaves dark, waxy green with angular-shaped divisions.
                .... *C. purpúreus*, 4-10", **W**, see no. 249

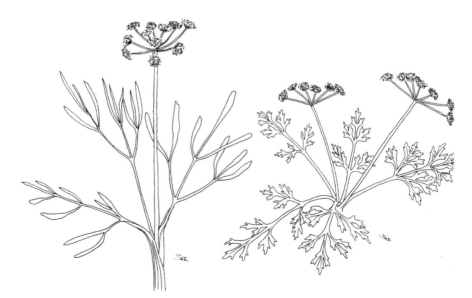

247: *Lomatium triternatum*   248: *Cymopteris fendleri*

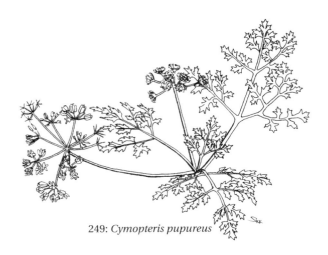

249: *Cymopteris pupureus*

FUMARIACEAE (FUM)   Fumitory Family

Corýdalis
Flowers are irregular with four separate petals; the outer two spreading with one spurred and the inner two small, narrow and united at the tip. Flowers have six stamens in two sets. Leaves alternate or basal, finely dissected. Fruits are capsules.

1a.   Low plants of dry, disturbed sites and forest openings from upper foothills to subalpine. Frequently found among oakbrush or on banks of dry arroyos. Flowers yellow. Leaves bipinnate; grayish.
.... *C. aúrea*, Golden Smoke, 4-16", see Plate 47

1b.   Tall plants in wet drainages of often steep and rocky upper montane and subalpine. Flowers pale pink, darker toward the center. Leaves two to three-times pinnately divided; green and thin.
.... *C. cáseana*, 2-6', see Plate 48

VIOLACEAE (VIO)   Violet Family

Vióla ....Violet
Flowers are irregular with the lower petal spurred. Flower parts in fives. Leaves alternate or basal and simple. Fruits are capsules.

1a.   Plants miniature. Inhabit alpine tundra. Flowers purple.
.... *V. labradórica*, 1/2-2"

1b.   Plants larger. Inhabit forested zones (2)

2a.   Flowers white (3)

2b.   Flowers shades of purple. Spur at base of petal is obvious. Found in moist montane. Most abundant species. .... *V. adúnca*, 2-10", see no. 250

3a.   Leaves large, some over 2 inches wide. Found in shaded, moist areas of montane. .... *V. rugulósa*, 6-16", **W**

3b.   Leaves small, none over 2 inches wide. Found in shaded, moist areas of montane. .... *V. rýdbergia*, 6-14"

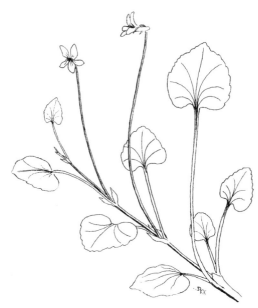

250: *Viola adunca*

FABACEAE (FAB)   **Legume Family**

Leaves alternate, usually compound. Flowers are irregular with five separate petals, however the tips of lower two petals join forming a keel. Stamens united. Fruits are pods with one row of seeds and usually splitting on two sides (a legume). Plants of this family have bacteria living on the roots which combine nitrogen with sugars to provide a form of nitrogen usable to plants. This relationship makes members of this family important for rejuvenating cultivated soil or disturbed areas where the loss of plant cover results in the loss of nitrogen in the soil.

Key to Genera

1a.   Leaves small, pinnate (crowded, appearing palmate) with three to six
         leaflets, sessile; flowers yellow and red-orange, spread along stems
         ....**LOTUS** p. 179
1b.   Leaves not as above (2)

2a.   Leaves palmate or trifoliate (3)
2b.   Leaves pinnate (9)

3a.   Leaves palmate, five or more divisions (sometimes three on some leaves)
         (4)
3b.   Leaves trifoliate (5)

4a.   Leaflets three to five; rather large plants with tiny flowers (less than 1/4
         inch) ....**PSORALIDIUM** p. 179

4b. Leaflets five or more; flowers large or if tiny then plants also tiny .... **LUPINUS** p. 179

5a. Flowers yellow or white (6)
5b. Flowers pink, purple or if white, then plants low (8)

6a. Leaves and flowers rather large and few; leaflets 1-2 inches long; flowers yellow .... **THERMOPSIS** p. 180
6b. Leaves and flowers small and numerous (7)

7a. Plants large and weedy; flowers yellow or white .... **MELILOTUS** p. 180
7b. Plants low and creeping; flowers yellow, minute .... **MEDICAGO** p. 182

8a. Leaves and flowers very small; plants large over 12 inches tall, clumped; flowers dark purple .... **MEDICAGO** p. 182
8b. Leaves and flowers large relative to the small size of plants; flowers pink, white or purple .... **TRIFOLIUM** p. 182

9a. Leaves with a tendril at the tip (may be short) (10)
9b. Leaves without a tendril at the tip (11)

10a. Stems vine-like; flowers purple .... **VICIA** p. 183
10b. Stems not vine-like; flowers purple or white .... **LATHYRUS** p. 184

11a. Fruits bristly, red-brown burs in clusters; found along ditches and river terraces of lower valleys .... **GLYCYRRHIZA** p. 184
11b. Fruits not as above (12)

12a. Fruit divided into segments like a chain .... **HEDYSARUM** p. 185
12b. Fruit not divided as such (13)

13a. Lower flower petals with a narrowed tip that curves outward .... **OXYTROPIS** p. 185
13b. Lower flower petals without such a tip .... **ASTRAGALUS** p. 186

Species

Lótus wríghtii .... Deervetch, 8-16", **W**, see no. 251
Flowers are red-orange and yellow; single or few together and axillary. Leaves sessile appearing palmate, the segments very narrow. Plants have many tufted stems. Common in rocky open areas or among oak and pine of foothills and lower montane.

Psoralídium tenuiflórum .... Scurf Pea, 8-24", **W**, see no. 252
Stems stout and branched and sparsely leaved. Leaves are three to five palmate. Plants spread by underground rootstalks, forming patches. Flowers tiny (less than 1/4 inch) and arranged in small racemes; deep purple to blue. Seed pods small. Found on dry foothill slopes.

Lupínus .... Lupine
Leaves are palmately compound. Flowers are arranged in terminal racemes or spikes. Bloom early in the season. Species hybridize often making them difficult to distinquish.

1a.   Plants annual; tiny. Two round seed leaves present at the base during
         bloom in spring. Flowers minute; deep blue. Found on dry, open
         ground under Piñon Pines in the foothills. .... *L. kíngii*, 2-8"
1b.   Plants perennial; stout (2)

2a.   Upper petal angled more than 45 degrees above the lower, joined petals (3)
2b.   Upper petal angled less than 45 degrees above the lower, joined petals (6)

3a.   Low growing in patches. Flowers purple and often whitish at the tip;
         bloom in spring. Plants dry up by summer. Common in open areas
         among sagebrush or oakbrush in the foothills.
         .... *L. ammophílus*, 8-20", **W**
3b.   Taller and clumped; often quite large (4)

4a.   Stem and leaf hairs spreading outward. Flowers bright purple with a
         contrasting bright white spot at the tip; fragrant. Bloom in late
         spring. Form thick uniform clumps. Common among sagebrush and
         oakbrush primarily in the far western foothills.
         .... *L. prunophílus*, 20-36", see Plate 49
4b.   Stem and leaf hairs not spreading outward (5)

5a.   Stem and leaf hair silky and pressed flat against the surface. Found in the
         upper Rio Grande Valley. .... *L. seríceus*, 12-40", **E**
5b.   Stem and leaf hair somewhat sparse; not silky and pressed flat. Flowers
         purple with whitish spot at the tip. Bloom in early to mid-summer.
         Form irregular clumps. Abundant throughout montane meadows
         and forest openings. .... *L. bákeri*, 12-40", **W**

6a.   Flowers with a small but definite spur at the base. Leaves often folded
         exposing the silvery undersides. Common to abundant in upper
         foothill and montane meadows and openings throughout the range.
         .... *L. caudátus* [L. aduncus], 12-40"
6b.   Flowers without a definite spur (may be a slight bump); small and many;
         light to dark purple. Leaves evenly hairy; usually folded exposing the
         silvery undersides. Hybridize with the above species creating plants
         with mixed characteristics. Found in dry montane and subalpine
         meadows; most common on the eastern slope. .... *L. argénteus*, 12-40"

Thermópsis montána .... Golden Banner, 12-24", see no. 253
Plants are showy, prolific early-season bloomers. Flowers bright yellow, in dense
racemes. Leaves trifoliate with leaflets 1-2 inches long. Seed pods erect; hairy. Often
form large patches. Common in moist or shaded areas of montane.

Melilótus .... Sweet Clover
Leaves are small and trifoliate. Form rather tall sparse clumps. Plants have a sweet
vanilla odor. Introduced for reseeding disturbed areas and rejuvenating cultivated
fields. Often abundant along trails and roads of montane and foothills. Annual or
biennial.
1a.   Flowers yellow .... *M. officinális*, 28-80"
1b.   Flowers white .... *M. álba*, 28-80"

251: *Lotus wrightii*

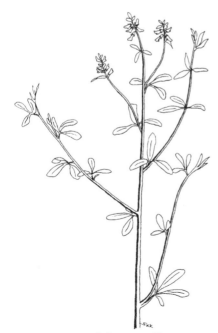

252: *Psoralidium tenuiflorum*

253: *Thermopsis montana*

Medicágo
Introduced plants.

1a.　　　Large dense clumps. Leaves small; pinnately trifoliate. Flowers dark
　　　　　purple to white. Cultivated for hay; escaped along roads and near
　　　　　fields in the lower valleys. .... *M. satíva*, Alfalfa, 12-40"
1b.　　　Tiny and ground-creeping. Leaves palmately trifoliate and finely serrated.
　　　　　Flowers minute in small ball-like clusters; yellow. Used abundantly
　　　　　throughout the mountains for reseeding road and trail sides.
　　　　　　　　.. *M. lupulína*, Black Medic, under 1"

Trifólium .... Clover
Leaves are trifoliate. Flowers usually in dense terminal head-like clusters.

1a.　　　Plants miniature. Found on alpine tundra. Form tight mats of tiny gray-
　　　　　green leaves. Flowers few together; erect, barely above leaves; red-
　　　　　purple, rose or pale pink-orange. .... *T. nánum*, 1/2-2"
1b.　　　Plants not as above (2)

2a.　　　Flower stems naked (3)
2b.　　　Flower stems with leaves (6)

3a.　　　Flowers dark purple to burgundy; several together, pendant. Dwarf alpine
　　　　　plants. .... *T. brándegei*, 2-6"
3b.　　　Flowers pale pink to rose-purple; many together; erect (4)

4a.　　　Plants form loose mats. Leaves narrow and long-pointed; gray-green.
　　　　　Found on gravelly open areas of subalpine.
　　　　　　　　.. *T. attenuátum*, 4-10", see plate 50
4b.　　　Plants do not form mats. Leaves broader with rounded tips; green (5)

5a.　　　Common in subalpine and moist tundra. .... *T. párryi*, 3-4", see no. 254
5b.　　　Found on wet tundra. Taller. .... *T. salictórum*, 4-8"

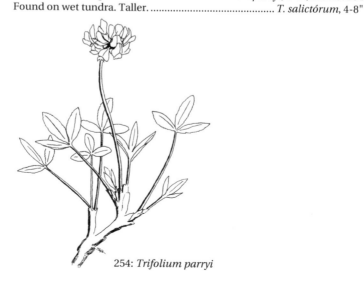

254: *Trifolium parryi*

6a. Stems with fused bracts below flower heads. Flowers whitish to rose. Found throughout the mountains.
.... *T. wórmskioldii* [T. fendleri], 3-20"
6b. Stems without fused bracts below flower heads (7)

7a. Leaves present immediately below flower heads. Leaves often bicolored; rather large. Flower heads very dense and large (1 inch or so) ball-like; pink. Plants tufted. Cultivated plants used in reseeding disturbed areas throughout the mountains and in fields of the lower valleys. .... *T. praténse*, Red Clover, 4-20"
7b. Leaves not present immediately below flower heads (distinctly stalked). Leaves small. Flower heads looser and smaller; white or bicolored, white and pink (8)

8a. Plants spreading in dense clumps or creeping. Introduced plants used in reseeding (9)
8b. Plants erect; not in dense clumps. Native. Flowers white to pink. Widespread in the mountains. .... *T. rúsbyi* [T. longipes], 3-16"

9a. Plants creep over the ground and root along stems. Flowers white.
.... *T. répens*, Dutch Clover, 2-12"
9b. Plants clumped, not rooting along ground-creeping stems. Flowers pink and white. .... *T. hýbridum*, Alsike Clover, 6-20"

Vícia americána ....Vetch, 4-32", see no.255
Flowers are bright purple and few in loose racemes. Leaves have a curled tendril at the tip. Stems few; climb over other vegetation, the tendrils wrapping tightly around stems for support. Common in montane meadows.

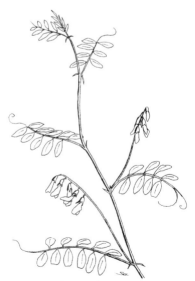

255: *Vicia americana*

Láthyrus .... Peavine
Leaves are pinnate with a tendril at the tip, though it may be very short and straight.
Stems several to many, not usually vining over other plants. Flowers have a sweet odor.

1a.   Flowers purple (2)
1b.   Flowers white; withering to ochre-rust. The following two may cross and
        mixed characteristics found (3)

2a.   Joined, lower petals definitely shorter than the two side petals. Leaves
        linear to ovate. Found in open woods and among oakbrush of upper
        foothills and montane. .... *L. pauciflórus*, 8-32", **W**
2b.   Joined, lower petals and two side petals approximately equal in length.
        Leaves oblong to linear. Found among sagebrush and oakbrush of
        foothills and in open montane woods throughout the range.
        .... *L. eucósmus*, 6-20", see no. 256

3a.   Leaflets less than six; narrow to oblong with tapered tips; leathery and
        gray-green. Tendrils barely curling. Found in woods of upper
        foothills and montane. .... *L. arizónicus*, 4-16", **W**
3b.   Leaflets more than six; oval with rounded tips; thin and green. Tendrils
        definitely curling. Found in woods from upper foothills to subalpine
        throughout the range. .... *L. leucánthus*, 5-20"

Glycyrrhíza lepidóta .... Wild Liquorice, 12-40", see no. 257
Leaves pinnate with many, narrow leaflets. Stems few to several together, spreading by
underground rootstalks to form colonies. Flowers yellowish to greenish. Fruits are red-
brown and bur-like. Common to abundant in moist areas such as along ditches and on
river terraces of the lower valleys.

256: *Lathyrus eucosmus*   257: *Glycyrrhiza lepidota*

Hedýsarum .... Chainpod
Large, densely tufted plants with showy, pink to purple flowers. Seed pods are pendulous and segmented like a chain. Found on embankments and in forest openings.

1a.   Upper sepals much shorter than lower ones. Seed pods without definite
        horizontal ripples on the surface. Flowers pink to purple. Found
        from upper foothills to subalpine. .... *H. occidentále*, 12-28"

1b.   Upper and lower sepals about equal in length. Seed pods with definite
        horizontal ripples on the surface. Flowers pink-purple. Locally
        common from foothills to montane. .... *H. boreále*, 10-24", W, see no. 258

Oxytrópis .... Locoweed
Most of the species are quite showy. The lower, joined petals narrow to a tip that
projects outward. Leaves are pinnate. The common name is misapplied to many of the
species in this genus.

1a.   Flowers some shade of purple or pink (2)

1b.   Flowers white in large, showy racemes (hybridize with *O. lámbertii*
        resulting in plants with pale purplish flowers). Plants are thickly
        clumped with numerous erect flower stems. Bloom in early summer.
        Abundant in montane and higher elevation parks, primarily on the
        eastern slope. .... *O. serícea*, 6-16", see Plate 51

2a.   Stems decumbent. Leaflets not whorled (3)

2b.   Stems erect; many, densely tufted. Leaflets whorled. Plants silvery and
        fuzzy. Flowers 1/2 inch; pink to purplish. Dry gravelly montane and
        subalpine meadows. Quite common on the eastern slope.
        .... *O. spléndens*, 4-14", see Plate 52

3a.   Stems and leaves gray and fuzzy. Flowers tiny (1/4 inch); purple. Flower
        stems leafy. Found scattered in montane meadows.
        .... *O. defléxa*, 4-16", E, see no. 259

258: *Hedysarum boreale*   259: *Oxytropis deflexa*

3b.   Stems and leaves not fuzzy. Flowers bright rose-purple to purple. Flower
        stems mostly without leaves. Common in grassy foothills and higher
        elevation parks; mostly on the eastern slope and northern end of the
        range. .... *O. lámbertii*, 4-12"

Astrágalus .... Milkvetch
Many of these species are quite showy, mostly spring blooming. The lower joined petals
are blunt-tipped to acute. Most bloom in spring. This is a large confusing genus until
one realizes that only a few species occur in any given area. With experience they can
be distinquished by habitat.

1a.   Inhabit dry foothills and lower montane (2)
1b.   Inhabit moist montane or subalpine. Stems rather low, sprawling and
        weak. Flowers small (less than 1/2 inch) (15)

2a.   Plants in tall, erect clumps of several to many stems (3)
2b.   Plants in low, compact clumps or sprawling (8)

3a.   Flowers bright rose-purple; showy. Form thick erect clumps. Leaves gray.
        Seed pods 1 inch long and 1/4 inch wide; slightly flattened from the
        sides; pendulous. Locally abundant among shrublands of the far
        western plateaus. .... *A. cóltonii*, 12-20", **W** , see Plate 53
3b.   Flowers white to yellowish (4)

4a.   Flowers pale yellowish to cream (5)
4b.   Flowers white (7)

5a.   Stems and leaves gray and fuzzy. Stems several to many in a clump; erect
        or somewhat leaning. Seed pods 1 inch long, narrow and pendulous.
        Abundant in eastern slope foothills. Also found among sagebrush on
        the mesas at the northern end of the range.
        .... *A. drúmmondii*, 10-24", see Plate 54
5b.   Stems and leaves not fuzzy (6)

6a.   Sepals are inflated and fuzzy, concealing most of the petals. Sepals persist
        and conceal seed pods as well. Leaves with numerous, linear leaflets.
        Form thick clumps. Found on rocky, selenium clay soils of the
        southwestern lower foothills. .... *A. oocálycis*, 12-24", **W**
6b.   Sepals not as above. Leaves with few, linear leaflets. Form large, robust
        clumps. Seed pods 1 1/2 inches long; flattened from the sides;
        pendulous. Found on slopes and embankments of foothills.
        .... *A. lonchocárpus*, 12-32", **W**, see no. 260

7a.   Flowers white with a purple spot on the lower petals; small (less than 1/2
        inch long) and numerous in narrow racemes. Seed pods less than 1/2
        inch long. Form thick, erect clumps. Found on selenium-clay soils of
        foothills and plateaus. .... *A. háydenianus*, 12-24", **W**, see no. 261
7b.   Flowers pure white; showy; larger (more than 1/2 inch long). Sepals rose-
        colored. Seed pods 3/4 inch long; cylindrical-oblong. Form thick,
        erect clumps. Locally abundant in selenium-clay soils such as in the
        gray hills directly west of Durango. .... *A. praelóngus*, 12-28", **W**

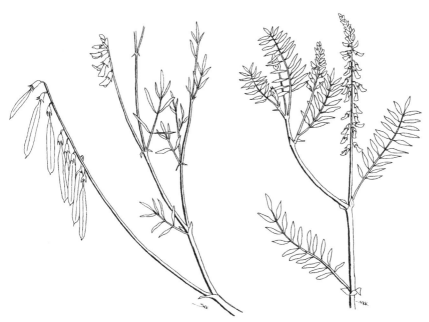

260: *Astragalus lonchocarpus*   261: *Astragalus haydenianus*

8a. Stems relatively few, elongate and sprawling or decumbent; sparsely leaved (9)

8b. Stems numerous, short and forming compact tufts or mounds (12)

9a. Stems decumbent. Flowers in dense, oval clusters; blue-purple or white. .... *A. adsúrgens*, 4-14"

9b. Stems elongate and sprawling; reddish (10)

10a. Flowers yellow to cream. Seed pods compressed from the sides; deeply grooved along the underside. Leaflets elliptic to oblong with tips pointed, blunt or notched. Abundant among sagebrush and oakbrush of the foothills. .... *A. scopulórum*, 12-24", see no. 262

10b. Flowers purple or bicolored, purple and white. Seed pods small; flattened from top and bottom sides. Leaflets oblong to oblanceolate; slightly notched or blunt tipped (11)

11a. Leaflets more than eleven. Flowers purple. Common scattered throughout the foothills and lower montane. .... *A. flexuósus*, 8-20"

11b. Leaflets less than eleven. Flowers white and purple. *A. próximus*, 8-20", **W**

12a. Flowers white or yellowish (13)

12b. Flowers purple (14)

13a. Found on western slope. Leaves gray. Leaflets small; narrow-elliptic to linear. Flowers whitish to yellowish with a rose tinge. Found in heavy, selenium-clay soil of the foothills. .... *A. flávus*, 6-10", **W**

13b. Found on eastern slope. Leaves green. Leaflets numerous; small, elliptic and notched at tip. Flowers tiny (1/3 inch); white with purple spot at tip of lower petals. Seed pods inflated, papery-thin and plum-shaped; pendulous on the undersides of stems. Abundant on rocky slopes of the lower, dry foothill grasslands.
.... *A. cerussátus*, 4-8", **E**, see no. 263

14a. Found on eastern slope. Leaflets oval; green. Seed pods flattened from top and bottom sides with tip strongly upcurved; 1 inch long and over 1/2 inch wide; plump when green. Flowers pink-purple spread out like flags on stems above the sprawling leaves. Found in sandy-loam soils of the foothills. .... *A. shortiánus*, 2-4", **E**, see no. 264

14b. Found on western slope. Leaflets elliptic; gray-green. Seed pods boat-shaped; about 1 inch long and less than 1/2 inch wide. Flowers lilac to bright purple. Found in clay soils of the upper foothills.
.... *A. amphióxys*, 2-3", **W**

15a. Leaflets elliptic-oval to obovate. Flowers bicolored, white and dark purple. Seed pods with black hairs; very small. Plants often forming loose continuous patches. Common along streams and in meadows of upper montane and subalpine. .... *A. alpínus*, 2-10", see no. 265

15b. Leaflets oblong to linear (16)

16a. Leaflets oblong, rounded at tip. Flowers purple. Found along streams of montane and subalpine. .... *A. eucósmus*, 8-24"

16b. Leaflets linear, pointed at tip. Flowers white or purple. Sepals with black hairs. Seed pods narrow; all pointing upward. Common in moist, montane meadows or under aspens. .... *A. míser*, 4-12", see no. 266

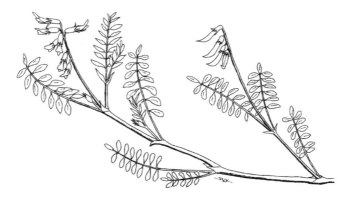

262: *Astragalus scopulorum*

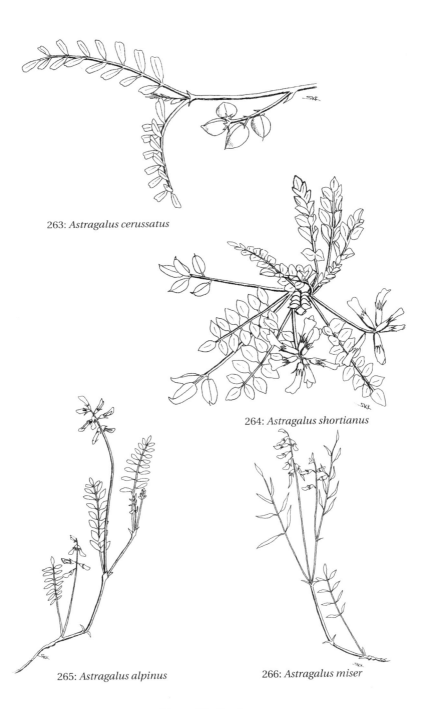

263: *Astragalus cerussatus*

264: *Astragalus shortianus*

265: *Astragalus alpinus*

266: *Astragalus miser*

HELLEBORACEAE (HEL)   Hellebore Family

Leaves usually compound. Flowers mostly irregular. Sepals are showy and petal-like. Petals are much smaller and usually hidden. Fruits are follicles (except *Actaea* has berries).

Aconítum columbiánum .... Monkshood, 24-60", see no. 267
Tall plants. Flowers are dark purple, arranged in rather loose terminal racemes or panicles. The upper petal-like sepal forms a hood, hence the common name. Leaves are palmately parted into three to five divisions, these further cleft and toothed. Found in moist forest openings and among willows of montane and subalpine.

Delphínium .... Larkspur
Flowers are arranged in showy racemes; blue to purple. Leaves are palmately divided.
1a.   Leaves mostly basal; deeply palmately divided with the segments further
         divided into very narrow segments. Stems usually short. Arise from a
         tuber-like root. Bloom in spring and die back to the root with the
         heat of summer. Flowers blue to violet. Common to abundant in
         open woods and meadows of foothills and montane; particularly on
         the western slope. .... *D. núttallianum* [D. nelsoni], 4-16"
1b.   Leaves not mostly basal; palmately divided with the segments cleft (2)

2a.   Flowers bicolored, pale blue and white. Uncommon in upper montane
         woods. .... *D. occidentále*, 24-80", **W**
2b.   Flowers solid purple to violet or deep blue (3)

3a.   Leaf divisions very narrow (4)
3b.   Leaf divisions broader. Plants large and robust. Abundant in moist
         subalpine; often forming extensive patches; found scattered
         throughout moist montane as well. .... *D. bárbeyi*, 20-80", see Plate 55

4a.   Plants less than 3 feet tall; rather slender; scattered in montane and
         subalpine meadows; common in certain locations. Flowers blue to
         violet. .... *D. ramósum*, 15-36"
4b.   Plants more than 3 feet tall. Found in broad canyons. *D. robústum*, 3-7', **E**

Psychrophíla leptosépala [Caltha] .... Marsh-Marigold, 6-12", see no. 268
Flowers white; several, regular. Leaves broad-oval. Extremely abundant in bogs of upper subalpine and lower alpine, often forming extensive, continuous colonies.

Tróllius albiflórus [T. laxus] .... Globe Flower, 8-24", see no. 269
Flowers large and regular; white to cream with many yellow stamens. Leaves are alternate and palmately divided. Common in moist areas and meadows of subalpine throughout the range.

Actaéa rúbra .... Baneberry, 20-32", see no. 270
Flowers are numerous, small and white arranged in short racemes. Petals are tiny and sepals drop early leaving the noticable stamens. Leaves twice ternately compound; large, thin and bright green. Fruits are large, shiny, oblong red or white berries; poisonous. Found scattered in shaded, moist, montane forests.

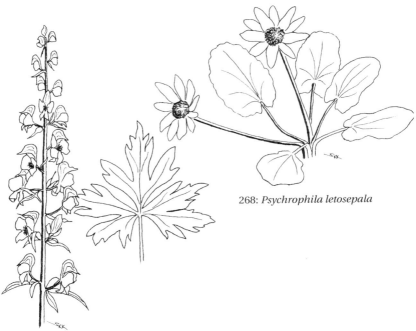

268: *Psychrophila letosepala*

267: *Aconitum columbianum*

269: *Trollius albiflorus*

270: *Actaea rubra*

Aquilégia .... Columbine
Petals are smaller than sepals and have spurs that protrude from the back of the flower.
Sepals are large and petal-like. Leaves two to three times ternately compound, the
segments roundish-lobed.

1a.   Flowers blue and white or more of one color. Quite variable due to
            hybridization with next species. Woodland plants tend to be tall and
            spindly with few flowers while plants of rocky, open areas are dense
            and compact with many flowers. Common in moist montane and
            subalpine woods and rocky alpine meadows.
            .... *A. coerúlea,* Colorado Columbine, 8-32"
1b.   Flowers red and yellow. Often form low dense clumps. Found on dry,
            shady, montane slopes and embankments and in subalpine woods. .
            .... *A. elegantúla,* Western Red Columbine, 4-16", see Plate 56

RANUNCULACEAE (RAN)   Crowfoot Family
Leaves re usually alternate; simple or compound. Base of petiole often dilated. Flowers
have numerous stamens. Some lack petals. Fruits are achenes.

Key to Genera

1a.   Vines (2)
1b.   Not vines (3)

2a.   Flowers numerous, small, white; stems densely leaved, climb into trees
            .... CLEMATIS p. 193
2b.   Flowers few, large, pale blue-purple; stems sparse, trailing on ground and
            over shrubs .... ATRAGENE p. 193

3a.   Flowers leathery, upside-down urn-shaped, dark brown-purple
            .... CORIFLORA p. 193
3b.   Flowers not as above (4)

4a.   Flowers with petals (5)
4b.   Flowers without petals, only whitish tufts of stamens; leaves very large,
            palmate .... TRAUTVETTERIA p. 194

5a.   Flowers rather large, white, rose or lavender (6)
5b.   Flowers smaller; waxy, bright yellow (7)

6a.   Flowers white or rose; seeds in round or cylindrical heads, not plumed
            .... ANEMONE p. 194
6b.   Flowers lavender, bloom in very early spring; seeds have showy plumes
            .... PULSATILLA p. 194

7a.   Stems stout, hairy and hollow .... HECATONIA p. 194
7b.   Stems not as above .... RANUNCULUS p. 192

Species

Clématis ligusticifólia .... Virgin's Bower, 12-18'
Large vine often climbing up into trees. Masses of small white flowers mature into seeds
with tufts of feathery plumes. Sepals and petals are not differentiated. Leaves pinnate
with five to seven leaflets, these lanceolate to ovate, incised and toothed. Leaves turn
scarlet in autumn. Abundant in lower valley bottoms.

Atragéne columbiána [Clematis pseudoalpina] .... Blue Clematis, 6-10', see no. 271
Sparse vine trailing along the ground or over shrubs and rocks. Flowers few and large;
pale blue-purple. Sepals and petals are not differentiated. Bloom early, followed by
tufted seeds with feathery plumes. Leaves are few and ternately compound. Found in
upper foothills and montane.

Coriflóra [Clematis] .... Sugarbowls
Flowers are leathery, pendulous urns; dark purple-brown. Petals and sepals are not
differentiated. Leaves pinnate.
1a.   Leaves appear further subdivided, the divisions linear. Stems in thick erect
           clumps. Found in forest openings and on slopes of upper foothills and
           dry, lower montane. .... *C. hirsutíssima*, 8-28", see no. 272
1b.   Leaves simply pinnate; leaflets elliptic. Stems sprawling. Common in
           montane forest openings. .... *C. scóttii*, 8-28", E

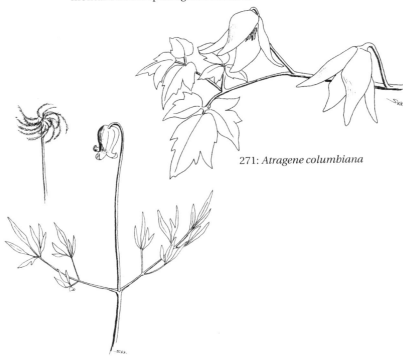

271: *Atragene columbiana*

272: *Coriflora hirsutissima*

Anémone
Flowers are single on long naked stems arising from a whorl of stem leaves. Petals and sepals not differentiated. Leaves palmately divided and further cleft and toothed. Seeds are many, compressed into heads.

1a.   Flowers white. Seed heads elongated and cylindrical. Seeds wooly. Found in montane meadows. .... *A. cylíndrica*, Thimbleweed, 12-24", see no. 273

1b.   Flowers rose. Seed heads short and rounded. Seeds hairy, not wooly. Common in dry forest openings and meadows of montane and subalpine. .... *A. multifída*, Windflower, 4-20"

Pulsatílla pátens [Anemone] .... Pasqueflower, 4-12", see no. 274
Bloom very eary in spring with large, lavender flowers, often when snow still lies in patches. Petals and sepals similar. Leaves often emerge later. Leaves and stems are densely silky-hairy. Seeds heads have tufted, showy plumes. Found in dry, rocky, open areas from sagebrush lowlands to timberline.

Hecatónia sceleráta [Ranunculus] .... Blister Buttercup, 6-20"
Stems robust, hairy and hollow. Petals are tiny; yellow. Leaves are palmately lobed to divided and further cleft and toothed. Found in muddy, disturbed areas such as around stock ponds and beaver ponds.

Ranúnculus .... Buttercup
Sepals and petals are different. Petals are waxy, bright yellow. Many species are quite similar or tiny and obscure. The more distinquishable ones most often encountered are covered here.

1a.   Leaves not divided. (2)
1b.   Leaves divided. Stems rather weak and tall. Petals tiny (little over 1/8 inch). Found in moist woodlands. .... *R. uncinátus*, 8-24", see no. 275

2a.   Sepals have dark, furry hairs. Flowers large relative to the short stems. Leaves oblong, blunt and toothed at the tips. Common meadows and forest openings of upper subalpine and alpine.
         .... *R. macaúleyi*, 4-6", see Plate 57

2b.   Sepals not as above. Flowers small. Stems taller. Leaves acute; lanceolate to ovate. Abundant in moist meadows of subalpine.
         .... *R. alismifólius*, 4-12", see no. 276

Trautvettéria carolinénsis .... False Bugbane, 12-40", see no. 277
Leaves very large (the size of your hand), palmately divided or cleft. Flowers lack petals. Sepals are petal-like, however they drop very early, leaving only the conspicuous ball of white stamens. Often abundant in subalpine forests or moist montane river gorges.

OXALIDACEAE (OXL)   **Wood-sorrel Family**

Óxalis violácea .... Violet Wood-sorrel, 2-4", **W**
Leaves trifoliate, the leaflets heart-shaped with the point at the base. Flowers are purple and clustered several together; five petals and five sepals. Fruits are capsules. Plants arise from tubers. Uncommon in moist montane woods on rock outcrops or cliffs.

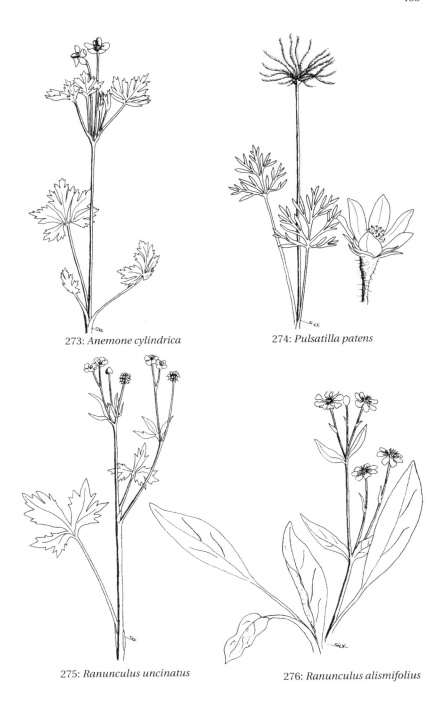

273: *Anemone cylindrica*

274: *Pulsatilla patens*

275: *Ranunculus uncinatus*

276: *Ranunculus alismifolius*

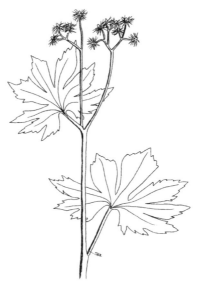

277: *Trautvetteria carolinensis*

CAPPARACEAE (CPP)   Caper Family

Cleóme serruláta .... Rocky Mountain Bee-Plant, 12-40", see no. 278
Rather weedy plants with branched stems of trifoliate leaves. Flowers are showy, pink-purple to whitish. Stamens protrude giving the flowers a feathery appearance. Racemes elongate during bloom so that fruits are maturing at the base while the top buds are first opening. Fruits are long and narrow, pendulous on long stalks. Found in disturbed areas; abundant in some locations.

PYROLACEAE (PYR)   Wintergreen Family
Leaves are evergreen, mostly alternate and simple. Flowers waxy with obvious thickened pistils. Petals open widely like saucers. Fruits are capsules. Inhabit shady forests.

Chimaphíla umbelláta .... Pipsissewa, Prince's Pine, 4-12", see no. 279
Leaves are thick, dark and evergreen; narrow kite-shaped and toothed. Stem leaves whorled. Flowers are white to pinkish and arranged several together in umbels. Found in shady montane and subalpine forests.

Monéses uniflóra .... Single Delight, Wood Nymph, 2-5", see no. 280
Flowers are white, single and nodding; fragrant. Leaves are small and round, mostly basal. Uncommon in cold, damp, subalpine forests.

Orthília secúnda [Pyrola] .... One-sided Wintergreen, 4-8", see no. 281
Flowers all hang to one side of the stem; white. Leaves are thin and bright green. They are not entirely basal, some up the lower part of the stem. Found in shady woods of montane and subalpine throughout the range.

278:*Cleome serrulata*

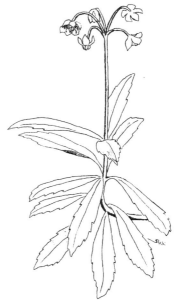

279: *Chimaphila umbellata*

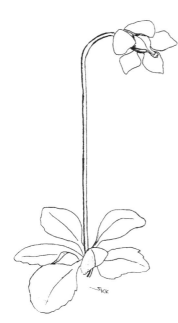

280: *Moneses uniflora*

281: *Orthilia secunda*

Pýrola .... Shineleaf; Wintergreen
Leaves all basal, thick, dark and evergreen. Found in shady montane to subalpine woods.

1a.   Leaves with cream-colored veins; acute. Plants partially parasitic, deriving nutrients from roots of other plants; sometimes lack leaves. Flowers white or tinged green to brown. Uncommon. .... *P. pícta*, 1/2-2", **W**
1b.   Leaves solid green; usually round to reniform (2)

2a.   Flowers greenish. Leaves 1/2 to 1 inch in diameter. Found in upper montane and subalpine woods. .... *P. chlorántha*, 4-8"
2b.   Flowers pink. Leaves over 1 inch in diameter. Found in moist woods and along streambanks. .... *P. rotundifólia* [P. asarifolia], 4-16", see no. 282

GERANIACEAE (GER)   Geranium Family
Leaves are usually opposite, palmately or pinnately compound or lobed. Flowers have five overlapping sepals and five petals. Petals drop early. Fruits are capsules with extremely long pointed tips that peel up from the base at maturity releasing the seeds.

Eródium cicutárium .... Crane's Bill, 2-6", see no. 283
Plants develop tight rosettes of finely dissected, basal leaves in autumn and bloom the following spring (winter annual). Flowers are tiny and pink. Abundant weed of disturbed, bare ground from the lower valleys to montane.

Geránium
Leaves are palmately lobed, parted or cleft. Basal leaves have long petioles. Flowers are rather small.

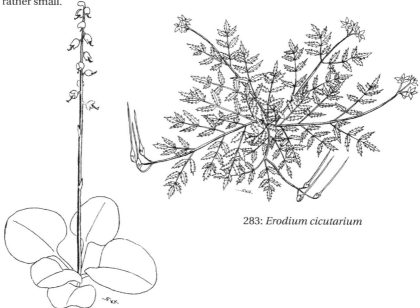

283: *Erodium cicutarium*

282: *Pyrola rotundifolia*

1a.   Plants with single or few erect stems. Flowers pale pink or white with
        darker veins. Abundant and widespread in montane and subalpine
        forests and meadows. .... *G. ríchardsonii*, 12-36"
1b.   Plants with many stems, decumbent or leaning; vary from loosely
        sprawling to densely clumped; sticky to some degree. Flowers
        numerous; either bright red-purple or pale pink. Red-purple-
        flowered plants tend to be sprawling and pink-flowered ones tend to
        be tightly clumped. One type or the other prevails in a given area.
        Common in open areas of upper foothills and montane.
        .... *G. caespitósum*, 4-24", see Plate 58

MALVACEAE (MLV)   **Mallow Family**
Leaves alternate and simple and palmately veined or lobed. Flowers have five petals
and five sepals that are more or less united and often encircled at the base by united
bracts. Stamens are united into a column. Capsules have seeds arranged in wheel-like
rings.

Málva neglécta .... Cheeseweed, 4-12"
Deeply rooted, weedy plants. Stems are low and sprawling. Leaves small and rounded.
Flowers are small; pale pink. Found on disturbed ground of the lower valleys and
foothills.

Iliámna grandiflóra .... Wild Hollyhock, 2-7', **W**, see no. 284
Tall, robust, showy plants with large flowers arranged in tall spikes; whitish to rose.
Leaves are deeply five to seven-lobed and toothed. Found in moist, montane forest
openings and roadsides; common in certain locations such as east of Ridgeway.

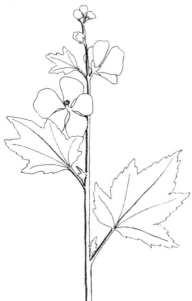

284: *Iliamna grandiflora*

Sidálcea .... Checkermallow
Plants erect. Flowers showy, in terminal racemes. Lower leaves roundish and the upper leaves palmately divided into narrow lobes.
1a.   Flowers white. Leaves smooth. Found in wet areas of montane.
           .... *S. cándida*, 16-36", see no. 285
1b.   Flowers purple. Leaves hairy. Found in moist areas of montane.
           .... *S. neomexicána*, 8-36"

Sphaerálcea .... Globemallow
Flowers in dense racemes; orange. Leaves are divided or lobed.
1a.   Plants low. Leaves silvery and grainy; palmately divided into narrow
           divisions. Found mainly on disturbed sites, roadsides and fields of
           the lower valleys and foothills.
           .... *S. coccínea*, Scarlet Globemallow, 4-10", see no. 286
1b.   Plants tall. Leaves green; shallowly lobed. Common in gravelly, open areas
           or woodlands of the lowest foothills. .... *S. parvifólia*, 8-40", **W**

HYPERICACEAE (HYP)   St. Johnswort Family

Hypericum formósum .... St. Johnswort, 8-12", see no. 287
Flowers have five petals and sepals with numerous stamens protruding; yellow. Leaves are opposite, small, elliptic with rounded tips; glandular dotted on the surface. Fruits are capsules. Wet areas of upper montane and subalpine.

LOASACEAE (LOA)   Loasa Family

Núttallia [Mentzelia] .... Blazing-Star
Flowers are large relative to the sparse stems and leaves. They are yellow and have five to ten petals and numerous stamens. Leaves deep green; pinnately lobed and very rough (can stick to clothing). Found sporadically on bare clay or shale slopes.
1a.   Leaves deeply lobed. .... *N. laciniáta*, 12-16", **W**, see no. 288
1b.   Leaves shallowly lobed. .... *N. multiflóra*, 12-32, **W**

ONAGRACEAE (ONA)   Evening Primrose Family
Leaves opposite or basal. Flowers have two or four sepals and petals and are arranged in axillary or terminal, elongating racemes (a few flowers open at any one time, the progression of bloom moving upwards). Fruits are four-celled capsules.

Oenothéra .... Evening-Primrose
Flowers with four relatively large, thin, petals open late in the day and wither by the heat of the next day. Each day new flowers open. Stamens and pistils are large and obvious. Sepals are united into very long tubes that appear as flower pedicels. Seeds are rather woody capsules.
1a.   Plants ground-hugging. Leaves in a basal rosette with flowers among
           them. Leaves somewhat pinnately lobed (2)
1b.   Plants with erect stems (3)

2a.   Flowers large; white, withering to pink. Spread by underground rootstalks
           forming loose colonies. Common on steep slopes and embankments
           of foothills and montane.
           .... *O. caespitósa*, Tufted Evening Primrose, 2-5", see no. 289

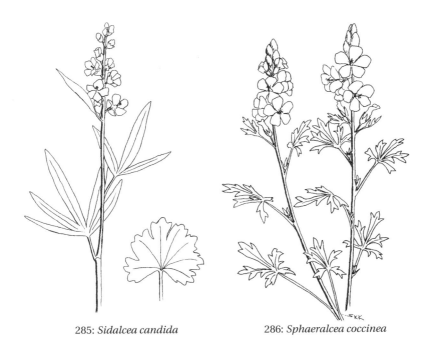

285: *Sidalcea candida*

286: *Sphaeralcea coccinea*

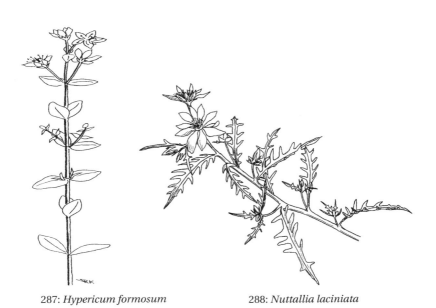

287: *Hypericum formosum*

288: *Nuttallia laciniata*

2b.   Flowers smaller; yellow, withering to pink-orange. Moist areas from
         foothills sagebrush meadows to montane throughout the range.
         .... *O. fláva,* 1-3"

3a.   Flowers white, withering to pink-red; 1 inch diameter. Stems rather short
         and slender. Leaves deeply divided into linear segments; form dense
         basal rosettes. Spread by underground rootstalks, forming loose
         patches. Found on gravelly ground in meadows and along roads;
         foothill and montane. .... *O. coronopifólia,* 2-10", see no. 290
3b.   Flowers yellow, withering to orange; 2 to 3 inches in diameter. Stems tall
         and leafy. Biennial or short-lived perennial; basal rosettes only the
         first year. Found scattered throughout the mountains and valleys in
         wet meadows and along roads. .... *O. eláta,* 1-5', see no. 291

Gaúra coccínea .... Butterfly Weed, 4-12", see no. 292
Plants delicately branched with small, narrow leaves. Flowers have tiny, white petals
that are narrowed at the base like pan handles. Petals wither to scarlet. Flowers fragrant.
Locally common on dry, disturbed ground and slopes of the foothills.

Epilóbium .... Willowherb
Flowers tiny and inconspicuous; white, or pink to purplish. Long, linear seed capsules
split open releasing seeds that are attached to white, cottony hairs. Plants usually turn
scarlet in autumn.
1a.   Plants dwarf. Inhabit alpine. Stems tufted, several to many. Flowers pink.
         Leaves elliptic. .... *E. anagallidifólium,* Alpine Willowherb, 2-6"
1b.   Plants taller. Inhabit lower elevations than alpine (2)

2a.   Flowers white. Leaves elliptic to lanceolate. Found in forest openings of
         subalpine. .... *E. hálleanum,* 4-16"
2b.   Flowers pink to purple (3)

3a.   Found in forest openings of subalpine. .... *E. hórnemannii,* 4-12", see no. 293
3b.   Found on disturbed ground of foothills and montane. Leaves narrow.
         Stems tall and branched with peeling outer layer.
         .... *E. brachycárpum* [E. paniculatum], 12-40"

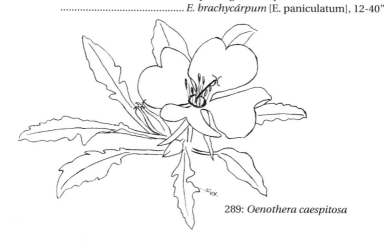

289: *Oenothera caespitosa*

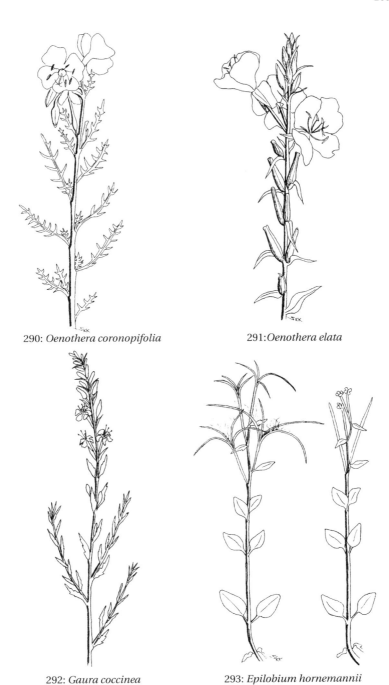

290: *Oenothera coronopifolia*

291: *Oenothera elata*

292: *Gaura coccinea*

293: *Epilobium hornemannii*

Chamérion .... Fireweed
Flowers showy pink-purple. Seed capsule long and linear, splitting open to release
seeds that are attached to white, cottony hairs. Plants turn scarlet in autumn.

1a.   Plants tall. Leaves green. Flowers many in long racemes. Spread by
        underground rootstalks often forming extensive patches. Abundant
        on open, moist, disturbed ground along roads, burned areas and
        clearcuts of subalpine.
                ... *C. dánielsii* [Epilobium angustifolia] Fireweed, 24-48", see Plate 59
1b.   Plants usually short. Leaves blue-green. Flowers few in short racemes;
        relatively large. Found in open, wet, gravelly ground of upper
        subalpine and alpine.
                .... *C. subdentátum* [Epilobium latifolium]Dwarf Fireweed, 4-20"

BRASSICACEAE [CRUCIFERAE] (BRA)   Mustard Family

Leaves alternate. Flowers have four petals and four sepals. Petals are usually narrowed
at the base like a pan handle. Stamens six; two shorter than the others. Flowers are
arranged in elongating racemes (the progression of bloom beginning at the bottom and
moving upward). Fruits are two-celled pods.

Key to Genera

1a.   Seed pods long and narrow (2)
1b.   Seed pods short and broad (10)

2a.   Petals dark maroon and yellow, narrow and pointed; seed pods flattened,
        rather wide, erect .... **STREPTANTHES** p. 205
2b.   Not as above (3)

3a.   Seed pods flattened (4)
3b.   Seed pods not flattened (6)

4a.   Sides of seed pods veined .... **BOECHERA** p. 205
4b.   Sides of seed pods veinless (5)

5a.   Leaves cordate; seed pods about 1 inch long; inhabit wet areas
        .... **CARDAMINE** p. 207
5b.   Leaves otherwise; seed pods shorter; inhabit drier sites .... **DRABA** p. 207

6a.   Basal leaves absent; flowers yellow .... **SCHOENOCRAMBE** p. 208
6b.   Basal leaves present; flowers variously colored (7)

7a.   Plants rooted in water. Flowers white .... **NASTURTIUM** p. 208
7b.   Plants not rooted in water (8)

8a.   Leaves divided (9)
8b.   Leaves simple; flowers relatively large and showy, yellow or lilac to violet .
        .... **ERYSIMUM** p. 208

9a.   Flowers white to pinkish; plants low; inhabit alpine ...... **SMELOWSKIA** p. 208
9b.   Flowers yellow, minute; plants rather tall and weedy; inhabit lower
        elevations .... **DESCURAINIA** p. 208

| 10a. | Seed pods inflated (11) |
| 10b. | Seed pods not inflated (12) |

| 11a. | Seed pods strongly inflated like a balloon constricted in the middle making it appear double .... **PHYSARIA** p. 208 |
| 11b. | Seed pods only slightly inflated, not appearing double .. **LESQUERELLA** p. 208 |

| 12a. | Seed pods oblong .... **DRABA** p. 207 |
| 12b. | Seed pods broader (13) |

| 13a. | Seed pods heart-shaped .... **NOCCAEA** p. 208 |
| 13b. | Seed pods round; cleft at tip .... **LEPIDIUM** p.208 |

Species

Streptánthes cordátus .... Twistflower, 12-36", **W**, see no. 294
Leaves in a basal rosette, blue-green to gray in color and coarsely-toothed. Flower stems very tall. Flowers are small and rather tubular with narrow pointed petals; deep maroon and yellow. Bloom in spring. Seed pods relatively wide, flat and erect. Common in sandy-loam soils or rocky hillsides of the dry, lower, foothill woodlands.

Boéchera [Arabis] .... Rockcress
Plants early blooming. Seed pods long, narrow and flattened, the sides veined. The foothill species are rather similar in appearance, having flowers that are few and small relative to the tall, wiry stems. In some of these species, the new leaves in early spring are covered with a yellow rust that make them appear to be flowers.

| 1a. | Seed pods erect; seeds in two rows. Flowers white to pink. Stem leaves auriculate. Common in meadows from montane to lower alpine throughout the range. .... *B. drúmmondii*, 12-24", see no. 295 |

294: *Streptanthes cordatus*

1b.   Seed pods spreading from stem or pendulous; seeds in one row or only partially in two. Flowers purple, pink to white (2)

2a.   Pedicels of mature seed pods spreading from stem at approximately right angles or reflexed downward against stem (3)

2b.   Pedicels of mature seed pods ascending (7)

3a.   Pedicels of seed pods reflexed downward against stem. Flowers white to purplish. Common in woods and subalpine meadows.
.... *B. retrofrácta* [A. holboelii], 8-36"

3b.   Pedicels of seed pods at nearly right angles to the stem (4)

4a.   Stems less than 8 inches tall. Basal leaves less than 3/4 inch long. Flowers pink to purple. Found in alpine areas of heavy snow accumulations.
.... *B. lémmonii*, 2-8"

4b.   Stems more than 8 inches tall. Basal leaves more than 3/4 inch long. Common in lower, foothill woodlands (5)

5a.   Flowers white. .... *B. púlchra*, 8-24"

5b.   Flowers pink to purple (6)

6a.   Flowers pink or purple. Basal leaves gray-green.
.... *B. lignífera*, 8-20", see no. 296

6b.   Flowers pink. Basal leaves green. .... *B. féndleri*, 10-24"

7a.   Basal leaves gray. Flowers pink. Stem leaves auriculate. Common in the lower foothills among Piñon Pines. .... *B. sélbyi*, 10-20", **W**

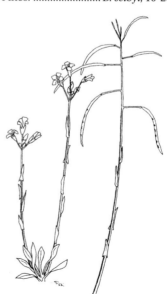

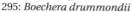

295: *Boechera drummondii*   296: *Boechera lignifera*

7b.   Basal leaves green. Flowers pink to purple. Found in open woodlands of
        foothills and montane. .... *B. divaricárpa*, 12-36"

Cardámine cordifólia .... Bittercress, 12-30", see no. 297
Flowers are white and usually numerous. Leaves cordate and toothed to elongated and
lobed; dark green. Seed pods about 1 inch long, narrow, somewhat flattened and erect
or ascending. Common along streams and seeps from montane to lower alpine; usually
growing in the water.

Drába
Plants are low. Leaves mostly in basal rosettes. Seed pods are flattened and short;
oblong to ovate. Many of the species are similar in appearance separated by technical
differences.

1a.   Flowers white. A species with grayish leaves, found on the eastern slope's
        rock outcrops is *D. smíthii.* Others found in rocky alpine areas are *D.*
        lonchocárpa and *D. cána.*
1b.   Flowers yellow. Among these are *D. hélleriana, D. streptocárpa* and *D.*
        crassifólia. The most widespread and abundant are as follows (2)

2a.   Leaves narrow, entire. Seed pods twisted. Abundant in rocky areas and on
        embankments from montane to alpine.
        .... *D. aúrea,* Golden Draba, 4-20", see no. 298
2b.   Leaves oval, slightly toothed. Seed pods curved, not twisted. Common to
        locally abundant from montane to alpine in meadows and forest
        openings. .... *D. spectábilis,* 4-16"

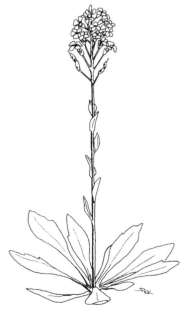

297: *Cardamine cordifolia*   298: *Draba aurea*

Schoenocrámbe linifólia .... Skeleton Mustard, 8-16", **W**, see no. 299
Stems are tall and wiry, single or several together. Stem leaves are narrow and few. Lack basal leaves. Flowers small and yellow. Bloom in late spring. Seed pods are narrow and long, not flattened. Common among brush or dry woodlands of the foothills.

Nastúrtium officinále [Rorippa nasturtium] .... Watercress, 4-8", see no. 300
Plant found in fresh slow-moving water from lower valleys to montane. Stems float on the water or loosely root in the soil. Leaves pinnate; segments round to cordate, the end segment larger. Flowers white.

Smelówskia calycína .... Fern-leaf Candytuft, 2-8", see no. 301
Leaves are pinnate, forming low mat-like mounds. Flowers white to purplish. Plant and leaf sizes vary drastically with the harshness of the site. Found in loose rock areas of alpine.

Descuraínia incána .... Tansy Mustard, 12-40", see no. 302
Plants tall and weedy-looking; biennial. Stems are branched and sparsely leaved; pinnate to further dissected. Flowers tiny, yellow and arranged in small, terminal clusters. Seed pods slim and 1/2 inch long. Found in montane and subalpine forests. There are several other similar species not mentioned here.

Erýsimum capitátum [includes E. nivale] ...... Western Wallflower, 2-28", see Plate 60
Flowers are showy, bright yellow at lower elevations and pale yellow to lilac or violet at higher elevations. Bloom early in the season. Leaves narrow, mostly basal. Seed pods long and linear with a blunt tip. Stem heights are quite variable with elevation. Found in meadows and forest openings from the foothills to alpine.

Physária acutifólia .... Double Bladderpod, 2-4", **W**, see no. 303
Leaves are arranged neatly in basal rosettes; gray, shaped like skillets except with pointed tips. Flowers are arranged in dense showy racemes; yellow. Bloom in spring. Seed pods are inflated like balloons with a constriction in the middle. Common on dry, lower foothill slopes.

Lesquerélla rectípes .... Bladderpod, 4-16", **W**, see no. 304
Leaves are tiny and gray; in basal clusters. Flowers tiny and yellow. Bloom in early spring. Flower stems branched. Fruits small and globe-shaped. This species hybridizes with one that occurs further to the east, producing crosses that have elliptical pods. Abundant on dry, lower foothill slopes.

Noccaéa montána [Thlaspi] .... Candytuft, 1-12", see no. 305
Stem leaves auriculate. Flowers tiny, in dense racemes; white. Fruits are elongated heart-shaped. Plants quite variable in size according to site conditions. Common and widespread from lower foothills to alpine tundra.

Lepídium montánum .... Peppergrass, 6-20"
Plants rather weedy. Stems widely branched. Flowers are tiny and abundant; white. Stem leaves short linear. Basal leaves pinnately lobed into linear segments. Seed pods are round and cleft at the tip. The species is quite variable with several subspecies recognized. Common in gravelly, open areas and parks of foothills and montane.

299: *Schoenocrambe linifolia*

300: *Nasturtium officinale*

301: *Smelowskia calycina*

302: *Descurainia incana*

303: *Physaria acutifolia*

LINACEAE (LIN)   **Flax Family**

Adenolínum léwisii [Linum] .... Blue Flax, 6-24", see no. 306
Plants have delicate stems with nodding flower buds. Flowers have five, bright blue to
whitish petals, opening in the morning and dropping by afternoon. Each day new
flowers open. Leaves are alternate, simple, entire and sessile; short and linear. Fruits
are globe-shaped, segmented capsules. Locally abundant in meadows from foothills to
upper montane, throughout the range.

CARYOPHYLLACEAE (CRY)   **Pink Family**
Leaves opposite, simple and entire. Stems have swollen nodes. Flowers have four to five
petals, these narrowed at the base like pan handles. Sepals united. Fruits are achenes
or capsules.

Anotítes ménziesii [Silene] .... Menzies Catchfly, 4-12"
Flowers white. Stems are repeatedly branched; sticky. Leaves narrow-elliptic. Common under oakbrush of upper foothills and in forests of montane and subalpine.

Gastrolýchnis [Lychnis] .... Campion
Flowers few, usually nodding at maturity. Sepals are inflated and striped with dark
vertical lines, resembling chinese lanterns. Petals inconspicuous. Leaves mostly basal,
narrow-oblanceolate.
1a.   Plants dwarf. Found on loose rock slopes of alpine tundra.
           .... *G. apétala*, 2-4"
1b.   Plants taller. Found in meadows from upper foothills to alpine.
           .... *G. drúmmondii*, 8-20", see no. 307

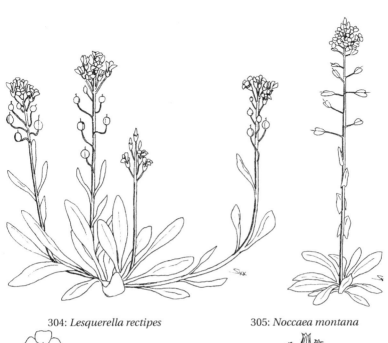

304: *Lesquerella rectipes*   305: *Noccaea montana*

306: *Adenolinum lewisii*   307: *Gastrolychnis drummondii*

Siléne acaúlis .... Moss Campion, under ½", see Plate 61
Leaves form tight moss-like mounds with small, five-petaled, pink flowers set among them. Leaves are acute and bright green. Common on alpine tundra.

Saponária officinális .... Bouncing Bet, Soapwort, 12-32"
Flowers are pink, often with double petals. Leaves oval to lanceolate. Spreads by underground rootstalks forming large, dense patches. Escaped from cultivation; often found near old homesteads in the valleys.

ALSINACEAE (ASN)   Chickweed Family
Plants low and mat-like, mounded or taller with few delicate stems. Stems have swollen nodes. Leaves opposite, simple and entire. Flowers white; four or five petals and sepals. Sepals are separate. Fruits are capsules.

Key to Genera

1a.	Leaves tiny (1/4 inch or less), linear to awl-shaped (2)
1b.	Leaves longer or broader (5)

2a.   Flowers inconspicuous among the moss-like mat of tiny blunt-tipped leaves; leaves with papery stipules equally as long .... **PARONYCHIA** p. 212
2b.   Flowers conspicuous on small stems above the leaves; no papery stipules; plants form tight mats or loose sprawling (3)

3a.   Sepals and leaves blunt-tipped .... **LIDIA** p. 213
3b.   Sepals and leaves pointed (4)

4a.   Stems unbranched .... **TRYPHANE** p. 213
4b.   Stems branched .... **ALSINANTHE** p. 213

5a.   Leaves linear, over 1/2 inch long .... **EREMOGONE** p. 213
5b.   Leaves broader or if linear then not over 1/2 inch long (6)

6a.   Leaves several inches long .... **PSEUDOSTELLARIA** p. 214
6b.   Leaves less than 1 inch long (7)

7a.   Petals not cleft, barely longer than sepals .... **SPERGULASTRUM** p. 214
7b.   Petals cleft (8)

8a.   Stems soft, with gummy hairs .... **CERASTIUM** p. 214
8b.   Stems wiry, without gummy hairs .... **STELLARIA** p. 214

Species

Paronýchia pulvináta .... Nail Wort, 1-2"
Form tight mats of tiny, blunt-tipped leaves with silvery, papery stipules equally as long. Flowers are inconspicuous, hidden among the leaves. Found on dry, gravelly alpine tundra.

Lídia obtusilóba [Arenaria] .... Alpine Sandwort, ½-2", see Plate 62
Form tight, moss-like mats. Leaves have rounded tips (unlike Moss Campion and
Alpine Phlox with pointed tips). Flowers are white on tiny, wiry stems, barely topping
the mat. Abundant on dry, gravelly, tundra ridges.

Tryphán̈e rubélla [Arenaria], 1-4"
Form loose mats of delicate, unbranched stems. Flowers white. Common, scattered
throughout rocky alpine areas and subalpine around timberline.

Alsinánthe macrántha [Arenaria], 2-4"
Stems are numerous, branched and spreading. Leaves short (less than 1/2 inch long),
linear, thick and soft; mostly basal. Flowers white. Common on tundra.

Eremogóne [Arenaria] .... Sandwort
Leaves are mostly in basal tufts; linear and grass-like, more than 1/2 inch long. Stems
are slender. Flowers white.

1a.   Flowers in an open, branched arrangement; stamens red; long blooming
            so that flowers and matured seed capsules are found on the same
            plant late in the season. Common in rocky meadows and on rock
            outcrops throughout the mountains. Form is quite variable
            according to site conditions; low and tightly mounded on alpine
            ridges and taller and looser at lower elevations.
            .... *E. féndleri*, 3-12", see no. 308
1b.   Flowers in tight ball-like clusters on slender stems. Leaves densely clumped at
            base. Found in gravelly meadows and forest openings from upper
            foothills to subalpine. .... *E. congésta*, 4-12", **W**, see no. 309

308: *Eremogone fendleri*   309:*Eremogone congesta*

Pseudostellária jámesiana .... Tuber Starwort, 8-20", see no. 310
Plants with tall and rather weak stems. Flowers are few and axillary and have white, lobed petals. Leaves are several inches long, tapering to a narrow point. Found in moist forest openings or under oakbrush of upper foothills and montane.

Stellária .... Chickweed, 2-20"
Flowers have white, two-lobed petals. Plants are delicate or miniature and often overlooked. Sizes vary according to habitat. The following species are similar and usually found in moist areas of subalpine and lower alpine; *S. crassifólia, S. longifólia, S. longípes* and *S. calycántha*. A species with widely branched flower stems is *S. umbelláta*.

Cerástium .... Mouse-ear Chickweed
Flowers have white, cleft petals. Plants are often rather gummy to the touch. Seed capsules have ten teeth at the top. The following two species hybridize where habitats come together producing plants with mixed characteristics.

1a.   Leaves small; elliptic. Sepals purplish. Form loose to dense mats on rocky
        areas above timberline. .... *C. beeringiánum*, 2-10", see no. 311
1b.   Leaves linear; soft fuzzy. Sepals green. Stems tufted; tall, erect or leaning,
        rather weak. Abundant in montane and subalpine meadows. Often
        on rocky or sandy soil. ...... *C. stríctum* [C. arvense], 4-12", see no. 312

Spergulástrum lanuginósum [Arenaria saxosa], 4-6"
Stems sprawling, forming mounds. Leaves elliptic and spread along the mostly un-branched stems. Flowers numerous. Petals are entire and rather short (barely exceeding the sepals); white. Found in rocky, open areas of montane and subalpine.

PARNASSIACEAE (PAR)   Grass-of-Parnassus Family

Parnássia .... Grass-of-Parnassus
Flowers have five, white petals. Five stamens alternate with five, yellow, fringed stalks. Leaves are basal except for a small, bract-like leaf on the stem. Fruits are capsules. Found in wet areas.
1a.   Petals fringed. Leaves reniform to cordate. Inhabit subalpine.
        .... *P. fimbriáta*, 4-12"
1b.   Petals not fringed. Leaves oval to ovate. Inhabit upper montane and
        subalpine. .... *P. parviflóra*, 4-12", see no. 313

SAXIFRAGACEAE (SAX)   Saxifrage Family
Plants have variously shaped and mostly basal leaves. Flower stems mostly tall and delicate. Flowers are small and have five petals or lack them entirely. Sepals are separate or united. Fruits are follicles or capsules.

Key to Genera

1a.   Leaves all basal (2)
1b.   Leaves not all basal (4)

310: *Pseudostellaria jamesiana*

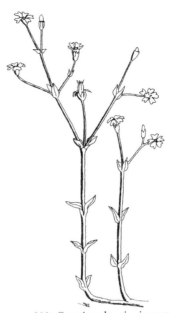

311: *Ceratium beeringianum*

312: *Ceratium strictum*

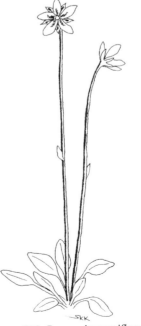

313: *Parnassia parviflora*

2a.   Leaves with even triangular teeth or thick and fleshy-textured
        .... MICRANTHES p. 216
2b.   Leaves with rounded teeth, not fleshy (3)

3a.   Leaves lobed and toothed; flowers with conical bases .. HEUCHERA p. 216
3b.   Leaves not distinctly lobed, only toothed; flowers with shallow saucer-like
        bases .... MITELLA p. 216

4a.   Leaves sharp pointed, stiff and awl shaped, arranged in tiny rosettes; form
        mats on rocks and cliffs; flowers white .... CILARIA p. 216
4b.   Not as above (5)

5a.   Leaves in tiny rosettes; form low patches on gravelly alpine tundra;
        flowers bright yellow .... HIRCULUS p. 216
5b.   Not as above; leaves ternately divided to compound (leaflets cleft and
        toothed); erect meadow plants; flowers white
        .... LITHOPHRAGMA p. 218

Species

Micránthes [Saxifraga]
1a.   Leaves few; oblong to obovate; entire to toothed; fleshy; short petioled;
        basal. Flowers in tight balls (loosening somewhat at maturity); white.
        Bloom early, soon after snowmelt. Common on gravelly, open
        ground from upper montane to alpine.
        .... *M. rhomboídea*, Snowball Saxifrage, 4-12", see no. 314
1b.   Leaves many; reniform with large, even teeth; long petioled; basal.
        Flowers few in diffuse panicles; white. Common along streams of
        upper montane and subalpine. .... *M. odontolóma*
        [S. arguta], Brook Saxifrage, 8-16", see no. 315

Heúchera parvifólia .... Common Alum-Root, 8-24", see no. 316
Leaves mostly basal, cordate at the base with scalloped margins and long petioles.
Flower stems rough and nearly naked. Flowers are tiny, tightly clustered at first and
later spreading; whitish. Variable stem heights and leaf sizes. Plants in the alpine are a
dwarf subspecies. Common rock outcrops throughout the mountains.

Mitélla stauropétala .... Mitrewort, Bishop's Cap, 6-20"
Leaves basal; cordate at the base with small teeth on the margins. Flowers have tiny,
white, oddly dissected petals (resembling T.V. antennae) encircled by saucer-like,
fused sepals. Found in moist, shaded upper montane and subalpine.

Cilária austromontána [Saxifraga bronchialis] .... Dotted Saxifrage, 2-6", see no. 317
Form mat-like carpets on rocks, composed of tiny rosettes of stiff, sharp-pointed
leaves. Flowers are few on wiry stems; white with red and orange dots. Found on dry
cliffs and outcrops from montane to alpine.

Hírculus serpyllifólius [Saxifraga chrysantha], 1-3"
Leaves are in many, tiny rosettes, forming patches. Flowers yellow; one to a few on short
stems. While the petals are still fresh the red, fleshy fruit is developing (obvious in the
center). Stem leaves very tiny. Found on gravelly tundra; common in certain areas.

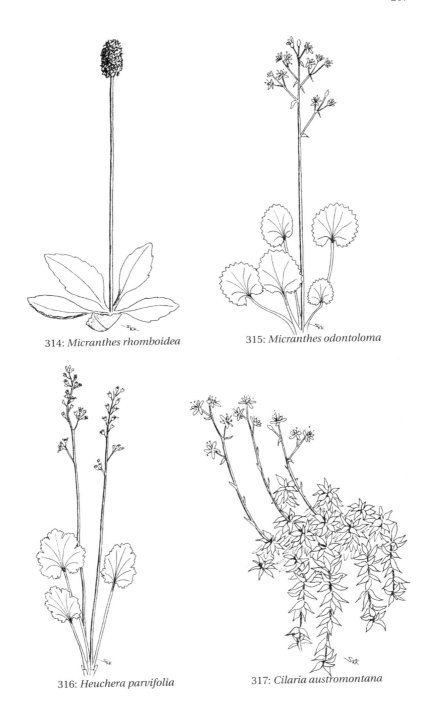

314: *Micranthes rhomboidea*

315: *Micranthes odontoloma*

316: *Heuchera parvifolia*

317: *Cilaria austromontana*

Lithophrágma .... Star Saxifrage, 4-10"
Plants are delicate and easily overlooked unless abundant and blooming. Flowers
small and white. Petals are deeply divided into three to five, pointed sections. Bloom in
spring. Leaves are deeply ternately lobed to compound, the divisions deeply cleft again
and toothed. Few leaves present on the flower stems. Three species are found from
sagebrush plateaus to montane meadows. They are especially abundant on the far
western plateaus.

1a.   Petals divided into three sections .... *L. parviflórum*, **W**
1b.   Petals divided into five to seven sections (2)

2a.   Petals divided into five sections; the end section larger than the bottom
         two. Tiny scarlet bulbs present at bases of petioles. .... *L. glábrum*
2b.   Petals divided into five to seven sections; all nearly equal.
         .... *L. tenéllum*, **W**, see no. 318

POLYGONACEAE (PLG)   **Buckwheat Family**
Leaves mostly alternate, simple, generally entire and often only basal. Many have
leaves that sheath the stem. Petals and sepals are not differentiated. Some species have
fused bracts encircling the flowers. Fruits are achenes; many are winged.

Key to Genera

1a.   Plants floating in ponds or rooted in mud along the edges; flowers bright
         pink .... **PERSICARIA** p. 218
1b.   Plants not as above (2)

2a.   Flowers clustered with fused bracts surrounding the base (3)
2b.   Flowers not with bracts surrounding them; leaf bases sheath the stem (4)

3a.   Flowers spread out and dangling along tall widely branched stems; leaves
         in a basal rosette .... **PTEROGONUM** p. 219
3b.   Flowers in compact clusters on shorter stems; leaves in mat-like clumps
         or spread along wiry to woody stems .... **ERIOGONUM** p. 219

4a.   Leaves reniform; found among alpine rocks .... **OXYRIA** p. 220
4b.   Leaves not reniform (5)

5a.   Leaves sagitate with lower two lobes bent outward .... **ACETOSELLA** p. 220
5b.   Leaves oblong elongate (6)

6a.   Plants very large and coarse; flowers in large clusters, greenish drying to
         rust-brown .... **RUMEX** p. 220
6b.   Plants small; flowers in small tight clusters, white to pinkish
         .... **BISTORTA** p. 220

Species

Persicária amphíbia [Polygonum] .... Water Smartweed, 4-36"
Plants float in ponds or root in mud along the edge. Flowers in thick, short spikes; bright
pink. Leaves elliptic. Found in montane.

Pterogónum alátum [Eriogonum] .... Winged Buckwheat, 12-40", see no. 319
Leaves form thick basal rosettes; oblanceolate and up to 4 inches long. Plants flower
after some number of years and then die. Flower stems are tall, few leaved and widely
branched. Flowers dangle along the branches; yellow. Seeds are winged. Common in
open dry areas of foothills and montane.

Eriogónum .... Wild Buckwheat
Flower clusters are surrounded by bracts and variously arranged. Leaves mostly basal
and have some degree of hairiness.

1a.   Plants shrub-like with wiry to woody intricately branched stems. Leaves
        small and narrow; spread along stems. Flower clusters very tiny;
        arranged in corymbs; whitish. Found in dry, lower foothills.
        .... *E. microthécum*, 4-24"

1b.   Plants not as above (2)

2a.   Flower clusters arranged in spikes or racemes on tall, naked, white stems.
        Flowers tiny; white tinged pink, drying to rust-brown. Leaves oblong;
        basal; long petioled. Common in foothills and dry montane
        meadows. .... *E. racemósum*, Redroot Buckwheat,
        12-32", see no. 320

2b.   Flower clusters arranged in dense corymbs or umbels on branched, low
        stems. Leaves mostly basal forming low mounds or thick clumps (3)

3a.   Leaves long, linear and acute; edges rolled under; quite variable in size
        from one location to another. Flowers whitish. Form thick clumps.
        Found on barren hills such as the shale slopes west of Durango or
        south of Pagosa Springs. .... *E. lonchophýllum*, 4-6", see no. 321

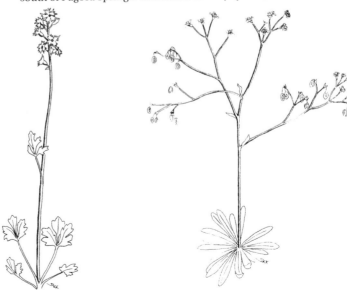

318: *Lithophragma tenellum*   319: *Pterogonum alatum*

3b.   Leaves shorter and broader creating mat-like mounds (4)

4a.   Flowers without hair on the surface; yellow, drying to orange-rust. Leaves
                obovate to spatulate. Common among sagebrush of foothills and
                dry, lower, montane meadows and forest openings.
                .... *E. umbellátum* Sulfur Flower, 4-12"
4b.   Flowers with hair on the surface (5)

5a.   Flowers white tinged pink, drying to brown. Leaves oblanceolate to
                obovate. Common on open, dry slopes from lower foothills to alpine.
                .... *E. jámesii,* 4-12", see Plate 63
5b.   Flowers yellow, drying to rust. Leaves oblanceolate. Found in dry, open
                areas from foothills to upper subalpine. .... *E. flávum,* 4-8"

Oxýria digýna .... Mountain Sorrel, 2-12", see Plate 64
Tufted, low plants of bare rock areas of alpine; common. Leaves reniform; deep green.
Flowers are small and in dense narrow panicles; greenish. Seeds rust-brown; winged.

Acetosélla vulgáris [Rumex] .... Sheep Sorrel, 4-24", see no. 322
Lower leaves are sagitate with the lobes bent outward. Flowers yellow-green turning
reddish with age. Plants spread by underground rootstalks. Quite variable in size
according to conditions. Common to abundant and widespread on moist, disturbed,
ground of montane and subalpine.

Rúmex .... Dock
Plants with large, oblong, basal leaves. Flowers in dense, thick spikes; pinkish drying to
rust brown. Seeds winged.
1a.   Stems with side shoots. Form sprawling patches in gravelly areas and
                roadsides of upper montane and subalpine; common.
                .... *R. trianguliválvis* [R. salicifolius], 12-32"
1b.   Stems without side shoots (2)

2a.   Plants introduced weeds of disturbed wet areas, fields and ditches from
                the lower valleys to montane. Leaf margins wavy. Seeds with
                enlarged bumps. Plants with several stems in a clump.
                .... *R. críspus,* Curly Dock, 12-40"
2b.   Plants native to boggy areas of subalpine. Leaf margins not wavy. Seeds
                without enlarged bumps. Plants spread by underground rootstalks
                forming large patches. .... *R. densiflórus,* Subalpine Dock, 20-40"

Bistórta [Polygonum] .... Bistort
Plants of high altitudes. Leaves are smooth and dark green; narrow to oblong. Flowers
white to pinkish; tiny and numerous in condensed racemes on naked stems.
1a.   Flower racemes very narrow (1/4 to 1/3 inch wide). Lower flowers are
                replaced by tiny bulbs. Plants slender and rather inconspicuous
                among other vegetation. Common in subalpine and alpine mead-
                ows. .... *B. vivípara,* 4-12"
1b.   Flower racemes thick and rounded (1/2 inch or more wide). Lower flowers
                are not replaced by bulbs. Plants larger and conspicuous. Abundant
                and widespread in subalpine and alpine meadows.
                .... *B. bistortoídes,* 10-24", see no. 323

320: *Eriogonum racemosum*

321: *Eriogonum lonchophyllum*

322: *Acetosella vulgaris*

323: *Bistorta bistortoides*

SANTALACEAE (SAN)   **Sandalwood Family**

Comándra umbelláta .... Bastard Toadflax, 6-10", see no. 324
Low-growing. Leaves pale green; alternate and sessile, simple and entire. Flowers are small pinkish stars in terminal corymbs. Petals and sepals similar in appearance. Plants spread by underground rootstalks. Partially parasitic on various plants' roots. Fruits are mealy drupes. Common in meadows of lower foothills.

INCONSPICUOUS-FLOWERED DICOTS

Key to Families

1a.	Vines, trailing over ground (2)
1b.	Not vines (3)

2a.	Leaves palmately lobed, dull, rough; flowers papery bracts in clusters ....**CAN** p. 223
2b.	Leaves trifoliate, shiny, smooth .... **Toxicodendron in ANA** p.18

3a.	Leaves simple (may be parted or lobed) (4)
3b.	Leaves compound (10)

4a.	Plants form tight moss-like mats on tundra; leaves with papery silvery stipules equally as long .... **Paronychia in ASN** p. 212
4b.	Plants not as above (5)

5a.	Leaves basal only (6)
5b.	Leaves on stems (7)

6a.	Leaves linear, lanceolate, elliptic to oval, entire and prominently ribbed; flower spikes cylindrical .... **PTG** p. 223
6b.	Leaves cordate, round or ovate, toothed or scalloped to lobed; flower spikes not cylindrical .... **SAX** p. 214

7a.	Leaves linear (8)
7b.	Leaves broader (9)

8a.	Plants with strong sage odor .... **Artemisia in AST** p. 92
8b.	Plants with tarragon odor .... **Oligosporus in AST** p. 113

9a.	Stem leaves simple, coarsely toothed; hairs stinging; flowers axillary in stringy spikes .... **URT** p. 224
9b.	Stem leaves pinnately parted; leaves with thin white edging ...... **VAL** p. 144

10a.	Leaves pinnate ....**Artemisia in AST** p. 92
10b.	Leaves ternate (11)

11a.	Leaves ternate several times, leaflets small and roundish; stems present; flowers composed of nodding tassels of stamens .... **COP** p. 224

11b.   Leaves once-ternate (12)

12a.   Plants with stems; leaves shiny .... **Toxicodendron in ANA** p. 18
12b.   Plants stemless; leaves not shiny, blunt and toothed at apex; flowers small,
            yellowish, clustered .... **Sibbaldia in ROS** p. 164

CANNABACEAE (CAN)   Hops Family

Húmulus lúpulus .... Wild Hops, to 12' or more
Vines trailing over the ground and rocks. Leaves opposite; palmately lobed. Stems have
weak spines making them very rough to the touch. Flowers lack petals though green,
papery bracts surrounding them are conspicuous; bracts dry yellowish. Locally common in rocky, open areas of montane.

PLANTAGINACEAE (PTG)   Plantain Family

Plantágo .... Plantain
Leaves are alternate basal, simple and prominently ribbed. Flowers tiny among bracts
in dense, cylindrical spikes. Fruits are capsules.
1a.   Leaves broad-oval; round at the base. Abundant introduced weed of
            disturbed meadows and lawns from lower valleys to montane. Quite
            variable in size. .... *P. májor* Common Plantain, 3-24"
1b.   Leaves narrower (2)

2a.   Leaves lanceolate; tapered at the base. Native of montane and subalpine
            meadows. .... *P. tweédyi*, 4-8", see no. 325
2b.   Leaves linear-lanceolate. Often form large clumps. Introduced weed of
            disturbed sites in lower valleys and foothills. .... *P. lanceoláta*, 4-24"

324: *Comandra umbellata*   325: *Plantago tweedyi*

URTICACEAE (URT)   **Nettle Family**

Úrtica grácilis ....Stinging Nettles, 3-6', see no. 326
Plants with stinging hairs. Leaves are opposite; lanceolate and coarsely toothed.
Flowers tiny and greenish, arranged in axillary, elongated clusters; no petals. Common
around rocks and logs, along trails and in disturbed, moist ground of the upper foothills
to subalpine.

COPTACEAE (COP)   **Meadowrue Family**

Thalíctrum ....Meadowrue
Flowers lack petals. Stamens are most noticable, forming pendulous tassels. Leaves
ternately compound several times; leaflets small, rounded and lobed (very similar to
Columbine). Fruits are achenes.

1a.	Plants small. Inhabit alpine.	*T. alpínum*, 2-8"
1b.	Plants tall. Inhabit forested zones (2)	

2a.	Upper edge of fruit bowed upward. Common to abundant in upper montane and subalpine.	*T. féndleri*, 12-24", see no. 327
2b.	Upper edge of fruit straight or concave. Less common. Found in shady montane woods and canyons.	*T. sparsiflórum*, 10-32"

326: *Urtica gracilis*   327: *Thalictrum fendleri*

APPENDIX I

Example of How to Use the Keys

A Colorado Columbine is the plant that is used for this example. Assuming that you do not have any idea in which family this plant belongs, start with the first key (Key to Major Groupings) on p. 12. Begin by reading both of the first set of opposing statements, 1a and 1b. Choose the one that best fits the plant at hand. The statement directs you to the next set of opposing statements to choose from (shown in parenthesis at the end of the statement). Continue in this manner through the key until a group name is given at the end of the chosen statement. The correct statements to choose for a Colorado Columbine are underlined in the sample key below:

KEY TO MAJOR GROUPINGS

1a.   Woody shrubs or trees with evergreen needles or compressed triangular scales .... **GYMNOSPERMS** p. 24

<u>1b.</u>   <u>Not as above (2)</u>

2a.   Reproduce by spores on the underside of leaf-like fronds; each frond directly attached to root crown (no main stem); frond axis (stipe) wiry, not juicy or green; plants without a strong odor .... **FERNS** p. 26

<u>2b.</u>   <u>Not as above (3)</u>

3a.   Stems cylindrical unbranched or with whorled branches; leaves are reduced to whorled united stem sheaths with tiny teeth .... **FERN-RELATED** p. 33

<u>3b.</u>   <u>Not as above (4)</u>

4a.   Grass, grass-like or plants with flower parts in threes or sixes and with parallel-veined leaves .... **MONOCOTS** p. 34

<u>4b.</u>   <u>Not grass-like; flowers with parts in fours, fives or multiples thereof; leaf veins not parallel (5)</u>

5a.   Flowers inconspicuous .... **INCONSPICUOUS-FLOWERED DICOTS** p. 222

<u>5b.</u>   <u>Flowers conspicuous (6)</u>

6a.   Flowers with petals united to one another (sometimes only near the base) **UNITED-PETAL DICOTS** p. 64

<u>6b.</u>   <u>Flowers with petals separate</u> .... **FREE-PETAL DICOTS p. 148**

You have been directed to the group, FREE-PETAL DICOTS. Following the same method of chosing between opposing statements work through this key until a family name is given. The correct route to take is again underlined in the sample key below:

FREE-PETAL DICOTS

Key to Families

1a.	Leaves large pads floating on the surface of ponds .... NYM p. 150
1b.	Leaves not as above (2)

2a.	Plants succulent to fleshy (note: some MONOCOTS also fleshy) (3)
2b.	Plants not succulent or fleshy (5)

3a.	Stems enlarged, succulent and spiny; no leaves (stems may be flattened pads that appear to be leaves) .... CAC p. 151
3b.	Not as above; leaves succulent to fleshy (4)

4a.	Leaves fleshy, in basal rosettes; flowers among them .... POR p. 152
4b.	Leaves succulent, in tiny basal rosettes or fleshy and larger, on stems; flowers on stems .... CRS p. 152

5a.	Plants woody, not vines (6)
5b.	Plants herbs or vines (12)

6a.	Plants small trees; leaves minute and overlapping; flowers in feathery clusters at the ends of branches; pink to whitish .... TAM p. 152
6b.	Plants shrubs (7)

7a.	Leaves opposite (8)
7b.	Leaves alternate or fascicled (9)

8a.	Leaves narrow; plants of dry foothills .... HDR p. 154
8b.	Leaves broad; plants of moist drainages .... COR p. 154

9a.	Flowers either tiny, yellow-green and axillary or small, white and in terminal clusters on thorny branches of low shrubs .... RHM p. 154
9b.	Flowers either larger or small, white and in clusters on thorny branches of large shrubs to small trees (10)

10a.	Plants low with large, spine-tipped, pinnate leaves or tall and spiny-stemmed with elliptic, simple leaves; flowers tiny, yellow, bell-shaped .... BER p. 154
10b.	Plants not with spine-tipped leaves; if branches spiny then leaves broader palmately veined or lobed and flowers not bell-shaped; white, pink, coral or yellow (11)

11a.	Flowers several together on twigs, petals usually smaller than the united sepals; stems with or without spines or thorns .... GRS p. 156
11b.	Flowers single or if clustered then many together and tall shrubs to small trees; petals larger than sepals; stems may have spines or thorns .... ROS p. 156

12a.   Plants with flowers arranged in umbels and leaves compound with enlarged petiole bases ....**API** p. 169
12b.   Plants not as above (13)

13a.   Flowers irregular (14)
13b.   Flowers regular (17)

14a.   Sepals and petals distinctly different in appearance (15)
14b.   Sepals and petals look similar ....**HEL** p. 190

You have been directed to the Hellebore Family as shown in the sample below. This family does not have a genera key since it has few genera. Read the first statement (or more if necessary) in the descriptions given for each genus until you find the one that fits your plant. The description for *Aquilegia* is the only one that fits. *Aquilegia* has two species. The key to species leads you to *A. coerulea*, Colorado Columbine.

HELLEBORACEAE (HEL)   Hellebore Family

Sepals are showy and petal-like. Petals are much smaller and usually hidden. Flowers mostly irregular. Leaves usually compound. Fruits are follicles (except *Actaea* has berries).

Aconitum columbianum ....Monkshood, 24-60"
Tall plants. Flowers are dark purple.

Delphinium ....Larkspur
Leaves are palmately divided.

Psychrophila leptosepala [Caltha] ....Marsh-Marigold, 6-12"
Flowers white; several, regular.

Trollius albiflorus [T. laxus] ....Globe Flower, 8-24"
Flowers large and regular, white to cream with many yellow stamens.

Actaea rubra ....Baneberry, 20-32"
Numerous, small, white flowers in a raceme.

Aquilegia ....Columbine
Petals are smaller than sepals with spurs that protrude from the back of the flower. Sepals are petal-like. Leaves two to three times ternately compound, the segments roundish-lobed.
1a.   Flowers blue and white or more of one color. Quite variable due to hybridization with next species. Woodland plants tend to be tall and spindly with few blooms while plants of rocky, open, alpine areas are dense and compact with many blooms. Common moist montane and subalpine woods and rocky alpine meadows.
         ....*A. coerulea*, Colorado Columbine, 8-32"
1b.   Flowers red and yellow. Often form low dense clumps. Found on dry, shady, montane slopes and embankments and subalpine woods.
         .... *A. elegantula*, Western Red Columbine, 4-16"

APPENDIX II

ACERACEAE ....ACE
AGAVACEAE ....AGA
ALLIACEAE ....ALL
ALSINACEAE ....ASN
ANACARDIACEAE ....ANA
APIACEAE ....API
APOCYNACEAE ....APO
ASCLEPIADACEAE ....ASC
ASTERACEAE ....AST
BERBERIDACEAE ....BER
BETULACEAE ....BET
BORAGINACEAE ....BOR
BRASSICACEAE ....BRA
CACTACEAE ....CAC
CALOCHORTACEAE ....CCT
CAMPANULACEAE ....CAM
CANNABACEAE ....CAN
CAPPARACEAE ....CPP
CAPRIFOLIACEAE ....CPR
CARYOPHYLLACEAE ....CRY
CELASTRACEAE ....CEL
CHENOPODIACEAE ....CHN
CONVALLARIACEAE CVL
CONVOLVULACEAE ....CNV
COPTACEAE ....COP
CORNACEAE ....COR
CRASSULACEAE ....CRS
CUPRESSACEAE ....CUP
CYPERACEAE ....CYP
ELAEAGNACEAE ....ELE
ERICACEAE ....ERI
FABACEAE ....FAB
FAGACEAE ....FAG
FUMARIACEAE ....FUM
GENTIANACEAE ....GEN
GERANIACEAE ....GER
GROSSULARIACEAE ....GRS
HELLEBORACEAE ....HEL
HYDRANGEACEAE ....HDR
HYDROPHYLLACEAE ....HYD
HYPERICACEAE ....HYP
IRIDACEAE ....IRI
JUNCACEAE ....JUN
LAMIACEAE ....LAM
LILIACEAE LIL
LINACEAE ....LIN
LOASACEAE ....LOA

The author has spent most of her life living close to the land observing the natural world. She has explored the landscapes of Alaska and many areas of the west becoming acquainted with the flora and fauna residing there. She is most intrigued by the Rocky Mountains and the southwestern deserts. Her knowledge of plant taxonomy and her artistic abilities are primarily self-taught. She obtained a B.S. in Wildlife Biology from Colorado State University. She currently resides near Durango operating a small native seed and plant nursery.

INDEX OF DRAWINGS AND PHOTOS

INDEX

A

Abbreviations, use of 10
Abies 26
Acer 16
Aceraceae 16
Acetosella 220
Achillea 88
Acomastylis 164. See also *Geum*
Aconitum 190
Actaea 190
Adenolinum 210
Adiantum 28
Agastache 118
Agavaceae 56
AGAVE FAMILY 56
Ageratina 94
Agoseris 116
Agropyron 44, 46. See also
   Elytrigia; Pascopyrum
Agrostis 41
Agyrochosma 28
Alder 22
Aletes 172
Alfalfa 182
Alliaceae 60
Allium 60
Alnus 22
Alp Lily 60
Alpine Avens 164
Alpine Forget-me-not 146
Alpine Parsley 172
Alpine Sandwort 213
Alsinaceae 212–214
Alsinanthe 213
Alum-Root 216
Amelanchier 164
Amerosedum 152
Anacardiaceae 18
Anaphalis 113
Androsace 144
Anemone 194. See also *Pulsatilla*
Angelica 172
Anisantha 50
Anotites 210
Antennaria 94
Anticlea 58
Aphyllon 118
Apiaceae 169–176
Apocynaceae 132

Apocynum 132
Appendix I 225–230
Aquilegia 192
Arabis. See *Boechera*
Arctium 113
Arctostaphylos 132
Area covered 7
Arenaria. See *Alsinanthe; Eremogone;*
   Lidia; Spergulastrum; Tryphane
Argentina 166
Argyrochosma 28
Aristida 39
Arnica 70
Artemisia 92, 113. See also
   Oligosporus; Seriphidium
Asclepiadaceae 116
Asclepias 116
Aspen 20
Asplenium 28
Aster 88. See also *Eucephalus;*
   Leucelene; Machaeranthera; Virgulus
Asteraceae 66–116
Astragalus 186
Athyrium 28
Atragene 193
Avens 166

B

Bahia 79
Ball Cactus 151
Ball-Head Gilia 138
Balsam-Root 80
Balsamorhiza 80
Baneberry 190
BARBERRY FAMILY 154
Bastard Toadflax 222
Bearberry 132
Bedstraw 142
Bee Balm 118
Bee-Plant 196
BELLFLOWER FAMILY 130
BELLWORT FAMILY 62
Bentgrass 41
Berberidaceae 154
Berberis 154. See also *Mahonia*
Besseya 124